Gwen John

1876–1939

Gwen John

1876–1939

Susan Chitty

Hodder & Stoughton
LONDON SYDNEY AUCKLAND TORONTO

British Library Cataloguing in Publication Data

Chitty, Susan
  Gwen John: 1876–1939.
  1. John, Gwen   2. Painters – Great Britain –
  Biography
  I. Title
  759.2   ND497.J6/

  ISBN 0-340-39215-0

For
Antoinette Grunelius
and
Marie-Odile Faye

Two friends in France who made this book possible.

People are like shadows to me and I am like a shadow.

Gwen John to Rodin

FOREWORD
to the original edition
by Sir John Rothenstein

'People are like shadows to me,' wrote Gwen John in a letter to a friend, 'and I am like a shadow.' In spite of the highly illuminating character of this book – and Susan Chitty has assembled an impressive range of facts, mostly hitherto unpublished – something of a shadow Gwen John still remains. It is significant that even the cause of her death and the whereabouts of her grave are unknown. This biography will, however, surely greatly increase interest in her work and her personality.

Forty-two years have passed since she died, yet no biography has been published. One early reason was the attitude of her brother Augustus. Although he ardently desired that a book should be written about her, his attitude was ambivalent. He insisted that the relevant material he had lent a writer be returned to him, and on several occasions proposed that my wife and I be entrusted with the task, only to withdraw on his recurrent impulse to undertake it himself. (I should add that this did not prevent him from according me the most friendly help with the chapter on his sister for my *Modern English Painters*.) Although his attitude no doubt discouraged writers likely to be interested, it cannot have been the primary reason why no biography was undertaken; after all Augustus died twenty years ago. This, I believe, was the sheer difficulty it would have involved.

Gwen John abhorred publicity and was reluctant even to exhibit her work. Had she not endured grievous and lifelong poverty, I doubt whether she would have exhibited at all, but as she only very rarely had an income sufficient to enable her to devote much of her time to painting and drawing, she was accordingly compelled to serve as an artists' model. She avoided, whenever possible, meeting – other than her friends – the few collectors of her work, even John Quinn, the wealthiest and perhaps the most enthusiastic among them.

With regard to her art, her only ambition was to paint and draw as well as lay in her power. About such power she had no doubt, no false modesty. Susan Chitty quotes from one of her innumerable studio notes: 'Don't be vague or wavering. Impose your style . . . Don't be afraid of falling into mediocrity. You would never.' Unlike most other artists she did not require recognition to give her confidence, very much the contrary. 'You are only free when you have left all,' read another of her notes. 'Leave everybody and let them leave you. Then only will you be without fear.'

It is therefore not surprising that she lived a life utterly remote from public view. Her passionate relationship with Rodin, with whom she was on terms of intense, though sporadic, intimacy for a decade following their meeting in 1904 became fairly widely known in the art world, but only somewhat vaguely. It was the author's access to the two thousand love letters – many of an extraordinary candour – which Gwen John wrote to Rodin that fired Susan Chitty's imagination and determined her to undertake the present book, one unlikely to be surpassed in its wide range and sympathetic perception.

Gwen John's intimate relationships with both men and women were often troubled; as were those with members of her own family, even with Augustus, a devoted and deeply admiring though unpredictable brother. Hardly less so were those with her cats; her devotion to one who strayed led her to search whole areas of Paris.

The crucial event of the latter part of her life was her conversion to Roman Catholicism. Paradoxically, perhaps, it was to Rodin, with whom her relationship had modified rather than changed, that she almost certainly owed her initial attraction. For he regularly attended Mass at Notre Dame, as did she, originally in the hope of catching sight of him. But she eventually became a devout, though never uncritical, daughter of the Church.

The combination of her feelings for Rodin, and for the Church, involved the beginning of her religious life in circumstances of extraordinary difficulty, but the courage and clear-sightedness with which she faced them made her will, already of exceptional strength, a formidable instrument. But the process was one of prolonged, unmitigated anguish. 'A beautiful life,' she wrote, 'is one led, perhaps, in the shadow, but ordered, regular, harmonious.'

The strength of her character is shown by the fact that neither of the scorching yet exalting experiences she underwent appear either to have hastened, or retarded, the serene progress of her art. It did indeed evolve; in its unhurried fashion, undergoing marked changes. In her early paintings she used glazes or else thin fluid paint, making gradual and delicate changes until the picture realised her vision of her subject. In her later work her procedure was radically different: she used thick paint, rarely touched her canvas more than once in the same place, preferring, in the event of failure, to begin again. She gradually ceased to use dark, almost black, shadows; as her tones became lighter and closer, her austerely simplified forms became simpler still. Her later works are marked by a heightened intensity and colour even more delicate. But no matter on how small a scale she worked – often it was tiny – this produced nevertheless an effect of grandeur. The wisdom she gained from her terrible poverty, and her emotional and spiritual ordeals, became even more firmly embodied in her art. In the chapter devoted to her in my book a sentence concludes: '. . . apart from her brother's eulogy [in the catalogue of her Memorial exhibition at the Matthiesen Gallery in 1948] and a discerning article by Wyndham Lewis [in *The Listener*], her work has received no serious consideration whatever; indeed it can scarcely be said to have been noticed at all.'

This exhibition did in fact establish her public reputation, though far from the extent it merits. I am confident that it will be radically enhanced by the present book, and that Gwen John will be recognised, as she so amply deserves, as a major British artist of her time.

JOHN ROTHENSTEIN

ACKNOWLEDGMENTS

At the outset I must record my indebtedness to the John family, in particular to Ben and Sara John, Gwen John's residual legatees, and to Romilly John and Mme Pol. Michael Holroyd, biographer of Augustus, gave me invaluable help, while Sir John Rothenstein shared the fruits of his research on Gwen John.

Also of great value to me were those who knew Gwen John or were members of her circle. Among these I am especially grateful to Mr Tom Burns, Mr Tristan de Vere Cole, Mrs Nicolette Devas, Mme Antoinette Grunelius, Miss Kathleen Hale, Lady Pansy Lamb and Mrs Vivien White.

In particular I was glad of the opportunity to talk to four Breton women who sat to Gwen John as children. They are Mme Basset (Simone Litalien), Mme Cardin (Odette Litalien), Mme Ferrec (Marie Hamonet) and Mme Lesage (Lucille Lejeune).

Others who gave generously of their time were: Miss Djuna Barnes, Mr Anthony d'Offay, M. and Mme Jean-Pierre Faye, David Fraser-Jenkins, Miss Germaine Greer, Miss Cecily Langdale and Mme Monique Laurent.

Of the multitude who gave help in different ways I can name but a few here. Professor and Mrs Gerald Aylmer, Professor Quentin Bell, Miss Mary Chamot, Miss Cordelia Chitty, Mr Michael Compton, the Mayor of Dieppe, Mr Julian Freeman, Mr Kenneth Garlick, M. Blaise Gautier, Mr Mark Glazebrook, Mr Rudolph Glossop, Sir Thomas Hopkinson, Miss Anita Leslie, Mrs Stephanie Maison, Miss Magda Polivanov, Admiral and Mrs Sinclair, Professor and Mrs Trotman-Dickenson.

I was particularly glad of the help of the following from Gwen John's native Pembrokeshire: Wing Commander J. R. Pike (postmaster at Amroth), Mr Powell (formerly of Lloyds Bank, Haverfordwest), Mrs Robins (proprietress of the Victoria Hotel, Tenby), and Mr and Mrs Thorne (of Begelly House).

The following institutions have also provided assistance: the Anthony d'Offay Gallery, the Ashmolean Museum, the Brighton Polytechnic, the Bristol Museum and Art Gallery, the B.B.C., the British Museum, the Centre Pompidou, Davis and Long Company, the Fitzwilliam Museum, the Houghton Library, the Leeds City Art Galleries, the London Library, the Musée Hébert, the Musée Rodin, the National Library of Wales, the National Museum of Wales, the National Portrait Gallery, the Pembrokeshire Countryside Museum, the Philadelphia Museum, the Sheffield City Art Galleries, the Slade School of Art, the Southampton City Art Galleries, the Tate Gallery, University College London, the Victoria and Albert Museum.

Finally I must thank my husband, Thomas, who did all he could for the book, short of writing it, and my typist and friend Miss Phyllis Jones, who knew the times of which I write, and some of the people, better than I. Miss Emma Glossop contributed the index.

I acknowledge financial assistance from the Arts Council of Great Britain.

CONTENTS

ILLUSTRATIONS

INTRODUCTION

I have treasured a postcard reproduction of the Gwen John self-portrait since I came across it as an undergraduate doing research on a quite different subject at the Tate. But I became really interested in the work of Augustus John's 'mysterious sister in Paris' in the early sixties. I was spending an evening with friends at an eighteenth-century château in Alsace, and over coffee my host asked me if I had heard of a painter called Gwen John. Naturally I told him that she was considered of great importance in England. He then brought out a portfolio containing no less than one hundred Gwen John watercolours, gouaches and drawings. For the next hour we turned over portraits of children and cats and the back views of nuns in church, all conveyed with the same reserved intensity that I had admired in the Tate self-portrait.

I was eager to know how my host had come to possess such a treasure. He explained that Gwen John had given the drawings to Véra Oumançoff, the sister-in-law of Jacques Maritain, the Catholic philosopher. When Véra died she had left the pictures to Maritain who had spent his long last years with my friends. 'The funny thing is', said my host, 'Jacques had no idea who they were by. There was a nun he knew who did little drawings, Christine van de Meer. He thought they might be by her.' Then a friend told Maritain they were by Gwen John, but he still had no idea she was a painter of importance.

The pictures had been no more valued during Véra Oumançoff's lifetime. In middle-age Gwen John, a close neighbour of Véra at Meudon, became deeply attached to her. When Véra could no longer stand Gwen John's attentions she rationed her visits to one a week on Mondays. After Mass Gwen John would walk home with Véra, carrying a little offering in the form of a watercolour, a gouache or a drawing. This Véra would toss into a cupboard at the end of the interview, no doubt with a sigh of exasperation. Thus was a fortune amassed.

The day after my visit to the château the pictures were removed to a safe in Strasbourg and, on my suggestion, advice was sought of Sir John Rothenstein, at that time director of the Tate. He suggested selling them a few at a time through Sotheby. The results of the sale of the first batch in 1968 caused widespread astonishment. A small gouache of a girl in church, for example (no. 244), for which £120 was expected, went for £2,000. The prices continue to rise and there are now fake Gwen Johns on the market, a certain sign of success.

Though several authoritative introductions to catalogues of Gwen John exhibitions have appeared over the years, notably by Mary Taubman, and although Sir John Rothenstein included a well-researched chapter on her in his *Modern English Painters* published in 1952, there has been no full-scale biography. Gwen John's obscurity is entirely of her own making. She did not want to be noticed. She lived quietly in Paris. Her pictures were small and few, almost always unsigned.[1] (Some can only be dated by the colour of the cats in them.) Until recently she was often left out of surveys of twentieth-century art. Even *The Penguin Dictionary of Art and Artists* (1959) only lists her as an appendix to Augustus (an insult not meted out to the sons of Pieter Bruegel). But times are changing. Rothenstein from the beginning insisted that Gwen was a better painter than Augustus. Augustus, to his credit, was of the same opinion. 'Fifty years hence', he said in 1946, 'I shall be remembered only as the brother of Gwen John.' There have been flattering references to her in several recent books, some of them lengthy, all of them, oddly enough, by women,[2] Germaine Greer in particular has championed each of her canvases as 'a sharp point of concentrated feeling'. Fourteen of Gwen John's pictures are now at the Tate and she is represented at many provincial galleries, including Sheffield, Leeds and Southampton. The largest collection, appropriately enough, is at the National Museum of Wales, in Cardiff. Apart from the paintings on display, one thousand of the drawings are in store there. In 1946 the Arts Council gathered two hundred of her works at the Matthiesen Gallery. Edwin John, her nephew, found most of these rotting in the garden shed she used for a studio when he went to France at the end of the war. There was another big exhibition at the Arts Council Gallery in 1968. Private galleries like Faerber and Maison and Anthony d'Offay also had shows. In New York, Davis and Long put on a major exhibition in 1975, appropriately enough since there are as many works by Gwen John in the United States as there are in Great Britain, if not more. This is because John Quinn, a New York lawyer, was Gwen John's chief patron. Cecily Langdale, co-director of Davis and Long, has written two masterly introductions to Gwen John catalogues, drawing on her knowledge of the American section of Gwen John's work. She is now composing a *catalogue raisonné*.

[1] A studio stamp of her signature was put on the drawings that appeared in the 1946 Exhibition.

[2] *Women Artists* by Karen Petersen and J. J. Wilson; *The Obstacle Race* by Germaine Greer; *The Camden Group* by Wendy Baron; and *Paula Modersohn-Becker* by Gillian Perry.

Although Gwen John was a contemporary of the *Fauves* and the *Cubistes* her work was essentially figurative. The mastery of anatomical drawing and the subtle use of colour that she retained until the end of her working life were the gifts of her earliest masters, Tonks and Whistler. It is perhaps surprising that no one of her group at the Slade should have produced anything that was experimental let alone abstract. Mary Taubman, the doyenne of Gwen John studies, makes the same point in her introduction to the Arts Council exhibition catalogue of 1968: 'Beside the Nabis at the Académie Julian a decade before, Augustus John and his circle at the Slade, enjoying a similar climate of confidence and enthusiasm engendered by so much mutual stimulus and support, may seem in comparison to have profited little by it in order to experiment and explore.' This failure to explore may have been because Roger Fry did not mount his revolutionary Post-Impressionist exhibition till 1910, when the members of the Slade group were already in their thirties.

Yet Gwen John's later work was sufficiently affected by the Fry revolution for two examples of it to be included in the Post-Impressionist exhibition at the Royal Academy in 1980. Between 1915 and 1925 (her most productive decade) the forms of sitters became increasingly simplified and pyramidal and detail vanished from their backgrounds. Some of the later gouaches of children showed a sense of line and simplicity learned from the Japanese prints she so much admired.

Gwen John was chiefly a painter of women. Other subjects were severely limited. She never painted a commissioned portrait or a portrait of a man. She often drew children and cats. Her only groups were of the backs of people in church and for landscapes she hardly went beyond the street corner and preferred the view from her studio window or the vase of flowers on the sill. She often portrayed the inside of her room.

The effect of a walk round a gallery of Gwen Johns is strangely calming. At Gwen John's 1926 exhibition, (the only one held during her lifetime), Sir William Rothenstein praised 'those cool nuns' who have found 'the wisdom of quietness and peace'. Fifty years later David Fraser-Jenkins, in the catalogue of the Cardiff exhibition of 1976, spoke of 'the sitters who never smile and rarely look directly at the artist . . . reflecting in their expressions their reactions to the artist's attitude towards them.' These entranced women had the same power over Sir John Rothenstein as they had over his father. It was he who first took up the cause of their creator and still insists that she is 'one of the finest painters of our time and country.'

Why is it then that there is still no book entirely devoted to Gwen John? Several have in fact been planned since the war but have never seen the light of day. Rothenstein himself was anxious to write one but was warned off by Augustus who planned to do the job. Edwin John, son of Augustus and heir to Gwen, remained anxious to see a biography of his aunt until his dying day. Sources, however, were hard to come by.

It was my admission to Gwen John's two thousand love letters to Rodin that made the book possible. These are written in French and are housed at the Musée Rodin in Paris. Perhaps one day they will be published. Also of great interest were the letters to John Quinn in the New York Public Library and the letters to a fellow artist, Ursula Tyrwhitt at the National Library of Wales in Aberystwyth.

From these various sources there emerges a portrait of a committed artist, a passionate woman and a self-denying mystic of extraordinary fascination. What biographer would not welcome a subject who, besides being a great painter, had a ten-year love affair with Rodin, became emotionally involved with several distinguished women, wrestled throughout her life with a famous brother and finally, in her desire to achieve sainthood, neglected herself and died a few days before the outbreak of the Second World War, after being picked up unconscious on the streets of Dieppe.

I

Haverfordwest

1876–84

When Gwen John heard the news of her mother's death she rushed madly round the house yelling, 'Mama's dead!' pursued by her younger brother Augustus, her older brother Thornton and her younger sister Winifred, who all took up the cry. She was eight years old at the time and the year was 1884.[1]

This heartless behaviour was due to the fact that Augusta John was a stranger to her children. For several years she had suffered from a mysterious disease which her doctors, almost certainly inaccurately, described as rheumatism. In search of a cure she travelled from spa to spa, only returning home for brief intervals.

Although the tumultuous Johns might rejoice in the death of a stranger, it was to have serious repercussions for all of them. Augusta had been a lively and generous woman. She was an accomplished artist, as is proved by her watercolours, one of which to this day hangs in an American art gallery, erroneously attributed to Augustus. The poet and art critic Arthur Symons admired others which hung in the family home. Augusta encouraged her children to draw, and a good drawing of a dog by Thornton survives. She was also a pianist. All these benign influences were withdrawn with her death. Her husband Edwin was by comparison aloof, concerned chiefly about keeping up appearances and covering up facts about his family.

The first of these facts was that he was descended from humble natives of Haverfordwest in Pembrokeshire, where he lived. Haverfordwest was in fact a town to be proud of. Situated at the head of the estuary on which Milford Haven stands, a meeting place of trade routes from time immemorial, it boasted a castle, several churches, a market place and

---

[1] Thornton was born on 10 May 1875, Gwendolen Mary on 22 June 1876, Augustus on 4 January 1878, and Winifred on 3 November 1879.

English-speaking pretensions. Nevertheless, Edwin was deeply ashamed of his connection with it, and there was a skeleton in the John family cupboard. Edwin's father was not only born of Welsh-speaking labourer stock but he was probably conceived out of wedlock. Augustus John's biographer, Michael Holroyd, has discovered evidence to prove that he was born between April 1818 and April 1819. But a search of the parish records of St Mary's, Haverfordwest, between these dates reveals no William John with a father bearing the surname John. The register does, however, record a boy called William born on 25 November 1818 to Anne John, single woman. It was perhaps for this reason that Edwin never told his children about their grandparents, merely informing them that they were descended from 'a long line of solicitors'.

For William John, for all his unpropitious origins, brought the family into the professional classes and founded the family fortune. Although he and his wife, Mary Davies, a seamstress, started their married life in a humble cottage in Chapel Street, they rose by degrees through Prendergast Place and Gloucester Terrace until they reached the summit of social ambition at 7 Victoria Place. The ladder by which William John rose slowly, a rung at a time, was the law. After many years as an attorney's clerk he was admitted as a solicitor and in 1854 started his own practice in Quay Street.

By the time he died William John had become a respected figure in Haverfordwest. For several years he had served as town clerk, he was agent to Lord Kensington, and he made stirring speeches in Welsh at Quarter Sessions. He also had an appreciation of the fine arts. He somehow found the time to travel through Italy collecting copies of Old Masters and imitation majolica. He also had a collection of books which included leather-bound editions of Scott, Dickens and Smollett, and a copy of the *Inferno* with the Doré illustrations.

Augusta John's antecedents were rather similar to her husband's. Her father, Thomas Smith of Brighton, also came from a working-class home. He followed in his father's footsteps as a plumber but rose to become master plumber, glazier and painter employing ten men and three boys. He was a cheerful plump man and much respected in Brighton. When he died he left £187,000, and half the shutters in the town went up.

No. 7 Victoria Place[2] was one of a row of terrace houses erected in 1839 to commemorate a new toll bridge over the River Cleddau. It was tall and narrow with an elaborate tiled passageway to take the place of a front hall. The house is now part of Lloyds Bank. The manager is a friendly

[2] Michael Holroyd points out that Haverfordwest Council have wrongly affixed a commemorative plaque to No. 5. They have also omitted Gwen John on the plaque.

man who will show the occasional visitor round the empty rooms which were once the family home.

Augustus recalled market day at Haverfordwest in the first part of his autobiography, *Chiaroscuro*.

The streets and squares were full of life and movement. Noise too, with the continual lowing of the cattle, the screaming of pigs and the loud vociferation of the drovers. Among the crowd were to be seen the women of Langum, in their distinctive and admirable costume, carrying creels of the famous oysters on their backs. Tramps, looking like the peripatetic philosophers of the school of Diogenes, would congregate idly at street corners. Gypsies arrived on the scene with their horses and light carts. Aloof, arrogant, and in their ragged finery somehow superior to the common run of natives, they could be recognised a mile off.

Gwen John has left no record of her childhood and once claimed in a letter to Rodin that nothing of importance happened to her before she was twenty-seven. She was born in 1876, when Thornton was one, but almost certainly her earliest memory was the birth of Augustus when she was two. Typically enough, Augustus caused the maximum amount of disturbance by being born in Tenby. The whole family removed to a superior lodging house there for several months to avoid an outbreak of scarlet fever at Haverfordwest. A year after their return Winifred was born.

It was after the birth of Winifred, her fourth child in five years, that Augusta John's bouts of illness became more disabling. From the age of three Gwen John was virtually motherless. Instead she had Mimi, her much-loved nurse. Mimi was a dark, handsome Welsh woman from the Presely Mountains in North Pembrokeshire. On occasion she had been allowed to take the children home with her. Augustus has described the cottage where the woodmen wore pointed clogs with brass toe-caps. 'We sat on our stools with our bowls of cawl and listened in wonder to the clatter of the clogs on the stone flags and the unceasing *bavardage* of our Welsh friends, few of whom knew a word of English.' A photograph of the children taken when Gwen John was five shows them grouped round Mimi who holds the two-year-old Winifred on her lap. Thornton, now seven, is in a Norfolk jacket and sits in a low basket chair. Augustus wears a sailor suit and Gwen John an elaborate Victorian dress with rows of dark satin trimming. There is a remarkable resemblance between the chinless yet determined faces and protruding ears of Augustus and Gwen.

After the death of their mother, the upbringing of the John children was entrusted to two of her sisters, the formidable Misses Leah and Rosina Smith. Aunt Leah was the cheerful one while Aunt Rosina, who had a ferret-like face, was lugubrious and suffered from indigestion. As her health varied she tried out different diets and different sects, including the Countess of Huntingdon's Connection and the Society of Friends. On two points, however, the aunts were united: their horror of Roman Catholicism (because of its emphasis on the cult of the Blessed Virgin) and their devotion to General Booth. They both held high rank in the Salvation Army.

The first act of the aunts was to dismiss Mimi, who was accused of allowing the children to become too fond of her. In her place they introduced morning prayers which both the children and the servants were expected to attend. At these sessions, besides leading the praying and the hymn singing, the aunts read aloud from such improving tracts for the working-class as 'Christy's Old Organ', 'Jessica's First Prayer' and 'The Lamplighter'. The children were already in the habit of going to church on Sundays, usually with their father to a church in Wales establishment, but occasionally with Mimi to a Bethel, a Sion or a Bethesda where the fervour of the singing and the preaching 'mightily impressed' them.

Edwin John, a solicitor like his father, like him practised his profession at Quay Street. This could be reached by a narrow alley leading from the back garden of No. 7. He walked this way to work every day. At weekends he took his children for long walks in the country. They followed strung out behind him like a row of ducklings as he strode ahead in silence. In his autobiography Augustus described the three favourite walks in surprising detail considering he was only six when he left Haverfordwest. The first followed the River Cleddau, which ran through the town and out to tidal flats from which the Norman castle above the town rose imposingly. Occasionally a train would apparently issue from an ivy-clad ruin, rumble steamily across the middle distance and vanish as suddenly into a hole in the hill with a despairing wail. The second walk led to a water-mill with a turning wheel. Here the children loved to see the miller, covered in flour from head to foot. Beyond the mill was a colonnade of tall trees where, in spring, it was the unvarying custom of Edwin to stoop and pick the primroses that were to be his daughter's favourite flower. The third walk took the little party up on to the bluff above the Cleddau where the girls of the workhouse, dressed in blue, took their exercise. The steep pathway back to the town passed a cottage which was inhabited by a witch.

Edwin, to his credit, made delightful summer holidays possible for his children by building a large stone house at Broad Haven, a cove on beautiful St Brides Bay, seven miles west of Haverfordwest. The house was named Rorke's Drift after the Zulu war defence (the name was later corrupted to Rock's Drift by a lawyer ignorant of military history). It was separated from the sea by a lawn and a brook. The only other building of note in the little settlement of fishermen was, and still is, a rather pretentious lodge which had been erected by a local benefactor who was later to supply the village with cholera-free water.

Broad Haven had a great advantage: it provided the aunts with a rich harvest of souls to save, and they swept the country in a wicker pony-chaise known locally as the 'Hallelujah Chariot'. Free from their super-vision, the three older ones ran wild. Even the drive to Broad Haven was thrilling. '. . . but our excitement reached its climax when the sea was first caught sight of over the flower-starred hedges. Once arrived, we lost no time in discarding shoes and stockings and raced past the *liac*, or brook, down to the sea.' So records Augustus who later drew this subject.

The world of Broad Haven went beyond the sea and the sand. There were also the cliffs and the beautiful hinterland, where a ray of sunlight sandwiched between the grey sky and the grey land of a distant prospect can still produce magical effects. Another easily available entertainment was watching baptism by total immersion in the *liac*. 'The Minister, up to his waist in water, would dip the neophytes, one by one like sheep, to the accompaniment of singing by the congregation on the banks. The girls with their skimpy black frocks, saturated and clinging, emerged like naiads from the ordeal.' Both Gwen and Augustus probably had their first revelation of the beauty of the female form on these occasions. Augustus later drew the subject.[3] Sometimes a landscape artist would set up his easel at Broad Haven and, filled with eager curiosity, brother and sister would approach as close as they dared to watch 'the mystery of painting'.

The Johns were not entirely without the companionship of children of their own class at Broad Haven. The handsome and haughty family of Georges used to come down to the beach and Teresa George was equally admired by Gwen, Augustus and their father. Edwin in fact, years later, sought her hand in marriage (without success). Even wet days at Broad Haven could be agreeable, for the kitchen was open to the children, who would crouch in a 'skew' by the kitchen fire and listen to the lively gossip of the servants. Here, too, the work of salvation went on. If a drunken man strayed in, the women would sing hymns to him and even dance 'until the wretch would at last subside in tears of sweet contrition'.

The last holiday at Broad Haven, in the summer that Gwen John was eight, was a sad one. William John died there on 6 July, of a disease

---

[3] Reproduced in *Augustus John: Drawings* by Lillian Browse, 1941.

known popularly as water on the brain. The distinguished old man had been living with the family for some time and growing increasingly senile. Now the children were led in to his room to see his corpse. Later they stood by his grave on a hill outside Haverfordwest. Few other members of the family joined them at the graveside, for there was a strong suspicion that Edwin had persuaded his father to all but cut out his oldest son Alfred, his youngest son Frederick and his daughter Clare from his will. It is true that Gwen John's youngest uncle, Frederick, who had lived with them at Victoria Place as a youth, had probably served a prison sentence and was eventually to die abroad. But her aunt Clare's only fault had been to marry a man who could support her. Alfred was a harmless eccentric much loved by the children. He was the black sheep of the family and, to avoid the law office in Quay Street, had run away to Paris to play the flute first in an orchestra and then in bed. He had haggard good looks and a charming sense of humour and came to fulfil the children's idea of a perfect gentleman in spite of his poverty, an idea that he encouraged by changing his name to St John.[4] In later years, when visiting Augustus on a hot day, he accidentally revealed that underneath his mackintosh he wore no clothes at all. Alfred, Clare and Frederick received only small annual payments under their father's will. Edwin now inherited the lion's share of his father's fortune.

Then came the dreadful news that Augusta had died suddenly among strangers, at Ferney Bottom, Hartington in Derbyshire. The cause of death, according to the death certificate, was rheumatic gout and exhaustion. She was thirty-five years old.

---

[4] It is under this name that he was buried at St David's Cathedral.

2

Tenby

1884–95

Edwin was deeply distressed by his wife's death and also embarrassed by it. People stopped him after church and pointed to the five-year-old Winifred. 'Is this the poor little motherless child?' they said. 'She does not know yet how terrible it is – *but she will later.*' Edwin decided to give up his practice at Haverfordwest, sell the house at Broad Haven, dismiss the aunts[1] and, taking with him only the two servants and the children, move to Tenby.

Tenby at that time was a fashionable resort where bathing machines, fancy goods emporiums and carriages supplied the needs of the English gentry on holiday. It boasted two long crescent-shaped beaches, North Sands and South Sands, intercepted by Castle Point and the harbour. Above Castle Hill, with its statue of Prince Albert, stood the church of St Mary's in a picturesque Tudor square. The other main feature of the town was the vast central fortress.

Victoria House was situated in a wide street of terraced houses running down to the esplanade at South Sands. Augustus remembered the house as dark and poky.

'It was like a cage . . . furnished without taste or imagination, its dull and uniform mahogany tables and chairs, its heavy shelves of law tomes and devotional works, its appalling conglomeration of unauthentic Italian pottery, pseudo-ivory elephants and fake Old Masters . . . contributed to the atmosphere of mediocrity and gloom. I felt at last that I was living in a kind of mortuary where everything was dead, like the stuffed doves in their glass dome in the drawing-room . . . This

---

[1] Both aunts later continued their work of conversion in America. Leah picked up an American accent and a band of marching disciples. Rosina married a druggist called Owen P. Bott in Nevada and, as an old lady, frightened Winifred's children with her steady grey eyes and humpback.

museum of rubbish, changing only in the imperceptible process of its decay, reflected the frozen immobility of its curator's mind.'[2]

Thornton, Gwen, Augustus and Winifred inhabited the two attics at the top of the house. From the mansard window of one the statue of Prince Albert on Castle Hill was visible 'as fresh as the day it came from the factory'. In winter these attics were bitterly cold and the children would pile not only the rugs and overcoats on their beds but even furniture. Winifred recalled years later the weary journey downstairs from these attics to breakfast.

The dining-room also was a singularly unprepossessing room. It stood on the right of the front door. The bow-windows were heavily curtained, the paint was black and much of the space taken up by a massive mahogany sideboard and a heavy dining-room table. The 'fleshless and abominable' skeleton clock, which Augustus particularly hated, ticked the weary seconds away on the mantelpiece. Nasty meals were eaten in that room under the supervision of Edwin. Gwen John was difficult about food and particularly hated rice pudding. She was forced to eat a great deal. Winifred, equally unwilling, was forced to swallow the bread and butter pudding provided for her because she was not strong. She was convinced the currants were dead flies. Conversation was not encouraged. Once, when Winifred hazarded some whispered remark, Edwin turned on her and asked, 'So you've found it at last, have you?'

'Found what?'

'Your tongue.'

After which silence was re-established.

It was now that Gwen and Winifred learned to speak by signs. This method of communication, however, was forbidden at table because the faces they made were so hideous. Instead they would go upstairs before each meal and rehearse suitable conversations to be held with their father. Winifred would make a suggestion and Gwen would say, 'No, I want to say that.' 'I thought of it first,' Winifred would reply. Gwen would conclude the argument by pointing out, 'Well, I'm the eldest.' When old William John had lived with the family at Haverfordwest he had found this silence well-nigh intolerable. 'Talk!' he used to say. 'If you can't think of anything to say, tell a lie.'

In the evenings Edwin used to read to his young children. He made an unusual choice of books for a group ranging in age from nine to five. There were *Jane Eyre* and *The Arabian Nights*, which were fair enough, but there were also the complete works of the obscure Belgian writer

[2] *Chiaroscuro* by Augustus John. Victoria House is now the Victoria Hotel, a remarkably light and cheerful place.

Henri Conscience in the original French, and Madame Blavatsky's *Isis Unveiled*. Helena Petrovna Blavatsky had founded the Theosophical Society in the year before Gwen John was born. Her 1,200-page book subtitled *A Master Key to the Mysteries of Ancient and Modern Science and Theology*, was a massive welter of theories cribbed from Eastern mystics and Western scientists and men of letters. Buddha rubbed shoulders with Faraday, and Comte with Bulwer-Lytton. Most were unacknowledged, only partially understood and imperfectly transmitted. It is hard to imagine what an eight-year-old girl can have made of it all.

The children seem to have had strangely little supervision at Tenby. No governess was hired to take the place of the aunts. Presumably Edwin, retired at thirty-seven, regarded himself as a substitute. However, they preferred the company of the two cheerful servants in the basement, the same two that had sung hymns in the kitchen at Broad Haven. Augustus and Gwen spent much time up in the attic drawing and painting.

Gwen John's education began three years after that of the average child. There is no mention of any instruction being supplied at Haverfordwest, although presumably someone must have taught her to write after a fashion: she never did it in any other way, and her spelling in later life must be ascribed to early neglect. When her education did start it was so sketchy as to be almost invisible. Edwin decided that the two girls should be sent to what he referred to as a private school a few yards away in Victoria Street. This school consisted of three pupils, the mother of the third one (a German lady married to a philosopher named Mackenzie) acting as teacher. The arrangement combined for Edwin the advantages of cheapness with social prestige. He could now claim for his daughters a foreign governess whom he always described as Swiss.

Mrs Mackenzie was a kind and homely woman who, to a limited extent, and more especially for Winifred, took the place of a mother. Her daughter Irene, who was younger than Gwen, became a particular friend of Winifred's and they were to correspond for the rest of their lives. The two of them laughed so much together that if one caught sight of the other even on the horizon she would be convulsed with giggles. Gwen, at this time, was considered to have faulty deportment. On doctor's advice she did her lessons stretched on her back on the schoolroom floor. The two younger girls insisted on joining her there.

The warm-hearted Mrs Mackenzie soon became a friend to all the repressed John children. She lived with her husband and her own children in a large house at Manorbier, a village west of Tenby on the coast. To most people Manorbier is famous for its great half-ruined castle. To the Johns it was the place where they could run wild during school holidays.

After a year or two the girls transferred to Miss Wilson's academy, a school that placed more emphasis on conduct than on scholarship. Miss Wilson had none of the motherly warmth of Mrs Mackenzie. She had a grim expression, and later committed suicide by striding into the sea. On one occasion she took Gwen, Winifred and some of their school friends on an excursion by wagonette to Manorbier Castle and on the way home they agreed to give three cheers for her. 'Hip, hip . . .' they began, as Miss Wilson stood stonily facing them, but half way through the cheer dried out into a series of frantic whispers.

'Why didn't you go on?'

'I was waiting for *you*.'

French was not on the curriculum at Miss Wilson's and Edwin, who spoke French adequately and read it better, arranged lessons outside school. Gwen and Winifred were for a time taught by a governess who was delighted by their progress and told their father it must be due to some French ancestry. This intended compliment so shocked Edwin that he discontinued the lessons and substituted in their place instruction (presumably from Mrs Mackenzie) in German grammar, a language which Winifred was to hate for the rest of her life. Gwen John never betrayed any knowledge of the language either.

It was probably at this time that Winifred started to take violin lessons. She had inherited a marked musical talent from both parents and was later to become a concert performer in Canada.[3] Gwen never showed the slightest interest in music.

By the time Gwen John was fifteen her education had virtually ceased. She had learned to read and write and she had mastered some arithmetic and some French. She had had some rather odd books read to her and had presumably read some more herself. And she had learnt a great deal about conduct, both from Edwin and Miss Wilson. She was, whether she liked it or not (and she didn't like it) a lady. She was so much a lady that for the rest of her life she would not go into the street without first putting on a hat, or fail to acknowledge the smallest favour with a thank-you letter. Winifred shared this primness. There was the famous occasion when she wrote to Irene Mackenzie in 1917 about the birth of one of her children. She used a code because she felt the subject was indelicate and as a result Irene (who was, of course, half German) was arrested by Scotland Yard for suspected collaboration with the enemy.

Yet beneath this ladylike exterior lurked twin passions for Art and Nature. Gwen had drawn ever since her mother first encouraged her.

---

[3] These gifts were handed down to the next generation. Her daughter, Mrs Matthews, is a cellist. Two of Augustus's sons were also musical. David was a professional oboist, Edwin an amateur flautist.

After Augusta died she and Augustus remained passionately addicted to drawing and painting. 'Wherever they went,' wrote her father in later years, 'their sketch-books went with them. In their walks along the beach, in excursions into the country, they sketched little scenes, people, animals . . . When they were a little older I sometimes used to take them to the theatre in London . . . even here the inevitable sketch-books turned up . . . Then in the few minutes' interval between acts they worked feverishly to draw some person who had interested them.'

As she grew older Gwen began to seek subjects in the countryside beyond Tenby. She and Winifred had bicycles and were allowed an unusual amount of freedom. The two girls formed a contrasted couple, for Gwen, the tall slim one, was dark and Winifred, who was shorter and plumper, had fair curls down her back. Both were intensely shy, but whereas Winifred was gentle and timid, with a self-deprecating sense of humour, Gwen's unobtrusiveness contained a far more intractable nature. Together they used to go for long bicycle rides along the Pembrokeshire lanes, climbing on to the stone walls whenever they met a flock of sheep, blushing furiously when a column of marching soldiers from Penally barracks divided ranks to allow them to pass through.

If Tenby was a prim and restricted little society, the wilderness was not far away. Scenery as beautiful and impressive as any in Europe can still be seen from the coast path. The Johns lived on the southern boundary of the town and almost at their doorstep were the bushy dunes known as the Burrows where Augustus as a boy first led his tribe of Comanches and later conducted experiments with his sister's friends and his friends' sisters. At the far end of South Sands was Giltar Point, a magnificent headland from the extremity of which Caldy Island floated like a cloud and the headlands of Lydstep and Manorbier stretched away to the right.

The unique Tenby daffodils grew here profusely in those days.[4] They were about the same size as the conventional wild daffodil but their trumpets pointed upwards. An expedition to collect them in early March must have been an annual necessity for Gwen John who had already begun her lifelong affair with flowers. She even dreamt of flowers at night and in winter, when there were none to be picked, would spend her halfpenny pocket money on a few precious blossoms.

The sea was Gwen's other great passion in Nature. The tame bathing below the promenade would no longer satisfy her. Now she sought wild and lonely beaches like Lydstep, with its palisade of cliffs[5] and its smugglers' cave with the blow hole that sent a plume of spray into the field

[4] Half a million bulbs were sent to London in the winter of 1895-6.
[5] These cliffs are now topped by a 'superior model-caravan holiday area', to the eternal shame of the Council.

above. Here she could bathe naked off the rocks and swim far out to sea, excited by the fear that she might not be able to get back. Augustus too liked to get his clothes off but not always in such suitable places. Sometimes, when walking along the beach in a school crocodile he would suddenly fling off his clothes and cavort before his school master, naked and noisy. It was the custom to ignore young John on these occasions.[6]

Gwen and Winifred went inland in search of flowers. A circular walk, which must have been a favourite, started near home at the village of Penally in its wooded valley where bluebell carpets were laid every spring. Above the woods was the ancient Ridgeway with the Atlantic on one side and the distant Prescelly Mountains on the other. In spring the verges of the Ridgeway were starred with bluebells, pink campion, primroses, purple orchids and rare white violets. Later came foxgloves, cow-parsley, meadowsweet, oxeye daisies and red sorrel. On the way back they passed Hoyle's Mouth Cave, hidden, as now, in beech woods and looking out over the marshes of the St Florence River. Augustus left enthusiastic accounts of the place as 'a narrow deep and devious cave, its walls polished by the shoulders of ancient hunters who had left their arrowheads and bones for us to dig up'. The children found that leading out of this cave there were others which they could only reach by crawling along a very low passage with a lighted candle. The main cavern was nearly one hundred and fifty feet in length. It must have been a relief to see the sunshine once more on the yellow flags and kingcups of the marsh.

There was another country house, beside the Mackenzies' at Manorbier, where the children were welcome. The Morgans at Begelly House often had them to stay. Begelly House stands half way up the village street at Begelly, five miles north of Tenby. It overlooks King's Moor, a small common where gypsies used to camp with their cattle and geese and still do. The house has rather the air of a tall stone town mansion with a steep flight of steps going up to the front door. It is approached by a steep circular drive which encloses a planting of exotic shrubs and palms. Here the rules and repressions of Tenby were forgotten, and the silent children of Victoria Street were transformed into a turbulent troupe of Johns.

At the time that Gwen John left school Augustus, now thirteen, was sent away, somewhat belatedly, to a prep school at Clifton near Bristol where he wore an Eton jacket, was partially deafened by a blow on the ear from a cricket ball but won a fair proportion of his fights. Often he came home at the end of term in a dangerous frame of mind. His first duty then was to set upon Gwen, rolling her on the ground and accusing

6 Paul Ableman covers this phenomenon in his book on nudism.

her of being an ignorant half-wit who would never be any good at anything. Gwen John had nightmares about these homecomings of her younger brother for the rest of her life.

Augustus was not sent away to public school. He went to a very small day school called St Catherine's in a neighbouring street, where he gave the boys to understand that he was descended from Owain Glyndwr. One of the masters (who, like Miss Wilson, later committed suicide) encouraged these fantasies by comparing him to a Welsh colossus astride Caldy Island and Lydstep Point.

When Augustus left school he showed no particular inclination to do anything, although the army and distant places (preferably very distant) were considered. He still drew all the time, but few steps had been taken to develop this talent. At St Catherine's he had won a Master Stumpers Certificate, third-class. Stumping consists of portraying cubes and spheres with a paper cone rubbed in pencil dust. Now he asked to fill in time at the local art school, run by Edward J. Head, R.A., whose pictures Edwin admired annually on his expedition to the Royal Academy Exhibition.

Gwen John's reaction to this piece of favouritism can only be imagined. She had not even been given a course in stumping. Nor was she in a position to accompany Augustus to the secluded bathing place on the north shore where young Father Bull encouraged him to make life studies of attractive young men. By way of consolation she turned the back attic into a studio and took models up there to draw. According to Augustus,

My sister was always coming across beautiful children to draw and adore. Jimmy was a boy of about twelve when we met him. He wore auburn corkscrew curls down to his shoulders, and his costume was of old grey velvet. His face was rather pale and beautiful. Jimmy stood on the sands at Tenby, where he made fairy structures of coloured paper, which he would cleverly snip and manipulate into changing forms, each more surprising than the last. Everybody applauded the sweet boy with his candid smiling eyes, and pennies were produced in quantities: these his mother collected. Soon we made friends with Jimmy, and invited him to our house to be drawn and painted. His mother would come too. Our father didn't approve of these strollers but, as usual, had to give way before our insistence. Our studio was an attic under the roof. Here we worked with Jimmy and only wished his mother wouldn't come. Perhaps she wasn't his mother, for there was no earthly resemblance between the two.

Few examples of Gwen John's work at this time have survived apart from sixteen rapid pencil sketches made at a concert for two violins and piano. One of these portrays a woman violinist, presumably Winifred, elaborately dressed in full sleeves and a full skirt, her hair piled high on her head.[7] The drawing is lively but superficial. The figure lacks the anatomical accuracy that training gave to later ones. An oil painting of a woman and child walking on the sand by Tenby harbour made at the same time is a more finished work. The figures are successfully conveyed but the water appears somewhat solid. Gwen John gave the picture to Augustus.[8]

Apart from drawing and painting Gwen's great love at this time was cats. At Victoria House she owned a mog called Mudge, a tom whom she refused to neuter. Not content with laying waste the back garden, he would wander in the town with crumpled bleeding ears and embarrass Edwin who, though a cat lover too, would look the other way and pretend to have no connection with him. Yet on less testing occasions he took an understanding attitude to his daughters' pets, and once sent the town crier out to announce the loss of Floss, Winifred's poodle.

Edwin's cult of respectability had now reached ludicrous heights. Although he had ceased to practise officially as a solicitor because he considered it ungentlemanly, the lack of a professional brass plate on the door did not mean that he would not give legal advice (for a fee). His straight back, commanding nose and heavy moustache gave him a military air and once, to his satisfaction, he was saluted by a soldier from Penally barracks who took him for a retired officer. In behaviour, however, there was little of the military man about him for he was pathologically shy and had few friends, and these he often found an embarrassment. Augustus described how 'walking at his side through the town, I would be surprised by a sudden quickening of pace on his part, while at the same time he would be observed to consult his watch anxiously as if late for an appointment: after a few minutes' spurt he would slow down and allow me to catch up with him. This manoeuvre pointed to the presence of a friend in the vicinity.'

In spite of his efforts to enter Tenby society, Edwin never succeeded. Though his children consorted with the best families, and the Swinburnes, the de Burghs and the Prusts asked them home, nobody asked Edwin home. Perhaps they had heard rumours of family scandals from Haverfordwest. Edwin tried further to enforce his reputation for

[7] 'A girl playing a violin', no. 2, 1976 Exhibition, Cardiff. Full details of Gwen John's exhibitions are listed on page 201.

[8] 'Landscape at Tenby with figures', no. 1, 1975 Exhibition, New York. Collection of Mr and Mrs Edgar Scott.

respectability by regular church-going. For a time he even considered taking holy orders. In the end he contented himself with playing the organ at the little church at Gumfreston. He was to walk out there every Sunday for the rest of his long life. He also attended matins regularly at St Mary's. When she was ten Gwen John had been baptised there with Augustus and Winifred.

It was a final shock when Augustus declared that he wanted to be an artist. Edwin was more than a little taken aback. He had, of course, observed his children's constant scribblings but he had never taken them seriously. True, it was uncommonly tiresome having Augustus always under his feet. And Edward J. Head, R.A. was an artist and he was *almost* a gentleman. Mr Head, to his eternal honour, recommended the Slade. Augustus insisted and at sixteen he went. Gwen, who was eighteen and every bit as talented, did not.

The last year at home was a bitter one for her. The departure of Augustus had left her without the support of a fellow artist. Thornton was no substitute. He had always been a quiet boy, slow in his speech and somewhat naive. He would rather be out of doors, preferably out at sea where he could be away from Augustus. Augustus had teased him unrelentingly, as he had Gwen, but when Thornton turned upon him, Augustus would reduce him to powerless laughter with acts of tomfoolery. Thornton's ambition was to prospect for gold. A few years later he left for Canada, taking no luggage, only coming back to enlist in the First World War, after which he returned to the gold fields.

Gwen was also having problems with her father. Edwin, now nearly fifty, was making embarrassing attempts to select a new wife from among her friends. The sly lust that caused him to hang pictures of naked women in his bedroom disgusted her. She was infuriated by his courtship of Ann Lloyd-Jones (to whom he was briefly engaged) and later of Teresa George (the friend from Broad Haven). Once, after mercilessly enumerating Edwin's failings, which included 'a hateful parsimony and a recurrent disposition to matrimonial adventure' she accused him of plotting the ruin of her very life. Winifred backed her up, although Augustus took the side of Edwin, thereby 'only winning the disapproval of all three parties'. The following day the young people were despatched to Begelly, 'a true haven after storm'. Edwin remained single.

Gwen's fury might have been less intense if her own life had been more satisfactory. Apart from attending Winifred's occasional violin recitals at private houses she had little social life and no romantic attachments. Tenby was a lively enough place in the summer season with balls at the Assembly Rooms, but these would hardly have been to Gwen John's liking. In winter the closed shops and desolate promenade were a depressing sight.

Painting was her sole interest and she was working in a vacuum without tuition or criticism. Increasingly she was finding it impossible to work at home. She blamed her failure on the 'relaxing air' of Tenby and claimed she could work well even four miles out of the town (probably at Begelly). Augustus was writing constantly to urge her to join him at the Slade. He now knew what expert tuition could make of her talent. She needed little encouragement. 'She wasn't going to be left out of it,' he wrote in *Chiaroscuro*. Edwin was no doubt unwilling to part with the money but in the autumn of 1895 Gwen John arrived in London.

3

Slade

1895–8

Gwen and Augustus took the London train from Tenby in time for the autumn term of 1895 at the Slade. Augustus was a spruce silent young man, clean-shaven and wearing a white collar. According to a fellow student, Ethel Hatch, he had chestnut hair and dark brown eyes and was meticulously polite. Gwen was small and neat beside him in her long-skirted travelling suit. Her eyes were grey and her hair under her large Edwardian hat was brown, but she still bore a resemblance to her brother, particularly in the matter of her receding chin.

For his first year in London Augustus had lived with the 'Jesus Christ Aunts', who were still preparing for their American adventure, in a villa in Acton. Now he had a room at 20 Montague Place in a superior lodging house. Gwen, after a brief stay at Miss Philpot's Educational Establishment at 10 Princes Square, settled at 23 Euston Square[1] just across the Euston Road from the Slade and next door to the station.

Brother and sister celebrated their liberation from Tenby with an evening at the theatre while their allowances were still intact. They saw Henry Irving in *The Knights of King Arthur*. Augustus was deeply moved by the tall black figure progressing deathwards to the sound of his own magnificent voice. Afterwards he became over-excited (he was still only seventeen). 'On reaching our lodgings, still under the spell of the Master, I seized a heavy walking stick, raised it above my head, while reciting appropriate lines, and smashed the chandelier!' he wrote in his auto-biography.

In 1895 the Slade was the most progressive art school in London. Its

[1] Euston Square has been destroyed. Augustus claims that he and Gwen always shared digs but in fact, according to Michael Holroyd, they only shared a flat twice, once in 1897 at Mrs Everitt's, and once briefly in 1900 when they had a flat over a tobacconist at 39 Southampton Street.

greatest period was dawning, its students were in a state of ferment and each of them felt he might be a Michelangelo. It had been founded twenty-three years earlier by a series of endowments from Felix Slade, a wealthy connoisseur, who wished to establish a London University Chair of Fine Arts. Money for the scheme was also voted by University College, London, to provide for the building of a school of art as part of the college. They sited it on the left side of their quadrangle in Gower Street.

From the start the new faculty dissociated itself from stagnant Victorian tradition of Alma-Tadema. Poynter, who had studied in Paris, was its first professor, Legros, who was French, its second, and Brown, who had also studied in Paris, its third. Frederick Brown,[2] a forceful somewhat military character, had been in charge for two years when Gwen John first crossed the quadrangle and entered the honey-coloured stone building, decorated with six Corinthian columns. To the right of the entrance hall were the stairs which led to the women's studio but she, as a freshman, was banished downstairs to the Antique Room with a sheet of Ingres paper and a piece of tomato-coloured chalk to draw the Discobolus and the Venus de Milo for a year. The Slade might be a progressive school that encouraged its students to draw what they saw, but it insisted that they saw nudes in the classical manner. This introduction was too much for some. Four years earlier young William Rothenstein, who was to become a close friend of both Augustus and Gwen, had walked out in disgust at such old-fashioned methods.

In the second year students progressed to the Life Class. Here old-fashioned customs were also observed. Women were strictly segregated, and the male nudes were never completely nude. Even when the model was a female the ladies, until very recently, had been required to leave the room when their instructor entered. He wrote his comments in the margins of their drawings. On their first visit to the Life Studio young artists were exposed to the living model for only twenty minutes. The shock of this was considered quite sufficient. 'Perfect beauty always intimidates,' Augustus wrote later of his own first experience of the Life Class. 'Overcome for a moment by a strange sensation of weakness at the knees, I hastily seated myself and with trembling hand began to draw, or pretend to draw this dazzling apparition.'

Gwen John's teacher in the Life Class was Henry Tonks. Tonks was an extraordinary man. Gaunt and fierce, dressed formally in grey, he resembled more the senior medical officer at the Royal Free Hospital that he had once been, than the greatest teacher of drawing in England that he

[2] Frederick Brown's paintings can be seen at the Tate. The teaching staff at the Slade were obliged to be practising artists.

had become. He was a confirmed bachelor and often reduced the women students to tears at their first lesson, for the Slade did not set an entrance examination and not all the freshers were gifted. He once stared down at a girl's drawing for several minutes before he spoke. Finally all he said was, 'Can you sew?' But if a student could stand up to this he would tell her all he knew. He found women were easier to teach than men. 'They do what they are told,' he said. 'And if they become offensive it is only a sign of love. They improve rapidly from sixteen to twenty-one. But then the genius that you have discovered goes off and they begin to take marriage seriously.'

Although Tonks himself never took marriage seriously he was not averse to a pretty face. New students were sometimes surprised to observe Mr Tonks following them down Gower Street. As a rule he only wanted them to model for his eternal paintings of pretty women in hazy hat shops. His mistress was the Slade and would be for forty years to come.

One of Tonks' favourites was Edna Waugh, a strikingly pretty girl of fifteen with long hair to her waist, who was in Gwen John's year. Tonks said she could draw like a man and had the imagination of a Burne-Jones. Her final achievement at the Slade was a large canvas, 'The rape of the Sabine women', a composition built up from the writhing bodies of countless nudes. By the age of nineteen she had become Lady Clarke Hall and was to devote the rest of her life to gardening and child rearing. Her incomplete set of ink illustrations to *Wuthering Heights* at the Tate is a proof of what was lost to art when she turned her back on it.

But the greatest favourite Tonks ever had was a man, Augustus John. By the end of John's first year Tonks was already proclaiming that he was the finest draughtsman Britain had produced. There are drawings of male nudes that Augustus made while still a student which jump off the page with their power.[3] Every time Gwen John and her friends walked up to the women's Life Studio they passed beneath a charcoal drawing by Augustus of a hairy model, his moustache bristling with masculinity.[4]

Tonks insisted that his students have a knowledge of anatomy approaching that of medical students. Skeletons were kept in the basement and reluctantly studied. Only when they knew how the femur rotated in the pelvic socket and the radius hinged on the ulna, he declared, could they understand the construction of living men and women. He also put great emphasis on the study of the Old Masters. When criticising the students' monthly compositions one day he told them that they should study the pictures in the National Gallery more

[3] *The Slade* by John Fothergill reproduces a fine male nude.
[4] See *Rude Assignment* by Wyndham Lewis, London 1950.

and the Beardsley drawings in the fashionable *Yellow Book* less. 'I cannot teach you anything new,' he told them. 'You must find that out for yourselves. But I can teach you something of the methods of the Old Masters.' The hint fell on fertile ground and both Gwen and Augustus learned to admire Rubens, Michelangelo, Rembrandt, Watteau and Ingres. Augustus also admired Reynolds, Gainsborough, Titian, Tiepolo, Millet and Goya and imitated most of them. Gwen was more discriminating. She took Rembrandt and the earlier Dutch masters as models.

There was one modern master whom the students were encouraged to admire and that was Whistler. He paid a visit to the Life Class one day in 1896, 'a jaunty little man in black, who had a white lock in his curly hair and wore a monocle. Mr Whistler! An electric shock seemed to galvanise the class.' Whistler, although an American, was now regarded as the leading English Impressionist. His battles had been fought and won. He had established the right to paint pictures with names like 'Nocturne' and 'Study', pictures which did not tell a story. He was founder and president of the International Society which staged vast shows of English and foreign pictures twice a year. Sickert was only the first of the young painters he was to influence profoundly. Gwen and Augustus John would one day be numbered as members of the school of Whistler.[5]

Painting was taught less well than drawing at the Slade. Wilson Steer was a good painter but a poor teacher. He was a bulky man with a fear of draughts. When he sat behind a student to criticise his work as often as not he proved to have fallen asleep. Augustus caricatured him mercilessly but in later years praised his technique in the painting of the nude. 'When in the Life Class, taking a student's brush and palette, he was moved to work on the defaced canvas before him with that flickering and voluptuous touch of his, it seemed as if a new and more enchanting world was blossoming before our eyes.'

Gwen and Augustus John returned to Tenby in December 1895 for their first Christmas vacation. They took with them Michel Salaman, whose sister Louise was also at the Slade. Michel came from a large family who spent the money they had raised from ostrich hunting on hunting the fox. Like his brothers and sisters, several of whom were at the Slade, he had red hair and good looks, and would ultimately devote himself to the chase. But he was a young man of extraordinary sympathy and generosity who corresponded not only with Gwen and Augustus John for many years but also with most of their friends. If he had a fault it was that he was a bore. At a concert he would distract his companion by making laborious attempts at describing how well the band had played

---

[5] *'Whistler and his influence in Britain'*, 1977 Exhibition at the Tate.

last time he took Edna Waugh to a concert. At Victoria House Michel made no attempts to describe anything. The silence silenced even him. Edwin, stately and upright, hardly spoke. Thornton, Salaman declared, was a hobbledehoy, miserable when not playing cards. Winifred was at all times extraordinarily dull and musical except in the presence of Gwen when the two girls giggled continuously. To escape from all this the two men visited Hoyle's Mouth. But this Michel found worse and he was sure the box of matches would empty before they regained the fresh air.

Gwen John's giggles may have betrayed a certain fondness for Michel. In a letter written two years later she confessed, 'I feel at ease with you and I should like you to read at will all my thoughts and feelings. Don't be bored, and whatever you do, don't *laugh*!!'

It was probably in her second year at the Slade that Gwen became intimate with Ida Nettleship. Ida was the daughter of the Pre-Raphaelite animal artist Jack Nettleship. She had a dark sensuous beauty and an untamed quality that expressed itself in silence. She described herself as 'tongueless' and when she did speak it was in a low voice and with a cultivated accent. She had been a Slade student since 1892 and went around with a group of girls younger than herself known as 'the nursery'. The best known of these were Edna Waugh and Gwen Salmond (the future Mrs Matthew Smith). Each member of the nursery took the name of a character from *The Jungle Book*. Ida, as Mowgli the man cub, gave advice to her jungle children. She wrote as follows to Bagheera (Bessie Cohen) on the occasion of her wedding. 'I think you are a charmer – but oh you *are* married – never girl Bessie again. Do you know you are different? . . . Mowgli will be so lonely in the jungle without the queen pantheress. Oh you're worth a kiss sweet, though you are grown into a wife.' Another letter was signed, 'Bless you with jungle joy. Your bad little man cub, Mistress Mowgli.' Gwen John never assumed a jungle name but she came to regard Ida as her closest friend. Ida in turn used to say that in times of real trouble she could speak only to Gwen.

Ida's parents lived in a flat in Wigmore Street and their home was one of the few open to Gwen and Augustus in London at this time. Ida's father made it a welcoming place even if her mother, a superior dressmaker, was somewhat formidable in her well-filled black bombazine. Jack Nettleship was an eccentric character with his bald head, his grey beard and his nose, according to W. B. Yeats, 'like an opera glass'. Years before he had broken an arm while hunting. 'A little whisky would always stop the pain,' wrote Yeats. 'Soon a little became a great deal and he found himself a drunkard.' He had been cured of alcoholism but always required a jorum of cocoa beside him to assuage his need to sip. At Wigmore Street the young Johns met celebrities like William Michael

Rossetti and Sickert, and writers like Yeats and Beerbohm. William Rothenstein, who liked to be where the famous were, was often at the apartment.

Rothenstein was a small man in horn-rimmed glasses who could only be described as bumptious. He had studied art at Julian's in Paris where he had met Rodin, Degas and even Picasso. Rodin was the artist who had impressed Rothenstein most. He had been invited to the sculptor's home at Meudon, near Paris, to make drawings and lithographs of the Master, and was full of enthusiasm for the famous head with the flowing beard and the hair that grew as strongly as the crest on a Greek helmet. He had also met Charles Conder, a blond and bearded Australian painter four years his senior who embarrassed him by bringing women to his studio for other purposes than art.

Rothenstein was now at work on his famous series of drawings and lithographs, *Oxford Characters*. And he had just married the beautiful Alice Knewstub, to the annoyance of Augustus. Alice was a generous and golden goddess. She was an actress but came from an artistic background. Her father had been Rossetti's assistant, and Wilson Steer had admired and painted her luminous hair. She shared her husband's determination to help people, particularly the Johns.

Ida's other close friend at the Slade was Ursula Tyrwhitt. She was an ecstatic, bird-like girl, rather vague. Her father was the vicar of Nazeing, in Essex, and she had to fight him for five years before she could come to the Slade. Only when she was twenty-three and presumably past hope of marriage did he let her go. As a result she was somewhat older than her contemporaries. She had officially left the school before Gwen came,[6] but continued to be closely associated with it and with Ida.

Ida's friends, Ursula Tyrwhitt, Edna and the two Gwens, now came to be recognised as an exclusive group at the Slade. Augustus wrote of them, 'In what I have called the Grand Epoch of the Slade the male students cut a poor figure, in fact they can hardly be said to have existed. In talent, as well as in looks, these girls were supreme.' Augustus proceeded to pay court to two members of the group in rapid succession. He started with Ursula Tyrwhitt who wasn't particularly interested in men. He used to walk her home in the evening but she could never remember whether she loved him or not. She blew hot and cold and the relationship for some time did not get far beyond an exchange of portraits. (Augustus's chaste drawing of Ursula's head can be seen at the Ashmolean.)

Augustus meanwhile had assembled his own group known as the Three Musketeers. Ambrose McEvoy and Benjamin Evans were the

[6] Ursula Tyrwhitt's dates at the Slade were 1893–4 and 1911–12.

other members. McEvoy was later to play an important part in Gwen's life. He was a strange-looking youth, extremely tall with long limbs that he arranged awkwardly. Large short-sighted eyes peered from under a Phil May fringe. There is a red chalk drawing of McEvoy by Augustus at the National Portrait Gallery. It approaches a caricature. He dressed always in evening-dress, not forgetting the dancing-pumps and the monocle. Some said this insistence on a scheme in black and white was in deference to Whistler who was a friend of his father's. McEvoy was a gentle, naive youth with few intellectual pretensions. He left the Slade a year after Gwen John arrived. Benjamin Evans, a gifted draughtsman, was the jester of the trio and had been at the same 'horrible school' as Augustus at Clifton. He later gave up art and became a sanitary engineer, to the disgust of Augustus who said he had gone down the drain.

On Saturday nights the Musketeers went to the music-hall at Sadlers Wells and were occasionally thrown out of it. This was the age of Marie Lloyd, Dan Leno, Harry Tate and that 'prince of buffoons', Arthur Roberts. They also went to see the 'celestial' dancing of Adeline Genée at the Empire and the acrobats at the circus. When they were out of funds on a Sunday they sometimes walked to Hampton Court or Dulwich to see the pictures, breakfasting in a cabman's shelter. Their free evenings were spent sketching in cafés.

Both Augustus and Gwen John continued to take their sketch-books everywhere. 'Do present-day art students bring their sketch-books with them to the cinema, night clubs or wherever they go in the evenings?' Augustus later enquired. 'I think not. For one thing, drawing seems to be out of fashion and the curriculum of the State schools, requiring the absorption of numerous learned works on Anatomy, Architecture, Economics, Stained Glass, Perspective, Illustration, Foundry-work, Enamelling . . . leaves the poor aspirant for a government grant pretty well exhausted by the end of the work.'

The cafés of Fitzroy Street were a source of more appealing subjects than the respectability of Gower Street on the other side of the Tottenham Court Road. Russian anarchists in frock-coats passed their evenings there with bearded Spaniards. In January 1897 Augustus and Gwen moved into a flat in Fitzroy Street and Gwen's most eventful year at the Slade began. The flat was the first floor of a brothel which had been converted into flats by Mrs Everitt, a warm-hearted woman, who had both a son, John Everitt,[7] and a niece at the Slade. She longed to be there too, but her clothes were eccentric and she distracted the students with her hymn singing so she was banished to the basement where the skeletons were kept. The students on the floor above could still hear her

---

[7] John Everitt produced paintings of ships for the rest of his life but never sold one.

singing down there while she made tea on a spirit stove. They used to join in the more stirring choruses. On Sundays the hymn singing at 21 Fitzroy Street was above ground and accompanied by cups of tea and bread and jam. Augustus and Gwen were painfully reminded of the aunts, but it was politic to join in.

Winifred John, who, at eighteen, had succeeded in escaping from Tenby, now joined her brother and sister in the flat. She was studying the violin in London. There was a third girl in the flat, Grace Westray,[8] also a student. It was Augustus John who dictated the diet upon which the four young people lived. He pronounced that fruit and nuts alone were sufficient for survival. Gwen was persuaded to join them for a time, 'subsisting like monkeys'. He insisted the diet was 'hygienic and cheap' but was always ready to accept a meal out if it was offered. Gwen went out less and Augustus became worried about her. He disapproved of the long hours she spent at her easel in Fitzroy Street. Surely, he suggested, *some* exercise was necessary for survival.

Winifred and Grace now became Gwen John's principal models out of school hours. Her ability to draw from life had greatly increased and it was in this year that she won the Slade certificate for figure drawing which Augustus had also won in his second year. Her drawing of Winifred, 'A woman asleep on a sofa',[9] was masterful and assured. The full-length portrait of Grace Westray in oils, 'Young woman with a violin',[10] is a more elaborate work. Grace is shown seated against the stark background of the room in Fitzroy Street, somewhat in the manner of Whistler's portrait of his father. Her instrument is tucked under her chin and she appears to be playing it, but her round face with its dark cap of hair is so pensive that it seems she must have ceased to play and fallen into a reverie.

There is a mystery about Grace Westray. Was she or was she not the young woman at the Slade for whom Gwen developed a passionate affection at this time? Augustus, in *Chiaroscuro*, would only refer to this friend under the pseudonym of Elinor. He described a complication in their relationship which now occurred. 'Elinor had formed a close attachment to an outsider. This young man was a curious fellow, giving himself the airs of a superman with pretensions to near immortality, but apparently only occupied for the present in some form of business. Gwen John decided that this affair must be stopped.' Her fury was unbounded. The same demon that had inspired her to tear her father from his intended

[8] This is how the name is spelt in the Slade records. Grace appears to have lived with McEvoy and his wife for some years to come.

[9] No. 34, 1975 Exhibition, New York. Collection of Mr and Mrs Paul Sylbert.

[10] No. 3, 1975 Exhibition, New York. Collection of Mr and Mrs Edgar Scott. Gwen John gave this picture to Augustus, who kept it by him all his life.

bride once more entered her heart and Augustus and Winifred could do nothing to calm her. She threatened suicide. 'The atmosphere of our little group,' Augustus wrote, 'became almost unbearable, with its frightful tension, its terrifying excursions and alarms. Had my sister gone mad? At one moment Ambrose McEvoy thought so, and, distraught himself, rushed to tell me the dire news: but Gwen was only in a state of spiritual exaltation and laughed at my distress.' Elinor's love for Gwen had now changed to hate and Augustus ended the matter by threatening to fight her lover who wisely retreated to his wife. If Elinor was Grace Westray it seems that she did not marry, but was destined to become a member of the McEvoy household.

In the summer of 1897 Ambrose McEvoy was in Tenby with Benjamin Evans and Augustus. The Three Musketeers were planning to walk diagonally across Pembrokeshire to St David's Head and were negotiating with Mr Lewis, a Tenby sweep, for the purchase of a donkey and cart to carry their canvases and camping equipment. On their way they visited Augustus's boyhood haunts at Haverfordwest. There were seventeen hills between Haverfordwest and St David's, and Augustus had to help the donkey pull the cart up every one of them, McEvoy and Evans 'taking care to be well ahead on these occasions and deep in discussion'. Tradition has it that they stopped at Broad Haven and painted a folding screen in return for their keep.[11]

McEvoy, who claimed to be an expert on food values, had decided that treacle and onions would provide a balanced diet, and took on the duties of camp cook. He was a strange figure at the smoky fire, his head hanging between his bony knees, his long hair incessantly in his eyes. On their way back through Haverfordwest they lost him and he did not catch up until they were camping on Begelly Common. According to Augustus, 'He greeted us with bitter accusations . . . Explanations followed and a bottle of whisky, with which, knowing the shortest way to his heart, we had wisely provided ourselves'.

Augustus and Gwen stayed on at Tenby. One day, with Edwin, Winifred and Winifred's friend Irene Mackenzie, they walked to the far end of South Sands to bathe under Giltar Point. Augustus decided to dive from a triangular rock off shore that can still be seen. 'The water below appeared to be deep enough for a dive,' he wrote later, 'but was by no means clear, the surface being encumbered with seaweed. Still, taking a chance, I stripped and made the plunge. Instantly I was aware of my folly. The impact of my skull on a hidden rock was terrific. The universe seemed to explode! Yet I wasn't stunned. Perhaps the cold water saved

---

[11] A giant flower fills each panel of the screen. The present owners ascribe the lily to Augustus, who is still known as Disgusting John in the neighbourhood.

me for I was able to get out of it, replace the flap of scalp I found hanging over one eye, tie the towel round my head, dress and rejoin my father, who was much alarmed at my plight. We made for home as fast as we could but did not take the nearest way up the cliff for that would have meant publicity.'

When Gwen John returned to the Slade for the autumn term of 1897 Augustus was still in bed, bored and writing long letters to Ursula Tyrwhitt with whom he had persuaded himself he was in love. He remembered parting from her at the college at the end of term soirée. 'How the strawberries sweetened one's sorrow – how the roses made one's despair almost acceptable.' As his passion increased his writing became wilder and was interspersed with drawings of himself unshaven with a bandage round his head. He demanded a pledge that she would keep him company that term.

When Augustus returned to the Slade his friends hardly knew him. The polite tidy youth had vanished and in his place was a red-bearded Bohemian who dressed in corduroy and wore a large hat and earrings. This young man claimed to have gypsy blood, got involved in outrageous exploits, drank and did not pay his rent. People thought the change was due to the knock on the head but it was more probably due to feelings of revolt against Victoria House where he had been so long imprisoned.

A new student, William Orpen, joined the Slade in 1897. He was a witty, slightly monkey-like Irishman with high cheek-bones and sunken cheeks, who came from the Metropolitan School of Art, in Dublin. A few months later William Rothenstein's little brother, Albert, (known as All But Rothenstein) also joined the school. Albert was small and pink and regarded as rather a rake. This pair became co-opted members of the Three Musketeers. At night, with Augustus, they would pick up a girl and take her to Augustus's room at 21 Fitzroy Street to draw.

It is unlikely that Gwen John would have assisted at these sessions since the model was nude, but the constant presence of McEvoy in the flat was to influence her work profoundly. McEvoy was obsessed with the techniques of the Old Masters of the seventeenth and eighteenth centuries. Although he had left the Slade, he continued to set up his easel daily in the National Gallery before the works of Titian, Rubens and, above all, Rembrandt. More than one lady had been touched by the sight of the young man with the poetic expression at work day after day. In this way he learned to build up a picture in the classical manner. First he made a preliminary brushwork study in black, white and ochre. Over this he applied a series of semi-transparent glazes which gave a translucent character to his canvases. His influence on Gwen John's painting was evident by the time she left the Slade.

Meanwhile Augustus had fallen in love with Ida. She had been briefly engaged to Clement Salaman in February 1897, and had gone to paint in Florence to forget him. She had returned enfolded by what she called an 'eternal ennui'. And now Augustus noticed her velvet beauty. He followed her everywhere, persistent as a dog. He even pursued her up a haystack at St Albans where she was trying to be alone with Edna Waugh on a picnic at Edna's home. When she repulsed him he tried to throw himself off and the girls only saved him by holding on to his trousers.

Gwen John won the Melvill Nettleship prize for figure composition in her last term at the Slade in 1898. It was a triumph for one whose natural tendency was to concentrate on single figures. But it could not raise her above the status of 'John's sister'. Augustus was to win three prizes that year – also his final one.[12] When Edna Waugh was decorating a gallery with roses for the leavers' soirée Tonks passed and pointed to an empty decorated pedestal. 'Is that for John?' he said.

[12] Augustus did a five-year course, Gwen only a four-year course.

4

Ambrose McEvoy

1898–1903

Edwin John had moved house, but only to an identical one round the corner in South Cliff Street.[1] The shades of Tenby began to settle once more round Gwen and Augustus. Augustus's description of the last summer vacation there could surely have been written by Gwen too: 'Rain has set in and I feel cooped up and useless. What we have seen of the country has been wonderful. But it is ten minutes to the rocky landscape with figures. The colloquy of the table compels in me a blank mask of attention only relieved now and then by hysterical and unreasonable laughter.'

In the autumn Augustus escaped to Amsterdam with McEvoy and Evans, to see the Rembrandt exhibition.[2] Gwen was not slow to follow his example. A letter from Ida summoned her to Paris where she was sharing a flat with Gwen Salmond. Edwin was appalled at the expense that would be involved, but Gwen sailed round the house singing, 'To Paris! To Paris!' and Edwin capitulated. 'Gwen is coming! Hurrah!' wrote Ida to her mother on 18 September. A week later she crossed the Channel for the first time.

In 1898 Paris was the Mecca of artists from all over Europe. Many of the greatest painters of the twentieth century were foreigners who had settled there. No self-respecting art student omitted to spend at least a few months at one of the great Paris schools like Colarossi's or Julian's (where William Rothenstein had studied). Life in the city was geared to the student. 'Its multitude of café terraces swarmed with people from every corner of the earth: it was still *la nouvelle Athènes*, divinely disputatious, with an immense student population for whom the publishers poured out "libraries" of masterpieces priced at a few francs . . . The

---

[1] Now Southcliffe.
[2] Stedelijk Museum, 8 September – 31 October 1898.

poorest student could sit all day long (and often did) for the cost of a cup of coffee.' In the workmen's bars, where the clients wore blouses and aprons, the cost of a glass of wine was even lower. Montparnasse was full of bare little rooms which could be had for thirteen francs a month and at a *prix fixe* restaurant a franc or two bought a three-course meal and all the bread you could eat.

Ida and Gwen Salmond were staying in 'a very old lady style' *pension* at 226 Boulevard Raspail,[3] close to the junction with the Boulevard Montparnasse with its far from 'old lady' bars, restaurants and *cafés-concerts*. 'Such a healthy part of Paris,' Ida assured her mother, who was convinced that the city was a sewer.

When Gwen John arrived carrying with her a marmalade cake, the three girls set about flat-hunting and saw many 'lovely bare places furnished only with looking-glasses.' They found what they wanted high up on the first floor of 12 rue Froidevaux.[4] The rue Froidevaux was close to the Boulevard Raspail, but it was slightly the quieter of the two streets and had two rows of trees down the centre. Ida hastily wrote to tell her mother about the salubriousness of the place. She assured her that the water in the taps did not come from the Seine and the concierge was 'exceedingly healthy looking', and as for the landlady she absolutely forbade gentlemen visitors. '*Les dames, oui! Les messieurs, jamais!*' The flat was over a café, but the entrance was round the corner from it, and as for the aspect, the windows looked over a large and most healthy open space. Ida omitted to mention that the open space was the South Montparnasse cemetery.

Gwen Salmond had developed as a painter since she had been a member of Ida's jungle nursery. 'The descent from the cross', painted in her last year at the Slade, had been a powerful composition which Augustus declared could have been by Tintoretto. She held strongly expressed and original views on art. She had become dissatisfied with the standard of work being done at the Slade and was seeking new inspiration. Writing, like everyone else, to Michel Salaman, she said, 'Of course we've gone down in art – and I shan't bring up the average. My four years show me that a sort of technicality is the wall I break myself against.' It was from this wall of technicality that she was seeking to liberate herself in Paris.

She had planned to study at Julian's, a more robust establishment than Colarossi's where Ida had enrolled, but then she heard about Carmen's, the extraordinary new school that Whistler had opened at 6

---

[3] Now destroyed and replaced by a block of modern flats.
[4] Sometimes misspelt Froidveau. The girls jokingly called it Cold Veal Street. The building still stands and has changed little. Students rent rooms under the roof to this day sharing a cold tap on the landing and a W.C.

passage Stanislas near the Luxembourg gardens. In 1898 everybody had heard about Carmen's and the schools of Paris were emptying themselves into it. The carriages of wealthy students blocked the narrow approach while their owners struggled in the glazed courtyard and on the staircase leading to the studios.

The school was the property of Carmen Rossi, an Italian beauty who had been Whistler's favourite model. He had agreed to teach there two days a week and this, of course, was the cause of the excitement. After a few lessons with him Gwen Salmond became convinced that Gwen John must also enter the school. Unfortunately Edwin had omitted to give his daughter enough money to study in Paris, only enough to live there, so the kindly Miss Salmond (who had wealthy parents) provided it and Gwen John went to study under Whistler in the afternoons. Edwin was given to understand that she had won a scholarship.

Gwen Salmond did more than she ever knew when she paid that thirty pounds to Madame Rossi. If Gwen John learnt to draw in four years at the Slade, she learnt to paint in four months at Carmen's. Whistler once said that his was 'a tonal modelling not a drawing school'. Elsewhere he declared, 'I do not teach art. I teach the scientific application of paint and brushes.' When teaching the painting of the nude he insisted that the three-dimensional form of the figure must be modelled in grey paint as a sculptor models with his clay. He had strong views on colour and considered that the artist's chief weapon was the palette, where the colours must be mixed and several brushes loaded before work commenced. Students were encouraged to arrange their palettes in a set order. As a result of Whistler's teaching an exquisite sense of tone values became one of the characteristics of Gwen John's work. She numbered her tones and made notes like the following on the backs of drawings: 'Road 32, roof 13–23, grass 23, black coats 33.' It was this sense of tone that Whistler recognised as Gwen John's chief quality. Augustus, on his way back from Amsterdam, met Whistler by chance at the Louvre. He ventured to suggest that Gwen showed a sense of character in her portraits. 'Character?' said Whistler. 'What's character? Your sister has a sense of *tone*.'

Augustus now insisted on calling on Whistler with Gwen at his studio near the school. Great windows gave a view over the Luxembourg gardens. It was Whistler's custom to keep all his canvases facing the wall. But Gwen and Augustus did see a pale self-portrait drowning in a surrounding sea of black. It was as if Whistler knew that he too would have withdrawn into the shadows within a few years.

Augustus, of course, could not visit the girls in their flat. No doubt he read the account of the life they led there which they sent home. 'We have a very excellent flat,' Ida wrote to her mother, 'and a charming studio room – so untidy – so unfurnished – and nice spots of drawings and photos on the walls – half the wall is covered with brown paper, and when we have spare time and energy we are going to cover the other half . . . Gwen John is sitting before a mirror carefully composing herself. She has been at it for half an hour. It is for an "interior".'

Sometimes they painted each other. 'The Gwens are painting me and we are all three painting Gwen John.' Other models were found at the anarchist restaurant where they ate and where beautiful but shabbily-dressed girls waited on each other on principle. Gwen John, who had at first been a little lonely, now made friends with several beauties. One of these, a golden girl called Marthe from Alsace, she brought back to the flat for everyone to draw.

The day at the flat started with readings from *King John* or *King Lear* at breakfast. Sometimes there were 'most comically unideal rubs . . . which made one feel like a washerwoman or something common,' according to Ida. In the evenings there were dressmaking sessions. It was the product of one of these sessions that caused the rift between Gwen John and her father. Edwin had come to Paris to look into the matter of Gwen's allowance. She had arranged a small supper party, putting on a new dress designed by herself from a dress in a picture by Manet. The picture was possibly the 'Bar at the Folies Bergères' and the dress probably displayed more of his daughter's neck and forearm than he was accustomed to see. He greeted her with the words, 'You look like a prostitute in that dress.' She replied, 'I could never accept anything from someone capable of thinking so.' It was from this time that she started to work as an artist's model to support herself.

Gwen John and Gwen Salmond returned to London in February 1899, leaving Ida to study in Paris a month or two longer. Gwen John took a basement room under a decorator's shop in Howland Street, W.1., where, according to Augustus, no ray of light ever entered. She acquired a cat and made some watercolours of it. The next four years of her life (1899–1903) she herself termed as her subterranean period, not only because she spent most of it living in basements but because it was an unhappy time about which not much is known. In the future she was to look back on it with horror. 'It was in London I saw nobody,' she told Augustus in a letter written a few years later. 'If to "return to life" is to live as I did in London, merci Monsieur! There are people like plants who cannot flourish in the cold, and I want to flourish.' Augustus called her the waif of Pimlico.

There was another reason for Gwen John's unhappiness. She was in love with Ambrose McEvoy, but there were many misunderstandings. McEvoy and Augustus were now living in their first studio. It was Constable's old one at 76 Charlotte Street, just down the road from 21

Fitzroy Street. They hired a red-haired model once a week with Evans, Orpen and Albert Rutherston,[5] who each paid sevenpence an hour until the model's red hair fell off and proved to be a wig. Augustus at least was beginning to make money. In the evenings they drank beer at the Café Royal. They were often joined by Ida and one-time members of her 'nursery'. Gwen John usually came with McEvoy.

The history of Gwen John's affair with McEvoy is obscure. The barrage of secrecy with which she liked to surround herself on this occasion appears impenetrable. There is no mention of her in Reginald Gleadowe's biography of McEvoy, published in 1923. All that appears sure is that she loved him and he, flattered by the attention of his friend's older sister, thought he loved her.

In the spring of 1899 McEvoy was evidently much on Gwen John's mind. Mrs Everitt had opened a boarding house called Peveril Tower at Swanage near Poole Harbour in Dorset and Gwen John had been invited there for a holiday. From there she wrote to Michel Salaman, giving a vivid picture of her state of mind in the early months of her love affair with McEvoy. She was listless and unable to work, wandered along the cliffs by moonlight catching fireflies and putting them in her hair. By day she went for long country walks.

> Yesterday I came to an old wood. I walked on anemones and primroses – primroses mean youth, did you know? I bathe in a natural bath three miles away. The rocks are treacherous there, and the sea unfathomable. My bath is so deep I cannot dive to the bottom . . . There is a delicious danger about it, and yesterday I sat on the edge of the rock to see what would happen – and a great wave came and rolled me over – which was humiliating and *very* painful – and then it washed me out to sea and that was terrifying – but I was washed up again.

Neither Gwen John nor McEvoy joined Augustus's painting party in Normandy that summer but one member, Orpen, when he returned, had work as a model ready for her. Orpen very much admired Gwen John's looks. 'She is a most beautiful lady,' he confided to Michel Salaman. He was working on his Slade summer composition, an elaborate set piece which represented the play within the play in *Hamlet*.[6] While the Player King and Queen display themselves on a lighted stage in the top left corner, the rest of the players, now the audience, disport themselves in the foreground. It was for one of these foreground figures

---

[5] William Rothenstein's brothers, Albert and Charles, changed their surname to Rutherston *c*. 1914.

[6] Reproduced in *The Slade* by John Fothergill.

that Orpen required Gwen John to model. The figure was Ophelia but when Gwen saw the pose, the maiden thrown backwards by Hamlet in the ardour of his embrace, she refused to take it. She broke her nose two days later and Ida took her place.

Gwen John was now homeless, as she was often to be in the next four years. She had left her basement in Howland Street and was at 122 Gower Street. But 122 Gower Street appears to have been an empty house at this period. It was officially inhabited by a woman, Annie Machew, who from October 1899 had paid no rates. The rating authorities who attempted to collect the money owing to them throughout 1900 reported that there were no effects there. Gwen seems to have spent short periods there from time to time.

Augustus also was homeless. His behaviour had become so scandalous that his landlady would not let him back into 76 Charlotte Street with McEvoy when he returned from Normandy. One night, simply to terrify her, he had danced on the roof of St John the Evangelist church next door. At other times he fraternised, long after hours, with nude models. After an unsuccessful siege he was forced to retreat to Orpen's cellar at 21 Fitzroy Street. William Rothenstein described these as 'comfortable quarters' now that Mrs Everitt had moved to Swanage. They had only one sagging bed between them and no armchairs.

The winter of 1899 was a cold one and the kind-hearted William Rothenstein took pity on the homeless brother and sister. He and Alice had recently moved into a 'delectable cottage' appropriately named 1 Pembroke Cottages, in Edwardes Square just off Kensington High Street. He was moving to Manchester to draw celebrities and proposed to lend it to the couple, hoping perhaps that they would also act as caretakers for his growing collection.

The experiment was not a success. For Augustus at least, Kensington was too far from Fitzrovia. He constantly missed the last train home and ended up on Orpen's floor. When Rothenstein returned to London suddenly for a night he sent a telegram ahead of him to the Johns. It had no effect. 'I found the house empty and no fire burning. In front of a cold grate choked with cinders lay a collection of muddy boots. Late in the evening John appeared, having climbed through a window; he rarely, he explained, remembered to take the house key with him. There were none I loved more than Augustus and Gwen John, but they could scarcely be called "comfortable" friends.' Alice would not live in the house again until it had been scrubbed and whitewashed throughout.

In the summer of 1900 the kindly Salaman had not only rented a flat at Le Puy and invited McEvoy to bring Gwen but he had supplied McEvoy with the money to do it. McEvoy's gratitutde was almost hysterical. On a nearly illegible postcard he described himself as, 'a mere wreck covered with gaping wounds from which the cheque hangs – a testimony to mankind in every way. How can I thank you? O, I cannot. But believe me telepathy or some such power is telling my feelings – such exuberance of spirits I have never known and I can say with Nietzsche, "I could not believe in a God who did not dance." I have told Gwen and I think she can come on Wednesday.'

The start of one of the pilgrim routes to Compostela, Le Puy is an ancient town perched above the pine woods and the mists of the Auvergne. 'There are most exquisite hills,' Augustus told Ursula Tyrwhitt, 'dominating valleys watered by pleasant streams, tilled by robust peasants.' He did not mention the most striking feature of the town, the one that had impressed Arthur Symons, the poet. 'Looking up I saw, horribly close above me, the great brown statue, the little doors opening in its body as the visitors climbed inside it.' This was the statue of the Virgin that still stands above the town.

Life was pleasant enough for Augustus, Gwen and McEvoy (Salaman had already left) once they grew accustomed to the richness of the food. The flat looked over a pleasant garden where a peasant girl sang at her work and a cock crowed. McEvoy and Gwen went for long walks every day and in the evenings they dragged Augustus from his easel to show him, as he wrote to Salaman, 'new and ever more surprising spots'. Then they came back to cook a dinner 'which is often successful in some items'. Afterwards they would go and listen to the band and Augustus and McEvoy, 'the absinthe friends', would go on somewhere to drink together. McEvoy had already started on a career of heavy drinking.

Idyllic though this existence sounds, McEvoy's letters to Michel Salaman are not as enthusiastic as they might be. He was living through 'a period of mental and physical bewilderment'. Augustus, he said, was 'a demon who refused to budge from his easel' but for him, 'Drawing is quite impossible . . . you arrive at a place with preconceived ideas about beauty and find a variety of beautiful things . . . What should an artist do? Should be proceed to introduce the wonders into his own little world?'

McEvoy did not tell Salaman the real reason for his 'mental and physical bewilderment'. During the month at Le Puy his relationship with Gwen had reached some kind of a crisis. By the end of it, according to Augustus, he was drinking and she was perpetually in tears. No doubt if he had been a more forceful character and she a less inhibited one their problem might have been solved in the conventional manner. When the trio returned to England they moved into a flat above the Economic Cigar Company at 39 Southampton Street.

Two months later McEvoy announced that he was engaged to Mary Spencer Edwards, a woman nine years older than him, who had studied at the Slade; and on 17 January 1901, he married her. 'Sister Gwen upset,' Augustus noted. She was more than upset. Not only she but all her friends had assumed she was McEvoy's friend. 'We all thought they were running around together,' wrote John Everitt in his diary. And now it appeared that McEvoy had been secretly engaged all along, even while sharing a flat with Gwen John.

Mary Edwards had first fallen in love with McEvoy at the National Gallery where Augustus had introduced them. It seemed that she had declared her love at the studio at 21 Fitzroy Street as long ago as 1897 when she broke off a previous engagement on account of him. Since then she had waited in the background. After the wedding the McEvoys lived squalidly in a patron's cottage in the country and then returned to the river, to live in a house with a fine studio. Gwen John never forgave Mary Edwards.

Once more Gwen was homeless. She could not stay in the flat above the tobacconist while McEvoy prepared for his wedding so she had to suffer the alternative humiliation of moving in with the parents of the man who had jilted her. Captain and Mrs McEvoy now lived at 41 Colville Terrace, in Bayswater, a house where the shutters were always closed to avoid paying the rates. McEvoy's kindly father, a friend of Whistler, had moved into London from Wiltshire after his financial ruin. Eventually Gwen took a room in Chatham Street. She was careful never again to part with her solitude.

Solitude, she began to understand, was the essence of her being. From Chatham Street she wrote to Michel Salaman. 'I don't pretend to know anybody well. People are like shadows to me and I am like a shadow. To me the writing of a letter is a very important event. I try to say what I mean exactly. It is the only chance I have, for in talking, shyness and timidity distort the meaning of my words in people's ears – that I think is one reason why I am such a waif.'

During the disturbed years after she left the Slade, Gwen John continued to paint. In 1900, the year when so much in her life had gone wrong, she exhibited for the first time at the New English Art Club. The New English Art Club, known to artists as the N.E.A.C., was founded in 1886 as a challenge to the Royal Academy by a group of French-trained artists who admired the French elective jury system of selecting paintings. Because Whistler, Steer and Sickert were early members of the jury the Club became closely associated with the Slade and was the natural place for ex-students to exhibit. But although it was only fourteen years old it was already approaching a somewhat conservative old age. Augustus had been showing there for several years when he finally persuaded Gwen to send two pictures. They were accepted and he rejoiced in 'a healthy inoculation of Celtic blood at the aged N.E.A.C. at last.'

One of Gwen John's paintings was of a crabbed 'Old woman wearing in a bonnet'.[7] Michel Salaman bought the painting, which is also known as 'Mrs Atkinson' or 'The Concierge'. The other was the famous portrait of herself wearing a red blouse that now hangs in the Tate. It is a picture that conveys her character perfectly according to people who knew her. The gentleness of the eyes is contradicted by the obstinacy of the mouth and yet an overriding impression of calm is given. Sir John Rothenstein wrote of the painting, 'This portrait – to my thinking one of the finest portraits of the time, excels . . . any portrait of McEvoy's.' Nevertheless Rothenstein pointed out that the picture owed the technical perfection of its glazes to McEvoy's knowledge, 'as generously imparted as it was laboriously acquired'.

The N.E.A.C. self-portrait was bought by Frederick Brown, Gwen's professor at the Slade, always a generous patron to his students. It appears in the background of his own self-portrait painted in 1920,[8] and was finally sold to the Tate by his daughter, Ellen Brown, in 1942.

After a disgraceful episode at Peveril Tower in which he had attempted to seduce Mrs Everitt's Austrian maid (a counterfeit countess), Augustus had declared that he was tired of the wild life and he begged Ida to marry him secretly and keep him out of trouble. Only Gwen, McEvoy and Benjamin Evans were present at the St Pancras Registry Office that foggy morning in the autumn of 1901. Afterwards they all went round to 1 Pembroke Cottages to tell William and Alice Rothenstein the news, and the Rothensteins gave an impromptu party. In his memoirs William wrote that Ida looked 'exquisitely virginal in her simple white dress'. Her parents, some of the Salamans, Tonks, Steer and Albert Rutherston with Gwen Salmond arrived. 'We had scherades towards the end of the evening – which were great fun,' wrote Albert to his parents. One of these charades represented Steer teaching at the Slade. A long silence, then, 'How's your sister?' This, Augustus swore, was a perfect example of Steer's methods. For their honeymoon, Augustus took his wife to Peveril Tower. Mrs Everitt had presumably dismissed the Austrian maid.

Soon after their marriage Augustus and Ida moved to Liverpool, where Augustus was to teach art at University College. On 6 January 1902 David was born and Gwen went to keep Ida company for a few weeks. She found Ida somewhat bewildered by the devastating new presence in her house. 'He howls,' she had written to Alice Rothenstein. 'He is howling now. I have done all I can for him and I know he is not hungry. I suppose the poor soul is simply unhappy. I think he would very much rather not have been created.' In another letter she said, 'Baby

[7] No. 2, 1975 Exhibition, New York. Private Collection, New York.
[8] Ferens Art Gallery, Hull.

takes so much time – and the rooms we are in are not very clean, so I am always dusting and brushing. Also we have a puppy, who adds to the difficulties. I think I enjoy working hard really.'

Another hazard of Ida's household was the old ladies. The wives of professors made it their duty to call regularly, carrying with them 'pieces of black net, flannel nightgowns, wool socks or torn lace, disused blankets, second-hand pin-cushions, half the veil of a deceased nun, a redundant stove for preparing baby's food and all manner of items pulled from old cupboards'. Perhaps it was on account of the old ladies that Gwen John spent much of her visit wheeling David John round the streets of Liverpool, accompanied no doubt by the dog. 'I am very busy with baby,' she wrote to Michel Salaman. She had the habit of sitting on the nearest doorstep when she needed a rest. Such behaviour would have been frowned on in a housemaid in Liverpool University circles, let alone a lady.

There was, however, one sympathetic university couple living in the same street. John Sampson,[9] known as 'the large and rolling rai', had become Augustus's closest friend. 'Rai' is the Romany word for king, and Augustus always declared that John Sampson should be the king of gypsies, not the university librarian. He was eventually to publish a masterpiece, *The Dialect of the Gypsies of Wales*. Already he had translated Omar Khayyám into Romany. Margaret Sampson, his sentimental little mouse of a wife, was also to become a close friend of all three Johns. Several of Gwen John's letters to her are preserved.

It was probably while Gwen John was in Liverpool that Augustus persuaded her to share his 1903 exhibition at the Carfax. The Carfax Gallery in Ryder Street, off St James's, had been recently opened by John Fothergill, painter, dandy and amateur innkeeper. Augustus had already had several exhibitions there. Now he groaned under the labour of hanging forty-five paintings. 'I'm devilish tired of putting up my exhibits,' he complained to Dorelia. 'I would like to burn the bloody lot.' Gwen's task was lighter for in the end she could only muster three pictures to hang. Nevertheless, in Augustus's opinion, 'Gwen has the honours or should have – for alas our smug critics don't appear to have noticed the presence in the gallery of two rare blossoms from most delicate trees. The little pictures to me are almost painfully charged with feeling even as their neighbours are empty of it. And to think that Gwen so rarely brings herself to paint. We others are always in danger of becoming professional and to detect oneself red-handed in the very act of professional industry is a humiliating experience.'

Gwen John also sent in paintings to the N.E.A.C. in 1903 but although

9 Grandfather of Anthony Sampson.

they were accepted they were not hung. Augustus was indignant and for once intervened in art politics. Orpen told Charles Conder in a letter of 2 May 1903, 'he demanded to know why they [the N.E.A.C. committee] had not hung them. But alas this question was out of order.'

On 22 March 1903 Ida's second son, Caspar, was born. Augustus showed little interest in the future admiral, for he had other things on his mind. He had fallen in love with Dorelia, whose legendary beauty was to change the course of his life. Dorelia was to play a brief but intense part in the life of Gwen John too. Indeed it was Gwen who discovered her. She had been born Dorothy McNeil, the daughter of a mercantile clerk and the granddaughter of a station master. She had a job in a solicitor's office, but she did not dress like the other typists. She dressed 'artistically' in a style entirely her own, for she felt that she belonged to the world of Art. After work she attended evening classes at the Westminster School (where Tonks had studied). Here she met a number of artists who invited her to their parties. At one of these she met Gwen John.

Dorelia was embarrassingly beautiful. According to William Rothenstein, 'one could not take one's eyes off her'. She had high cheek-bones and slanting eyes. Augustus painted her tall with a swan-like neck but in fact she was rather short. What was uncommon about her was the enigmatic power that gave her beauty its depth. She was not particularly witty. Indeed she was barely articulate, but people in trouble came to her hoping to share her calm.

Augustus fell in love with her and wrote her long letters in Romany (he appended word lists). He was anxious to transform her into a gypsy, and so dissociate her from her humdrum forebears. In Romany he told her she made him think of, 'The sea that sings and cries in the old way, my own great sad mother.' He signed his letters Gustavus Janik.

But a sea of another sort was rising in Ida's heart, a tidal wave of understandable jealousy. Augustus had not disguised his love of Dorelia from Ida and she had attempted to accommodate it in the overcrowded Fitzroy Street flat, to which they had now returned from Liverpool with the two babies and the dog. It was in this flat, with home-bred canaries intermittently landing on people's heads, that Albert Rutherston recalled a momentous occasion on 8 August 1903. Dinner was over when Dorelia entered with Gwen John. 'She and Miss John were about to start for Bordeaux from whence they intended walking to Rome!!!!'

The two girls, Albert declared, behaved like an eloping couple, flushed with excitement and disapproved of by Augustus. The plan was impossible, he insisted. It was also mad. But Gwen John brushed aside his objections and would not even listen to his arguments – 'She never did.' She was 'fat in the face and merry to a degree,' Albert declared.

5

Toulouse

1903–4

Gwen John and Dorelia took ship for Bordeaux under heavy loads. Unlike the Three Musketeers, they had no donkey-cart for their canvases. Augustus had provided them only with a small amount of money and some cakes. At Bordeaux they started to walk up the valley of the Garonne. Gwen wrote Ursula Tyrwhitt a long letter from La Réole, thirty miles out from Bordeaux. She was sitting at the roadside beneath a line of trees looking over daisy-starred meadows with the white Pyrenees beyond.

They earned their living, she explained, in the cafés. They would arrive, dusty and laden, at the principal bar of a village and offer to draw all comers for two francs a head (the price of a dinner). If the client did not wish to be drawn they would sing to him (for this purpose they practised singing as they walked). Often they were teased. One man told Gwen John she could not draw. She asked him if he were an artist and he said he was a sculptor. She believed him. 'It is good to have things pointed out,' she told Ursula. 'He said my lines were too short and choppy.' When they left that café late at night they were pursued by drunks to the haystack under which they hoped to sleep. Only by speaking to them like 'an angel' could Gwen John get them to go away.

The nights were cold under the stars. Once they lay on stone flags by the Garonne. The stones were 'like ice'. They lay on each other to keep warm, with their portfolios on top of them. There were sometimes strange noises in the dark. Once there was 'a huge black thing' that made a rhythmic sound as if it 'were peopled by phantoms'. By daylight it turned out to be a simple piece of farm machinery. They always woke to a row of men staring down at them. Sometimes the girls were so tired that they didn't care if they had the 'whole world' looking at them. At others they pretended to sleep to avoid the necessity for answering questions.

They ate little, for often in the cafés the men looked so disagreeable that Gwen could not pluck up the courage to tell them she did portraits. Fortunately the valley of the Garonne is closely planted with fruit trees and market gardens, and the famous Entre Deux Mers vineyards on the northern side supplied grapes, though these were not quite ripe. Apart from stolen fruit they lived chiefly on bread.

On one occasion Gwen John fell in love with an innkeeper's wife. She was 'young and intensely interesting and took an affection for us'. But her husband thought they were 'bad girls'. At the next village a family at table refused them bread. Gwen John shouted through the door that they were savages, and they pursued her down the road denying the accusation and offering her food. 'Of course we would not touch it.' A young man of the family overtook them later and walked to Meilyan with them. He turned out to have been the lover of the innkeeper's beautiful wife. Her maiden name had been Madeleine Latari, 'so we could send messages to her'.

La Réole, where Gwen was writing the letter, turned out to be a nice town on a hill above the Garonne. People gave them food and work and even bunches of flowers. There was 'a beautiful stable' to live in where 'people came to look at us'. A young artist came to look and stayed to admire. 'He gave us his address in Paris so that we can be models if we like in Paris.' The young artist was a Belgian farmer called Leonard Broucke and he fell deeply in love with Dorelia. There were to be tragic consequences.

At Agen, half way between Bordeaux and Toulouse, there was a letter waiting for Gwen from Ursula. A five-centime piece fell out of it and the girls ate a 'good dinner' and found the courage to ask their fellow diners to have their portraits drawn. They worked there all afternoon. There were also letters for the 'crazy walkers' from Augustus, whose disapproval of their 'wild and unprecedented travels' was increased by his frustration at being deprived of the 'Divine Ardor'. 'With all my growing sedulity,' he wrote, 'I find it difficult to believe you are really growing fat on a diet of wine and onions and under a burden of half a hundredweight odd.' He congratulated them on having escaped the advances of an old man in a barn 'with true womanly ingenuity' and enclosed five pounds for Dorelia which was indignantly returned. Meanwhile he bullied Gwen John about the winter exhibition of the N.E.A.C. The sending-in date was 9 November and she had promised a portrait of Dorelia. 'I hope Gwen will do a good picture of you,' he confided to Dorelia, 'and that it will contain all the genius of the Languedoc. I hope it will be as wild as your travels.' It was impossible to undertake a portrait on the road, so Gwen and Dorelia decided to hurry on through the pilgrim town of Moissac to Toulouse. They accomplished the second seventy-five miles of their journey in a matter of days, and did not refuse lifts in carts. Once they went in a car 'till it broke down . . . Every lift seems saving of time and therefore money too so we always take them,' Gwen told Ursula Tyrwhitt. By the time they reached Toulouse they had covered one hundred and fifty miles, averaging five miles a day. They may not have covered much ground, but for several weeks they had been more genuine gypsies than Augustus was ever to be with all his convoys of caravans and his copy-book Romany.[1]

Toulouse, Gwen declared, was a beautiful place, and a visit of weeks extended into months, for the fourth city of France and the capital of the Languedoc does not pall easily. The splendour of the Romanesque basilica, built to house a thousand pilgrims, contrasted pleasantly with the busy tree-lined squares and the mediaeval streets of mellow brick. With so many distractions it is no wonder that the portrait of Dorelia progressed slowly.

They found a cheap room where the furniture consisted chiefly of a bed, two chairs and a table. The landlady was a tiny old woman with a black handkerchief over her head. 'She is very very wicked, everyone says so in this house and the next where we go to dine sometimes,' Gwen told Ursula Tyrwhitt. 'There is something strange about her face. I cannot look at her she frightens me so but she is very civil, in fact very nice.'

Gwen John had a strange experience with the old lady who was 'frightfully particular' about their paying their rent daily. They had not been at home for three or four days and as a result she had been unable to collect it. On the fourth night, Gwen was woken by a dog barking. The old woman was standing in the open doorway of their room staring at her. This was more than a little surprising since the door had been locked on the inside when the girls went to bed. It was still locked in the morning. Gwen took the incident calmly. 'I suppose she was thinking so hard about the rent that she appeared there,' she told Ursula. 'I don't know why she bothered to open the door. I suppose it was a habit.'

As soon as they arrived in Toulouse Gwen John started to paint the ancient brick-built city from the hills to the north. 'Toulouse lies below, and all around we can see the country for many miles and in the distance the Pyrenees. I cannot tell you how wonderful it is when the sun goes

---

[1] In 1911, eight years later, Augustus was to set out from Effingham with a team of 'six sturdy omnibus horses', a sky-blue van, a canary-yellow van and a light cart. He had with him his family, a groom and a 'stray boy', both called Arthur, and a great number of letters of introduction from 'puissant personages' for the reassurance of 'corrupt policemen' in the matter of camping sites. He had not travelled beyond Cambridge before he had a fight with his groom and dismissed him. As a result most of the horses died and the vans were abandoned.

down, the last two evenings we have had red sun – lurid I think the word is, the scene is sublime then, it looks like Hell or Heaven.'

Augustus wrote again to Dorelia, saying 'The New English sending in day is next Monday and Gwen's picture doesn't seem to arrive.' The ninth of November came and went and, relieved of the pressure of sending-in day, Gwen John began to work at her own pace. The portrait of Dorelia was eventually sent to an N.E.A.C. exhibition six years late.[2] It was entitled 'The student' and shows Dorelia standing at the table in the room in Toulouse. She wears a simple check cotton dress in the 'Dorelia' style and her dark hair is drawn back. Her face is pensive. It is illuminated from below by an oil lamp that casts dark shadows on the wall behind.

There is something curiously tender about this first painting of Dorelia. Gwen John has emphasised her youth and innocence, her almost flower-like vulnerability. Her eyes, both in this picture and in the companion piece, where Dorelia is seated reading,[3] are cast down. (Augustus bought the painting.) Gwen John also painted 'Dorelia in a black dress' at this time, a painting that she sold to Ursula Tyrwhitt. It can now be seen at the Tate. In this portrait only the upper half of Dorelia is shown and her head is turned over her shoulder to face the viewer. The face is broad, the eyes focussed dreamily on some distant spot and the hair piled on top.

The critics repeat after each other that these Toulouse portraits of Dorelia were executed straight on to the canvas without preliminary studies. (By studies they in fact mean sketches, since a study is technically a detailed portrayal of a part of a larger composition.) In fact several preliminary sketches in charcoal for 'Dorelia in a black dress' were found in Gwen John's studio after her death and one was exhibited in New York in 1975, another in London in 1976.

It is interesting to notice the different treatment brother and sister gave to this same model, Dorelia. There seems little connection between Gwen John's innocent young girl with the downcast eyes and the slant-eyed houri Augustus was waiting impatiently to portray. 'Your fat excites me enormously,' he told Dorelia. 'I am dying to inspect it. I am itching to resume that glorious counterfeit of you which has already cost me too many sighs.' To Gwen Dorelia was a girl. To Augustus she was already a woman.

Gwen John appears to have been working on another painting at Toulouse, for she spoke of five paintings that must be completed before she could leave. The fifth was probably of a model she and Dorelia hired to come to their room. Gwen never liked this model, complaining of her 'vulgar red lips' and it was probably for this reason that the portrait, like

[2] Charles L. Rutherston, Albert's older brother, bought this picture at the N.E.A.C. exhibition of 1909. He presented it to the city of Manchester Art Galleries in 1928.
[3] 'Dorelia by lamplight at Toulouse'.

the landscape of Toulouse, does not appear to have been finished. Three completed paintings in three months was nevertheless a triumph by Gwen John's standards.

As Christmas approached Augustus continued to wait anxiously for news of Dorelia and finally received a parcel of 'beautiful toys and bonbons' for David and Caspar, and elaborate cakes for himself and Ida. The only news he could glean was that the girls had a dog who was 'naughty *always*'. Gwen and Dorelia were in fact leading a Spartan existence to save money. They bathed, when it was not too frigid, in the Garonne and lived mainly on stale bread, cheese and figs. They dined occasionally at the little bistro next door, but then they only took a bowl of soup and a bottle of local wine. Dorelia recalled, however, that Gwen John was always light-hearted on these occasions and took much trouble with her appearance before any outing.

Meanwhile Augustus's impatience increased. 'It was a bloody long time before I heard from you,' he wrote to Dorelia. 'Gwendolina says that you get prettier and prettier. When are you coming back again? You are tired of running about those foreign places, I know.' In fact they were.

As the three months at Toulouse passed a tone of *ennui* began to enter Gwen John's letters to Ursula Tyrwhitt. She looked back to the days on the road 'trudging from village to village . . . Our adventures now are not of such a thrilling nature as . . . we have a room to sleep in like any other *bourgeoise*.' She had developed a brief passion for a handsome married girl in the neighbourhood, but she was now tiring of her and dreamed of more stimulating company, preferably that of 'Miss Ursula'. 'I long sometimes to be in London,' she wrote, 'and to go to some exhibitions together.' She even referred to London as 'the dear old place'. 'I am hurrying so because we are so tired of Toulouse – we do not want to stay a day longer than necessary – I do nothing but paint – but you know how slowly that gets on – a week is nothing. One thinks one can do so much in a week – if one can do a square inch that pleases one – one ought to be happy – for after all to do in a year something beautiful . . . would be splendid!'

In February Gwen John and Dorelia set off, not for Rome but for Paris. 'We shall never get to Rome, I'm afraid,' Gwen wrote to Ursula. 'It seems further away than it did in England.' They planned to meet Leonard Broucke in Paris and earn their living for a few months modelling before returning to London in the autumn. It seems unlikely that they travelled on foot considering the time of year.

Dorelia anyway was tired of acting as a beast of burden to Gwen. She later confessed that Gwen had displayed a very bossy side of her nature on the walk and had often made her carry the heavy sack of equipment, arguing that she, the artist, must be fresh for her work. If there was only enough money for one meal it was Gwen who had the larger part of it.

In Montparnasse the girls found a furnished room round the corner from the flat Gwen had shared with Ida and Gwen Salmond. It was at 19 Boulevard Edgar Quinet, a pretty street with trees down the middle and a market. It was flanked by the cemetery for part of its length and is now somewhat dwarfed by the Montparnasse tower which stands at the end. Number 19 was (and is) one of a row of family hotels with shops below them and a little triangular park behind. Gwen and Dorelia's room was small. 'You must not mind the somewhat poverty-stricken appearance of everything in the house,' Gwen John wrote to Ursula – 'we have a hard time sometimes to get enough money to live.' They quickly acquired a tabby and white cat called Tiger who made the place look more homely. The dog who was 'naughty always' appears to have been left behind at Toulouse.

The two young women now set about the task of becoming artists' models. Leonard Broucke gave them introductions. They quickly discovered that the demand was for nudes and, in the interests of survival, they undressed. When Augustus, back in London, heard of it, he was furious. He wrote to Dorelia in Romany, 'You sit in the nude for those devilishly foreign people, but you did not want to sit for me when I asked you, you wicked little *lubni* that you are. You exhibit your naked fat body for money, not for love. So much for you! How much do you show them for a franc? I'm sorry that I never offered you a shilling or two for a look at your *minj*.' Unfortunately he forgot to append a word list.

Gwen John had also been followed to Paris by an admirer. The beautiful girl from Toulouse had now left her husband to be with her, but Gwen refused to see her. 'She was extremely strange and hard,' Dorelia told Michael Holroyd, 'always attracted to the wrong people for their beauty alone. But her work was more important than anyone.' Gwen John wrote to Alice Rothenstein, 'I am getting on with my painting and that makes me happy.' She had decided not to send to the summer N.E.A.C. exhibition and this also made her happy. On 8 July she wrote to Ursula Tyrwhitt, 'I think I can paint better than I used – I know I can. It has been such a help not to think of the N.E.A.C. – and not to hurry over something to get it ready. I shall never do anything for an exhibition again but when the exhibitions come round send anything I happen to have.'

But people would keep breaking in. No sooner had the Toulousaine been shaken off than Miss Hart appeared. Miss Hart was neither young nor 'intensely interesting'. She was a loud and leathery Lesbian from London who thundered continuously against the half of the human race that had had the misfortune to be born male. Like so many foreign painters living on a small allowance in Paris at the turn of the century, she hung on year after year in a small furnished room, hoping for fame, dreading the return to a family in Edwardian England. She had the room next to Gwen and Dorelia at 19 Boulevard Edgar Quinet.

When Gwen and Dorelia were not modelling or painting they were sewing. 'The room is full of pieces of dresses – we are making new dresses,' Gwen told Alice Rothenstein. 'Dorelia's is pink with a skirt of three flounces. She will look lovely in it. Our two painters will want her as a model I am sure when we go home.'

The exhibition, *Les Primitifs Français* at the Pavilion de Marsan[4] was the talk of Paris that season. In the second week of May Augustus arrived, in search both of primitives and Dorelia. What he found did not please him. On hearing of his approach Dorelia had eloped with Leonard Broucke to a secret address in Bruges. For a time Augustus seemed incapable of action. Then Ida, back in England, took the initiative. She wrote to Gwen insisting that Dorelia should come to live with her and Augustus. Encouraged by the letter, Gwen swung into action and drastically changed the lives of four people.

She was at her most formidable when she was tearing lovers apart. As a girl she had successfully prevented her father's second marriage and as a student she had prised Grace Westray from her married suitor. Now in a series of scorching letters addressed to a *poste restante* in Bruges she set to work to prevent Dorelia from becoming the wife of Leonard Broucke.[5]

Dorelia, something has happened which takes my breath away so beautiful is it. Ida wants you to go to Gussy – not only wants but desires it passionately. She has written to him and to me. She says, 'She [Dorelia] is ours and she knows it. By God I will haunt her till she comes back.'

'Gus loves you in a much more noble way than you think . . . You are necessary for his development and for Ida's, and he is necessary for yours – I have known that for a long time – but I did not know how much. Dorelia you know I love you, you do not know how much. I should think it is the greatest crime to take with intention anyone's happiness away even for a little while – it is to me the only thing that would matter . . . I am sorry for Leonard, but he has had his happiness for a time what more can he expect? We do not expect more. And all the future is yours to do what you like. Do not think these are my thoughts only – they are my instincts and inspired by whatever we

---

[4] April to July 1904.
[5] Michael Holroyd has worked out that Leonard and Dorelia were in fact staying at his parents' elegant house at Kraanplatz 5 near the Théâtre Royal Communal. Gwen John's letters to Dorelia and Leonard Broucke's to her are quoted in his *Augustus John*.

have in us divine. I know what I write is for the best, more than I have known anything. If you are perplexed, trust me. But I know you know what I do. Gussy is going home tonight. Come by the first train to me. I shall be at the *gare* to meet you. When you are here you will know what to do and Ida.

Do not put it off a minute . . . because I shall then think you have not understood this letter – that it has not conveyed the truth to you. I fear that, because I know how weak words are sometimes – and yet it would be strange if the truth is not apparent here in every line.

You will get this tomorrow morning perhaps – I shall be in the evening at the Gare du Nord. I would not say goodbye to Leonard.

Your Gwen

When Gwen went to the Gare du Nord the following evening, Dorelia was not there. She had written a letter. To come back, she claimed, would be for ever to curtail her freedom. With Leonard she was free because she was not acting selfishly, but thinking of Leonard's interests too, helping him to develop his talent. Gwen had written her letter in an 'ecstasy'. It was not reasonable. She must not come to her in Bruges.

Gwen was not discouraged. She wrote again, reminding Dorelia of her duty to Art and to her destiny, the twin pillars of her life.

Leonard cannot help you. He would have to know Gussy for that and Ida and you a long time, he never could understand unless he was our brother or a great genius . . .

Strength and weakness, selfishness and unselfishness are only words – our work in life was to develop ourselves and so fulfil our destiny. And unless we do this we are of no use in the world, then *only* can we help our friends and develop them. I *know* that Gussy and Ida are more part of you than Leonard is for ever. When you leave him you will perhaps make a great character of him . . .

While Gwen was writing this to Dorelia, Leonard had posted an answer to her first letter, which, disobeying Gwen's instructions, Dorelia had shown him.

Dear Miss John.

Dorelia got your letter yesterday and showed it to me. Your letter forces me to explain to you several things you forget as well as I can do.

Of course you do not know me neither do you know my sentiments to Dorelia; but this is the other side of the facts, at which you did not like to look, anyway it exists and it is true as your words, if I allow myself to talk a little bit to myself.

You say Leonard had had his happiness for a time, what more can be expect? Do you really think . . . Dorelia's feelings are small enough to love a man like this? People like me don't love often and a woman like Dorelia will not pass my way again, you would better understand, if you would know my life.

Your letter is full of love, the love of a woman for another one, now imagine mine if you can. I am no ordinary man who loves a girl because she is beautiful or whatever. I tell you and you are Dory's friend so you must understand it, I am an artist and cannot live without her and I will not live without her. Very right if you say, 'It is the greatest crime to take with intention anyone's happiness.' You might say as you did I had my happiness. Do you think happiness is a thing that you take like a *café* after dinner, a thing that you enjoy a few times and something you can get sick of? Not my happiness by God: I suffered enough before and I don't let escape something from me that I created myself with all my love and all my strength.

Leonard's letter to Gwen arrived before she had posted her second one to Dorelia so she slipped in an extra page, addressed to Dorelia. Leonard's letter she confessed had disappointed her, had made her 'more certain if certainty can be more certain of everything I have told you'. Leonard's love was, after all, nothing better than possessiveness, like that of the pebble in Blake's *The Clod and the Pebble*,[6] while Augustus's resembled the little clod of clay's. For whatever his faults, Augustus was an artist, while Leonard, as yet, was a part of the bourgeoisie . . .

He limits the laws of nature . . . The laws of nature are infinite and some are so delicate they have no names but they are strong. We are more than intellectual and animal beings we are spiritual also. Men don't know this so well as women, and I am older than Leonard.

[6] Love seeketh not itself to please
   Nor itself hath any care
   But for another gives its ease
   And builds a Heaven in Hell's despair.

   So said a little Clod of Clay,
   Trodden with the cattle's feet,
   But a Pebble of the brook
   Warbled out these metres meet:

   Love seeketh only Self to please
   To bind another to its delight
   Joys in another's loss of ease
   And builds a Hell in Heaven's despite.

He said, 'I could not live without her and will not live without her – this is clear.' Well a man who talks like that ought to be left to walk and stand and work alone – by every woman. Only when he can will he do good work.

Ida now added her entreaties to Gwen's. She had begun to identify her feelings for Dorelia with Gwen's and to suspect that she loved her. 'For the last time, oh my honey . . . I *crave* for you to come here . . . it is all I want. I now feel incomplete and thirsty without you . . . only you needn't come for ten days as I am curing freckles on my face and shall be hideous till I blossom again.' Augustus limited himself to sending poems. This pressure by post built up to a steady bombardment. Augustus, who had left Paris, now returned, prepared to bide his time. At last Dorelia wrote to Gwen John, 'I have given in and am going back with Gus soon.' Augustus at once advanced into Belgium, effected the capture and returned to London on 1 August 1904. As she stood on the platform at Bruges station Dorelia wrote a card to Gwen breaking a long silence. It read, 'How is the cat? Dorelia.'[7]

Gwen John might also have been expected to return to London at this stage. Before Augustus's arrival in May she had suggested to Ursula that they attend the Chelsea Art School, which Augustus had just opened with Orpen in Flood Street.[8] She had again begun to feel homesick for London, she told Ursula. 'We are always talking about beautiful places we know of beyond the suburbs of London. Fitzroy Street and Howland Street seem to me more than ever charming and interesting.' But since then something had happened which would cause her never to wish to leave France again.

---

[7] Leonard visited Gwen John in Paris in the autumn. 'I should write him a nice letter,' she advised Dorelia. 'He will get very ill otherwise.' After that no more was heard of him.

[8] The school was not a success.

6

Rodin I

1904–6

Gwen John met Rodin at the studio of a sculptor called Flodin. She afterwards told him she had sought him all her life on country walks but she would have fled if she had met him in the road. As it was, she agreed to show him her body with a view to work.

The prospect of visting Rodin had been awe-inspiring. Rodin, at sixty-three, was at the height of his fame, honoured and decorated far beyond the bounds of France. The days of the controversial statues 'The Bronze Age' and 'Balzac'[1] were far behind. At the Universal Exhibition of 1900 an entire pavilion had been devoted to works like 'The Kiss', The Burghers of Calais and Eve. Now he could demand what money he liked from prospective clients; celebrities flocked to his Saturday afternoon receptions, and women fought, sometimes literally, for his favours. Many received them.

The studio at 87 rue de l'Université was a vault of a place, in a tall sombre street near the Seine. It was sited at the government marble depot. But inside it marble was transformed into something warm and living, for Rodin's growing preoccupation with the sexuality of women was apparent also in his work. On the studio floor they squatted like toads, stretched like cats, threw their legs above their heads or flung them rudely apart. They twisted into a hundred attitudes, always 'turning upon the central pivot of the sex'.[2] Paul Claudel, more crudely, called the ensemble, 'a banquet of buttocks'. It was into this banquet that Gwen John stepped one cold spring morning in 1904.

Rodin, advancing across the studio towards her, resembled a prophet from another sphere. He had a powerful nose which dominated a bushy

[1] In the former case Rodin was accused of casting a figure from life, in the latter of making the great novelist look like an up-ended seal.
[2] *From Toulouse-Lautrec to Rodin* by Arthur Symons.

white beard and he was draped from head to foot in the white linen smock he wore for work. His hooded grey eyes dilated like those of a parrot.

Gwen John never forgot the tenderness with which this terrifying person drew her towards the stove on that first day, dusted an old wicker chair for her and sat her down. Only when she was rested and warmed through did he ask her to come to the model's couch and take off her clothes. There were screens round the couch and stand. They were supposed to provide privacy from the assistants who were always at work in the studio, but they did not. Young men on high ladders were frequently distracted from their work by what went on behind the screens.

For Rodin the moment when a stranger's nakedness was revealed for the first time never ceased to inspire awe. 'A woman undressing,' he wrote in *The Cathedrals of France*. 'What a gorgeous vision! It is like the sun breaking through the clouds. The first sight of that holy body comes as a blow, a shock. Momentarily taken aback, the eye glances off. The whole of nature resides in the body of every model.' By Rodin's standards Gwen John was thin. He preferred well-built women between thirty and forty. 'It is then that they are at their highest and most vigorous power of expression. Their flesh is firm and the modelling at its fullest development. A young girl is a poor thing in comparison, her flesh and muscles eaten up by anaemia.' Gwen John, however, looked larger with her clothes off and she had good legs and a graceful neck. Rodin was impressed. He told her that she had *un corps admirable* and that she might put her clothes on and start work the next day.

The happiest weeks of Gwen John's life were about to begin. Rodin had been commissioned to execute a memorial to Whistler by the International Society of London.[3] After the controversy surrounding his memorials to Victor Hugo and Balzac, he had decided to represent in the memorial not the subject, whom he had never liked, but the Muse who had inspired him. Gwen John was to be that Muse. As Rodin's own powers declined his models were encouraged to take increasingly athletic poses. In Gwen John he found the supple subject who perfectly fulfilled his requirements, for her body naturally fell into attitudes that few classical models were able or willing to take. From these poses Rodin selected the one now familiar to visitors to the Musée Rodin. The Muse stood with her right foot on a high rock, her head bowed, her mouth open.

Rodin always made small clay models, or *esquisses*, for his statues, which were later enlarged and translated into plaster marble or bronze by

[3] The International Society of Sculptors, Painters and Gravers.

his assistants, some of whom, like Maillol and Bourdelle, were in turn to become famous sculptors. He would build up a figure from a skeletal base with small lumps of clay, his blunt workman's fingers hovering and darting like humming birds over the work. Sometimes he advanced upon the living model with a pair of iron compasses and took a measurement or ran his hand over the flesh. Occasionally he took a mouthful of water and spat it at the clay to keep it pliable. It was not unknown for one of these mouthfuls to miss the clay model and spray the living one.

Gwen John began to fall in love with the great man who, although at the peak of a dazzling career, could concern himself with a little model's welfare.[4] She felt only pleasure in her nudity. As she stood before him naked in the flesh she felt she was naked in the spirit as well. A new peace and happiness welled up inside her. She waited for the best moment in the day when the assistants were dismissed and Rodin lit the candles that he kept in wine bottles.

Rodin always preferred candle-light to the flat brightness of gas jets, and liked to prowl the studio, peering at his work transformed. It was probably by candle-light that they first kissed. What followed was to be the supreme experience of Gwen John's life.

As the days passed work on the statue began to slow down. There was a large Norman cupboard in the studio and in this the lovers kissed before they started work. In the evening, as soon as the assistants and the workmen were sent home and the sculptor's hands were washed, the Muse's celestial pose was abandoned for more earthly ones. Her master took her repeatedly. Waves of pleasure passed through her. She moaned that her little *affaire* was tired but begged for more. Occasionally the concierge came in and Rodin became instantly calm.

The concierge was not the only third party present on these occasions. Gwen John's friend Flodin was one of Rodin's assistants. She was an attractive Finn convinced of her own ugliness, a former mistress of Rodin. So much did she admire Rodin's physique that she happily watched it engaged with another of equal beauty. On occasions she joined in, as Gwen recorded in her graphic letters to Rodin.

The daughter of Edwin John made no judgments on these unusual practices, apart from remarking casually that the French do not consider love outside marriage wrong. She now entered into a playful relationship with Flodin, while remaining involved with Rodin. It was as if the two girls, both in love with the same man, derived some satisfaction from each other's bodies in his absence. When Rodin did not require Gwen John as a model Flodin booked her for herself, although she claimed that

[4] All references to Gwen John's relationship with Rodin are taken from Gwen John's letters to Rodin at the Musée Rodin in Paris.

friends made bad models. She always knew if Gwen John had come from Rodin's embrace. On one occasion she asked her to take the Muse pose. When Gwen John obeyed she cried, 'When you took that position your little heart was on fire, wasn't it?'

Flodin encouraged Gwen John to draw. She even invited her to share a model in the evenings. But Gwen preferred her own little room and her cat, saying that if the cat wouldn't keep still she could draw flowers. She was happier at home surrounded by all that pleased her. Sometimes Flodin came to Gwen John's room and posed in return for a drawing. Once Gwen John infuriated Flodin by drawing her with a deep décolletage. She swore she'd draw her nude next time. Then Flodin threw herself on the bed and Tiger scratched her. She told Gwen it was a good thing she had a cat and not a baby. She'd look a fool going around with Rodin's brat on one arm and a cat on the other. Gwen John agreed it *was* a good thing.

Flodin was the only person, other than her sister Winnie, who brought out the girlish side of Gwen's character. One Sunday they went to the Bois de Clamart together and mislaid Tiger. Inevitably, a *rôdeur* (bad type) appeared. Gwen John's country walks were bedevilled by *rôdeurs*. At the turn of the century, perhaps because of a repressive moral code, Paris appears to have had a large population of unsatisfied men who prowled the outer suburbs in search of unaccompanied women. This one was particularly offensive.

'I'm looking for a pussy, too,' he said to Gwen John. She returned to Flodin who was waiting on the path.

'Did he show you his *thing*?' asked Flodin.

Gwen John went back into the woods, calling the cat. The *rôdeur*'s head was obscured by branches but his thing was not.

'I thought so,' said Flodin. 'Can't a girl have some peace in full daylight?' They both collapsed in giggles.

But while love made Gwen young it made Rodin old. He began to complain of his declining powers even at the height of the affair. He said that sex gave him a headache which lasted two days, that it made him stupid for his work and should be limited to once a fortnight. Gwen promised to behave more like a Muse next time she came to the studio so that both they and the Muse might benefit. She suggested they should confine themselves to kisses alone. When the next day came, they made love not once but twice.

By now Gwen John was deeply enthralled. She wrote Rodin passionate letters, speaking of 'things I never thought of before', letters that were 'to be burned at once'. Rodin was with her constantly during the many hours they were apart. When she walked alone in Luxembourg gardens his imaginary hand was in hers. At night she imagined he slept beside her in her narrow bed.

Now she knew that her life was at last beginning. Before she had come to France she had been a child lost in the woods, a little solitary person, unawakened and unhelped, a waif and a vagabond, a stranger in this world. What had happened to her before she left England was no longer interesting. Now he who was interested in all beauty made the world beautiful to her. With mysterious words he, a man, had broken down the walls of her prison. He was more than her master, he was her god. In his embrace she performed acts of worship, for he knew the Eternal, he almost *was* the Eternal.

For the next ten years Rodin, whether he liked it or not, was to take control of Gwen John's life. She looked to him as to a father, only making the provision, 'If you chide me do it gently as to a child.' At her request he planned almost every hour of her day. He knew that indolence was her chief enemy. 'I do only what pleases me and I don't even know my duties . . .' He insisted that she was to take one if not two modelling engagements every day and on Sundays was to walk in the country and visit the public baths in the rue d'Odessa. The rest of her time must be spent in drawing. But how could a woman in love draw, she enquired. To make a drawing you must put a morsel of your heart on one side. A work of art is a little beating heart. But her heart was elsewhere. She had wanted once to be a famous artist but the women artists she worked for had made her disgusted with ambition. She wanted only to bask in the sunshine of love. She thought of herself only as Rodin's model. If she couldn't model for him she would button his boots, brush his coat, light his stove, sweep his floor. Anything but draw. The box of pencils he gave her stayed on the mantelpiece in the room in the Boulevard Edgar Quinet. It was only slowly and reluctantly that she let him force her to draw, by scolding her if she did not bring one work with her each time she came to the studio. Also she hoped that by drawing she could prove she was not stupid in one thing. She wanted Rodin to be proud of her.

Rodin believed in work. He himself had been a workman most of his life and he expected others to be the same. From him Rilke was to learn the lesson of hours of daily work. Gwen John learnt the same lesson and her drawing improved. Her model continued to be her cat. Gwen found Tiger incomparably beautiful as she sat with her head turned; half-beast, half-girl, 'guarding the mysterious soul that haunts the body of a cat'. She drew the cat so that Rodin might know how beautiful she was and to preserve her from mortality. But she never felt anything she drew came near to conveying her.

Tiger was not an easy model. At the sight of pencil and paper she would start a game and become impossible to draw. She would only arrange herself when Gwen had given up and put on her hat to go out.

There are fifteen watercolours of Tiger among Rodin's drawings,[5] falsely attributed to him, some with and some without a kitten under her paw (Tiger had litters in August 1904 and 1906). They are natural in style, no doubt because they were intended as records and because they were painted for a man who claimed that the secret of art is in portraying life.

It was also Rodin who encouraged Gwen John to take an interest in her appearance. He had been known to turn away a model if she had an unbecoming hair style or shadows under her eyes. Gwen now brushed her long hair tirelessly and peered into the mirror for signs of pallor. She pinched her breasts to make sure their size was not diminishing and collected compliments from other patrons and from the men who followed her in the street to pass on to Rodin. And she started to buy clothes. She visited Liberty and Samaritaine. She combed her local department store, the palatial Bon Marché with its tiers of galleries, for hats, gloves, *bottines*, jackets, umbrellas and above all dresses. She spent many hours selecting a particularly pretty grey one with a tight bodice and a full skirt in the Dorelia style. She feared it might have a slightly arty flavour, but she counteracted this with a worldly hat. In Flodin's opinion she was a thorough-going '*cocotte*'. But then it was Flodin who had complained that she was a dowd when she first came to the studio. Another client complimented her on the fact that her hair style and her costume were 'all of a piece'.

It was Rodin's habit to employ his mistresses as secretaries, but he was to have little success with Gwen John for neither her French nor her English was good enough for correspondence. But she did attempt to translate some cuttings about Rodin's work from English newspapers. Rodin was not satisfied. He criticised not only the quality of the French but the choice of extracts. Why all this stuff about a collector called Yorke Towell? Gwen hotly pointed out that there would be no interest in knowing that Towell owned one of his heads if he knew nothing about Towell.

More successful was the course of reading Gwen embarked upon under her master's guidance. She was not a natural reader and found that reading confused her. 'We have a source in us,' she once wrote, 'that can only produce its own fruits. Instinct is our genius.' Rodin, although not a literary man, was a keen reader. Late in life he came upon Fielding and Richardson and his eyes would open wide as he compared the good nature of the one with the interesting cruelty of the other.

As a sculptor he was fascinated by classical Greece, so Gwen was encouraged to read Greek poetry and drama. She liked to select stories from mythology that she thought might prove suitable subjects for

[5] There are several thousand Rodin drawings in the Musée Rodin, Paris.

Rodin's sculpture. In a letter she related the tragic story of the death of Procris, the subject of her favourite painting in the Louvre. She also learned passages from the Greek plays in translation by heart in order to recite them to Rodin during intervals from posing. *Iphigenia* was her choice. Rodin asked her for a critical comment on its author and she said that Euripides, like Rodin, believed that everything had beauty. The characters said what they thought even if it was inconvenient, and the heroes even dared to cry and were egoists. She learned the whole play by heart, to recite to Rodin, but, owing to her poor French, the recitation was cut short.

During the summer two old friends from the Slade took rooms at the Hôtel Edgar Quinet. Gwen Salmond came to see the *Primitifs* exhibition, as Augustus had done, and stayed on to revisit the Louvre. The days were hot and the girls used to walk at night. 'The sky was a deep blue with some great clouds. The Luxembourg gardens looked beautiful without a soul there. So quiet and peaceful. And the trees are so beautiful down the streets, occasionally lit up by a lamp . . . I sometimes sleep in the gardens in a little copse of trees,' Gwen John told Ursula Tyrwhitt.[6]

Then Ursula herself came, on her way home from painting in Athens. She was the only one of Gwen John's women contemporaries at the Slade who was to remain a painter even after her marriage, perhaps because that marriage was late and childless. Her visit went well, apart from the fact that Gwen John was somewhat encumbered by a midsummer cold. 'What a lot depends on one's body,' she remarked afterwards. Ursula, who was accustomed to the comforts of her father's rectory at Easton-in-Gordano (a name Gwen John could never spell), found her room at the hotel small and bare. Gwen John's room was no better, and the constant presence of the gruff man-hating Miss Hart next door was irksome. Nevertheless the girls amused themselves. Ursula bought a hat at Samaritaine and thought she detected a fake Titian at the Louvre which Gwen John later proved was painted under the influence of Giorgione.

It was to Ursula Tyrwhitt alone that Gwen John confided her thoughts about painting all through her life. To Rodin she never admitted to being more than an amateur with a box of watercolours. 'I think I can paint better now than I used,' she wrote to Ursula, 'I know I can. It has been such a help not to think of the N.E.A.C. and not to hurry over something to get it done.'

Ursula was also the only person, either friend or relative, to whom Gwen John wrote about Rodin. She seldom spelt out his name and never indicated that there was an intimate side to her relationship with him.

[6] To sleep in the gardens it would have been necessary to hide in the copse until the gates were closed for the night.

Nevertheless she gave orders that any letter mentioning the name R. . . . was to be consigned to the rectory fire as soon as read.

Ida also had planned a visit to Paris but a third pregnancy (Robin) prevented her, and instead Gwen visited her, for Ida's letters were becoming desperate. Now that Dorelia was sharing Augustus's life at her request she no longer felt necessary and was often very near the laudanum bottle. With nothing but braying babies for company, she declared she was as square as a box and mad as a lemon squeezer. She longed for another woman who would share 'things beyond the ordinary aspect of things'. In short she longed for Gwen, beside whom she felt 'dreadfully feeble', for Gwen, she imagined, had no one at all now. She did not know about Rodin.

In September 1904 Gwen John stayed in Augustus and Ida's new house at Matching Green in Essex although only for three days, probably because she could not bear to be away from Rodin longer, and because she did not enjoy the life of a lady slavey, made necessary by the resignation of the nursemaid on moral grounds. Ida described a typical day in the life of the household. 'About 7 David and Caspar wake and say silly things and get dressed and have a baked apple and play with toys and run up and down. Breakfast about 8.30. D and C out for a walk. We have dinner about 1 and so on and on till 7 when they go to bed, sometimes dancing about and shouting, sometimes going to sleep.' It is unlikely that Augustus did much to lighten this diet of domesticity for he usually avoided 'the unspeakable fireside, the gruesome dinner table' and stormed through the rooms driving the children before him, or retired to bed with a concertina.

When Gwen John came back to Paris Rodin took up serious work on the statue of the Muse, for the opening of the 1904 Salon[7] was not far off and he wanted something to keep 'The Thinker' company. Gwen turned to her full programme of work as prescribed by Rodin. But there was a problem. She was beginning to lose weight. 'I feel I am getting quite thin,' she told Ursula. 'R. says I am too thin for his statue and I don't eat enough – but I rarely have time to eat.' The programme of modelling, drawing and taking exercise continued unabated.

There was another reason why Gwen John was growing thin. She pined to be Rodin's wife. She longed to be with him all the time, to sleep with him, to button his boots, to prepare his bowl of morning milk. As it was, he passed out of her life each evening after the walk to the station together. Sometimes she did not see him again until the following afternoon.

[7] The Paris Salon was the huge annual show organised by the Société des Artistes Français and more or less equivalent to the Royal Academy Summer Exhibition.

One day Rodin made a promise to Gwen John. After the Muse was finished they would go to Rome together. 'We'll have no headaches,' Gwen wrote in joyous anticipation, 'there will be fine weather and I'll wear the red frock if you like. I'll look after all the practical matters while you admire Nature. We'll come home to my room and all will be in order.'

But the Muse was not finished. Although a plaster maquette of the statue appeared at the Salon of 1904 at which 'The Thinker' was shown, it lacked arms. The reason for its armless state was that another Muse had appeared upon the scene. Her name was the Duchesse de Choiseul, and she arrived in the studio at an inconvenient moment. Calm as always, Rodin showed his drawings to the Duchess. Gwen John, trembling all over, pulled on her clothes while a female studio assistant attempted to console her.

The Duchesse de Choiseul was an American woman, the daughter of a New York lawyer named Coudert. Unknown to Gwen John, Rodin had already met her at her husband's château in Brittany and there she had fallen noisily in love with him. Rodin's friends were appalled. She looked like a painted weasel, they declared. Her hair, if it *was* hair, was red, her hats were awful and she was foreign. After her first visit to the studio she more or less installed herself, calling herself Rodin's inner voice. She brought a wind-up gramophone and danced with a shield and a shawl in the Grecian manner. Sometimes she fell, for the Norman cupboard where Rodin and Gwen had kissed now held many bottles.

Rodin appeared to be mesmerised by this creature. Some people even said she had put Red Indian poison in his milk. She did what she liked with him. She replaced his box-like tweed suits and black felt hats with toppers and tail-coats. She ordered his models from the studio and told the concierge to turn away his assistants Maillol and Despiau. She distracted him from his work and persuaded him to visit cathedrals with her.

She was not without wit however, and Gwen John feared her as one of those *grandes dames instruites* who can always think of something to say. The writer, John Marshall, who met her in Rome in 1912, declared 'she told me everything with such go that I seemed to see it all.' As an unpaid secretary she succeeded in selling seventeen pieces of Rodin's sculpture to the New York Metropolitan Museum.

The peaceful afternoons in the studio were now over. Gwen longed for an invitation to model for the arms of the Muse. It never came. Another now took her place. If she came to the studio it was as an ordinary visitor and as often as not the concierge, whom she detested, asked her if she had an appointment and told her that Monsieur was engaged and she must wait. When she did get in, he would treat her distantly, as if he were ashamed of her, or call her 'Mademoiselle' which made her suicidal. Finally he took to barking orders at her like, 'Use the other door', or 'Come at one o'clock', as if she were a child. She decided not to visit him privately again since it was not *plein de dignité*.

There was nothing left but to visit the studio on Saturday afternoons when Rodin was at home to society. On these occasions he was invariably surrounded by women. Once he insulted Gwen by giving her money in front of one of these. Often he paid no attention to her, and if she did get his ear she would be able to think of nothing to say and would end up by being rude in her efforts to hide her shyness. She always claimed she had been brought up in ignorance of good manners. She usually came away from one of Rodin's Saturday afternoons feeling that she had made a poor showing, which she probably had, considering that her sole interest in the proceedings was to hold the master's hand without being seen. On one occasion during a piano recital, she managed to squeeze his fingers. She begged his pardon afterwards and assured him that the lady pianist had not noticed for she had spoken nicely to Gwen John about her mignonette button-hole. On another occasion she had hidden behind the door as Rodin shepherded the company out of the studio. She was hoping that he would come back to kiss her but he merely shut the door behind him.

Eventually she ceased to attend the Saturday receptions but stood about outside waiting for Rodin. He was an energetic man and usually walked the distance to the station at Montparnasse. It was Gwen John's greatest joy to take his arm and go with him. If he was in a good mood at the station he would give her one of his warm looks and let her share a bench with him.

One Saturday she had to wait three hours in the doorway of the laundry opposite. ('It was all right,' she assured Rodin. 'Nobody said anything because I was wearing my best blue and white dress.') Finally the great doors of the studio opened and Rodin came out accompanied by 'That Woman'. The Duchess wore emerald-green velvet and a plate of mixed flowers on her flaming hair. The neat person in the laundry doorway could no longer contain herself. She rushed across the road and accused her rival of monopolising Rodin, of cruelly exhausting him with foreign travel and high living, of distracting him from his art and driving away his friends. Rodin, outraged, swept Choiseul off to the station. Gwen 'went crying home like a little weeping machine' and wrote a letter. She accused Rodin of having ceased to love her and of cruelly ignoring her in favour of his American friend. She said he had not even invited her to see her own statue at the 1904 Salon. She asked if it were true that they 'chase your women out of France'. She said that rather than accept another penny from him she would wear a cotton dress all winter.

Rodin replied with expected fury. She was jealous, she had 'unreasonable desires', made intolerable scenes. She was not to come to the studio again without an invitation.

With Rodin's door temporarily closed to her, Gwen John was obliged to set about the job she most dreaded: knocking on doors and asking for work from artists who were coming home from their vacations. She was always ashamed of being a model and, in obedience to Rodin, never let her concierge know her profession but always let it be understood that she was a sort of artist. She found the concierges at the studios pleasant enough once they knew she was a model and not an artist looking for a studio. The occupants of the studios were not so nice. Some didn't even bother to come to the door when they heard it was only a model. A German with 'a nasty face' was cross because she had disturbed him and then suggested she should move in with him and share his 'ideas.' An American at Auteuil apologised for being a landscapist but nevertheless put his hand on her breast 'to see if it was developed'. In all she visited four men and three women and was too upset to eat for two days afterwards.

She became increasingly unwilling to model for men after an unfortunate experience with Rodin's friend the painter Jacques S̩. He had admired the spiritual beauty of her body, and had offered her a higher fee than the women painters. At first she was impressed by the delicacy of his approach. He did not even touch her to indicate the pose. When he began to touch her feet, something unknown went wrong. She left the studio and wrote a frantic note to Rodin commanding him to recover her wages.

Soudbinine however was a male artist who never gave her trouble. At their first meeting she found him ill and wrapped in rugs beside his equally sick dog. He did a bust of her for the 1906 Salon. Indeed she appeared three times at that Salon, portrayed separately by Rodin, Soudbinine and the sculptor Miss O'Donnell.

Miss O'Donnell, like Flodin, was one of Rodin's assistants and also in love with him. But, unlike Flodin, she was a lady of high birth and doomed to perpetual virginity. Rodin used to imitate the way she shook hands with her finger crooked. Gwen John first saw her at Rodin's studio. In Gwen's words, 'She first admired, and then hired my face.' Later she made a complete statue of Gwen and, unlike Rodin, succeeded by dint of many extra sittings in finishing it. Rodin admired the work.

O'Donnell was dominating and overbearing. Yet she could be kind. Sometimes she went shopping with Gwen, helping her seek out 'good form' at the Bon Marché. According to Gwen, she was better able to choose clothes for others than herself. Through O'Donnell Gwen met and modelled for several other English ladies, all strictly celibate, all temporarily residing in Paris in pursuit of Art. One of them was Miss Bowser, sister-in-law of the poet Arthur Symons, who became a kind and faithful employer and used Gwen whenever Miss O'Donnell didn't need her. Gwen John always referred to these ladies collectively as 'the English' and never used their Christian names.

She always preferred to sit for women. They were more considerate. They seldom asked for difficult poses and they usually remembered the rest periods. Women made tea and conversation during the intervals. The first at least was always welcome. Most of Gwen John's clients talked to her solely of painting, knowing she was uninterested in gossip, even the art gossip of Montparnasse. Only Flodin discussed all subjects like an equal.

Modelling, even for female clients, could be risky, for there was always the danger of male visitors to the studio, dreaded by most female models. On one occasion a married couple arrived. The painter took the wife into the kitchen to make tea leaving Gwen naked and alone on her stand with the husband. He did not hesitate to make the most of his opportunity. Having remarked that English breasts were flat he passed his hands over Gwen John's body to test his thesis. For half a minute she couldn't speak, then she screamed. The women rushed from the kitchen but refused to believe her.

Meanwhile Miss Hart was becoming more insistent than ever and found her way into Gwen John's bedroom more than any of the other ladies. When Gwen was ill and could not pose she drew her in bed, pronouncing her 'extraordinary', ('whatever that means' Gwen John commented). Her conversation was over-vivacious and vulgar and punctuated with volcanic bursts of laughter. Always there were warnings about the danger of associating with the dirty, egotistical and brutal male, Rodin. 'Aren't you *ashamed* to stand naked before that man?' she said. 'Oh no,' said Gwen, 'I like it very much.'

Almost all Gwen John's employers were admirers of Rodin, if not in love with him, and the fact that she was his model impressed them. Every now and again she would obtain permission for a party of them to be brought to the studio and introduced to him. These were great occasions when the ladies would put on their best hats and dresses and hire a cab to take them to the rue de l'Université. The concierge would admit them to the ante-room and they would wait until the master was ready to receive them in his studio. He would then say a few words to each of them and, as Gwen John put it, 'even the one in the blue dress received a handshake that was strong and kind.' Miss Hart, needless to say, was left behind on these occasions.

For Gwen John being an artist's model was, and always would be, a chore. *Fragments*, a book she found in Miss Bowser's studio, was of some help. It consisted of brief extracts from a German philosophical author. Some of these Gwen John did not understand and, having translated them from English into French, she sent them to Rodin with *pas compris* written beside them. Others she learnt by heart and said over to herself while she posed. They were mostly precepts for the leading of the good life, and encouraged her to meditate.

But no amount of bracing precepts could persuade her to get up in the morning for a modelling appointment. She often woke before dawn, but then she lay naked and thought of Rodin. Soon the intimate part of her body was on fire and, like Sappho, she would turn and 'spread her tender limbs' and do 'what only Rodin should do.' Afterwards she always wrote and confessed to Rodin. He was invariably angry and ordered her to sleep with her hands crossed on her chest.

Ida's arrival in Paris in the August of 1905 was the result of a long period of unhappiness. At Matching Green Dorelia had become pregnant and Ida's liking for her had vanished. She found Dorelia's cow-like presence intolerable and could not bring herself to speak of the future child. Suddenly, late in her pregnancy, Dorelia left and Pyramus was born in a caravan on Dartmoor. Then Ida fell in love with her.

Dorelia, whom she had described as 'one of those fantastics whose bosoms stick out abnormally', was now 'the prettiest little bitch in the world'. She longed for her 'burning hot, not to say scalding' body next to her own in bed. 'I do not know rightly whether Ardor and I love each other. We seem to be bound together by sterner bonds than those of love,' she wrote to Augustus. 'With her I feel like a champagne bottle that wants to be opened.'

After a summer together in the caravan, they both decided to leave Augustus. Like Gwen John, Ida felt she could not live or paint near him. 'I feel so stifled and oppressed,' she wrote. 'It isn't that Augustus is difficult or unkind. It's the mental state. I can imagine going to the Louvre and then back to a small room over a restaurant or something. Think of all the salads and the sun, and blue dresses and waiters. And the smell of butter and cheese in the small streets. I think to live with a girl friend and have lovers would be almost perfect.'

By October the two women, with David, Caspar, Robin and Pyramus had settled in a barely furnished flat in the rue Monsieur-le-Prince. There was also a dog called Bolster. They had only one bed between them. The children slept in boxes and the babies slept in baskets. Soon 'another beastly boy, a coarse looking blockhead', arrived in spite of Ida's attempts to dislodge him. He was named Edwin. But still the women were happy. 'Imagine me in bed, with Ardor looking after the four others . . . Cheerful, patient, beautiful to look upon. Ready to laugh at everything and nothing. She wheels out two in the pram, with David and Caspar walking. She baths them, dresses them, feeds them and smacks them.'

Ida and Dorelia saw more of Gwen John than anyone in the next year or two. They came to her room to sew dresses and shared meals of salami, eggs and spinach, avoiding Miss Hart whom they still found 'embarrassingly attached' and the 'horrid cat'. Gwen John gave them 'three beautiful pictures' for their bare flat.[8] Ida declared she was 'always the same strange reserved creature.' It was typically secretive of Gwen to make no mention of Ida and Dorelia's visit in her letters to Rodin. When Dorelia made her a black velvet jacket for a hundred francs she told Rodin it had been made by a dressmaker.

The arrival of Ida and Dorelia as fugitives in Paris brought back terrible memories of Augustus's cruelty as a boy in Tenby; the fights on the first day of the holidays and the constant teasing. Gwen John began to have a nightmare in which she beat Augustus continually with her fists while he smiled. She began to realise that her self-imposed exile was an escape from Augustus.

In February 1906, perhaps as the result of Ida and Dorelia's persuasion, Gwen finally moved out of the sordid Hôtel Edgar Quinet. Ursula Tyrwhitt and Rodin had also been pleading for a move. Finally Gwen announced the good news to Ursula. 'Rodin suggested my leaving my room today and taking an unfurnished one – wasn't it kind of him. He thought it would be nicer to be *chez moi* and he is going to pay three months rent which one has to pay in advance, also to furnish it if I will allow him but I don't think I shall allow that. I shall be able to get all I want very soon gradually, as you said.'

The rue St Placide, her new address, was a wide friendly street of little shops at the northern extremity of Montparnasse, near the Luxembourg gardens and the river. Gwen's room at No. 7 was large and square, overlooking a courtyard where Tiger could take exercise. It was Gwen John's first real home. 'My room is so pretty,' she wrote to Rodin. ' "Pamela" is in the bookcase, my drawings are above the bed and there are flowers on the mantelpiece. I will draw it for you reflected in the wardrobe mirror with me doing something in the Dutch manner.' The drawing turned out to be the study for a well-known painting, 'Lady reading at a window'. It represented a slim girl in a black dress standing in the Muse pose with one foot on the famous wicker chair that appears in several of Gwen John's paintings and which her nephew Edwin preserved until recently. Her face is pensive and innocent like that of a girl of fifteen and her long hair is surmounted by a black bow. The room in which she stands is almost bare of furniture. Apart from the wicker chair, only a small round table and a hanging bookcase are shown. A French

[8] One of these was probably 'Dorelia in black'.

window with a billowing curtain and a papered wall form the background. There are watercolours of Tiger hanging on the wall.

An observant admirer of this picture, which now hangs at the Tate, will notice that the face of the young woman is not that of Gwen John but of a Dürer Madonna. She told Ursula Tyrwhitt that she had not wanted to have her own face there, but admitted that the deception had not succeeded and had been a silly thing to do. When she painted the same picture again several years later to send to America she put her own face in. This version can now be seen at the Museum of Modern Art, New York.

Gwen John painted a variant on this picture,[9] originally entitled 'La chambre sur la cour'. The subject is perched serenely sewing in an upright chair and Tiger has the basket chair with the cushion. The interior of the room across the court is plainly visible.

Now at last Gwen John had a room where she could receive a gentleman. Rodin visited one morning a week, although Gwen John stayed in every morning. In preparation to receive him she swept and polished, she arranged flowers in the exact centre of the mantelpiece and tied a bow around Tiger's neck. She washed and brushed her own hair until it gleamed 'a little' and ironed her skirt and belt. Then she waited for the step on the stair, never to be confused with the booted clump of a woman. Would he find the room dirty? Suddenly she felt 'as shy as a sheep'. It was surely not possible that such a man had ever been present in this room or ever would be. Then he was there. All too soon the hour of ecstasy on the solid mahogany bed was over. As she heard his steps descending she knew she was alone in the world for another week.

It was in this room at night that Gwen John held imaginary conversations with Rodin. After her modelling session was over she would stop for bread at the bakery in the rue Cherche-Midi and at the *charcuterie* in the rue St Placide for a slice of ham and then climb the stairs, avoiding the talkative concierge. Tiger would be waiting. She did not light the lamp or the fire. A full moon was shining straight through the window. She made sandwiches and a cup of tea, forgot to eat them and settled down at the round table by the window. Now she could fix on paper the remembered joy of the morning's embrace, that otherwise existed only in the air. In Rodin's presence she had been tongue-tied. She felt like Hans Andersen's little mermaid who was dumb, and could only dance before the prince. Now she could wait for the sentences to come of their own accord:

> Moon lightens the room
> My soul is calm like a lake

[9] 'Girl reading at a window', 1968 Arts Council Exhibition. Collection of Mrs Joseph L. Henderson. Referred to from now as 'La chambre sur la cour'.

Always without light or noise
Then my love has no fear
He rises from the depths of my heart
To keep me company.

During 1906 and 1907 Gwen John wrote three letters a day to Rodin, unable to resist the temptation to talk to him. Because she wrote them at times when she felt she should have been drawing, she wanted the letters to be works of art. They carried no date or address for she considered such conventions suitable only for ordinary people. When she made fair copies of them she cried at how few of her thoughts they conveyed. 'My heart is filled with beauty and I can only write down trivialities.' She blushed to think of Rodin reading such stupidity. 'I'm selfish to make him read them,' she confessed. 'But lovers are egoists (I read that in a famous author). And at least they're short.'

Certainly the letters were monotonous at times, either rejoicing at love recently received or lamenting love too long withheld. Complaints of his indifference to her unhappiness were frequent. In his studio he had ignored her six times when she had complained. In her room he had stood by the table and laughed at her sorrow. Yet she was not totally without an author's pride in her work. She once said of her letters, 'They are a part of me that lives for ever.' In another she informed Rodin that whatever they were they were not *jolies* and she was not 'a charming little woman'. She added, 'I may be timid but I am never humble.'

For a timid woman she discussed the physical aspects of sex with surprising frankness. She was discreet only in the use of names. Just as she called her clients 'the English' or 'the Germans', so she referred to Rodin's 'thumb' and her 'affair'. The conjunction of these was 'the thing'. Yet she did not hesitate to describe 'things'. She told Rodin how much she had bled after he had visited her on one occasion. She had had her *règles* at the time and had hardly been able to walk to the shops afterwards. Modesty only afflicted her when she was describing a case of cruelty to an animal. Then she would become almost speechless.

She had by now learned to tolerate the Duchess and several others besides, but she still considered herself Rodin's only true wife. She tried to believe what he told her, that a man could love many things in many women and there would always be a corner for her. But unconsciously she was still tormented by jealousy as a dream proved. She dreamed that Rodin was on the point of making love to her when her sister Winnie arrived from Canada with another woman. The other woman took him away and Gwen became hopelessly entangled with her clothes in her effort to pursue him. By the time she was ready to set off the guilty couple were no longer visible. After this dream Gwen John implored

Rodin not to show love for another woman in front of her. At times her jealousy would get the better of her. In a letter she told how the beauty of a morning walk in the woods near her beloved's home at Meudon was destroyed by a 'mad rage mounting from the heart to the brain. Is this monster in all women's hearts to devour them and tear them to pieces?' she cried. Sometimes, when she was tired or had her period (which always strongly affected her), she would let fly without restraint, accusing Rodin of criminal cruelty and thoughtlessness. She dreamed of a perfect existence with him in a small boat far out to sea or in a castle surrounded by high walls without gates. In the castle she would be his little maid.

Often it was only in her letters that she was alone with Rodin and she made sure they arrived when he was alone. She delivered them in person to the box at the studio lodge, disguising her writing to allay the suspicions of the concierge. Sometimes she wrote her letter at a café table opposite the studio and handed it to Rodin as he came out. Once she chased him all the way to Montparnasse station with one. Thinking she had said 'Meudon' not 'Rodin' the guard pushed her into a train which was just leaving.

Rodin reacted with marvellous patience to this bombardment. In two years he received close on two thousand letters from Gwen John. Whether he read them all is unknown. Certainly he opened and preserved them. His letters in reply were short but affectionate. They often contained good advice about her health and bad news about his own (he was usually *grippé* or *enrhumé*). He admonished her frequently. 'You must change your room which is damp and sunless.' 'Look after yourself. You are too pale.' 'This letter is to remind you to go for your walks always, and to look after yourself.' 'I beg you, *chère amie*, don't make yourself ill.' He praised her 'little heart, so patient, devoted and gentle'. He spoke of her 'great powers of feeling and thought'. He always ignored her complaints of neglect and often sent her money. Gwen John treasured these letters above all worldly possessions. She slept with one in her hand and painted Rodin a gouache of herself pressing another to her breast, her lips parted and her eyes dreaming.[10]

A strange aspect of Gwen John's letters to Rodin was the change in her handwriting.[11] The early letters were written in a neat but fast adult hand. The letters after 1904 were in what one can only describe as board-school copperplate. A spluttering nib describes large uncertain loops with an occasional blot which is apologised for in the margin. This change in handwriting must have been the result of the emotional shock caused by the intrusion of the Duchesse de Choiseul into Rodin's life. Perhaps

[10] Now in the Musée Rodin.
[11] See pages 202-3.

unconsciously Gwen John adopted a childish hand to ensure that even if Rodin abandoned her as a lover he could not abandon her as a father.

An odd aspect of all these letters was that she never settled upon a name by which Rodin should call her. She signed them variously, Mary, John Mary, Marie, or just Your Obedient Little Model. The name Gwen never appeared. But perhaps the strangest thing of all about these letters was that half of them were addressed to a woman who never existed. Her name was Julie. She was Rodin under another name and it may well have been Rodin who invented her. On several occasions he had complained that Gwen John's letters were monotonously emotional. He wanted to know more about the everyday events of her life. She complained that her life consisted of trivial joys and chagrins which could only be told to a woman, someone like her sister Winnie. And so it was that Winnie was transformed into Julie and started to receive a letter every day.

An elaborate deception heralded the birth of Julie. On the last day of February 1906 Gwen John claimed to have found a fragment of a letter addressed to someone called Julie lying under a tree in the Bois de Boulogne. She forwarded it to Rodin, enquiring whether he liked it. It ran as follows:

Dear Julie,
I have dressed and washed today and was with my master by 5.0. I will not talk of our lovemaking for you have a lover of your own. The concierge, as so often, disturbed us, but Rodin was calm at once. Anyway, I have promised to tell you of daily events, and not to speak too much of love.
When Rodin and I left he took my coat and said, 'Are you coming with me Mademoiselle?' (Because we were in front of the concierge.) We walked side by side to the station, having a most interesting talk. As usual he said he was old but for me he is young. When I got back to my room I went on my knees and gave thanks.

From the beginning Gwen John frequently put the Julie letters to the use for which they were not intended. She spoke about Rodin in them, instead of describing 'with truth my own existence', for she had no intimate woman friend apart from Flodin with whom she could discuss her lover, and Flodin, like most of the women she knew, was in love with him herself. Keeping a picture of Winnie's face with its small friendly eyes in her mind, she felt safe, even bold as she wrote. She confided her two chief fears about Rodin: that he would find her unintelligent and that she lacked the coquetry of a French woman which kept a man interested. She would even describe her night thoughts or specify which part of her body she wanted *Mon Maître* to kiss next time they met, and on more than one occasion she worked herself into such a fever of passion while writing that she would beg Julie to hug her and bring the letter to an early close.

In some of the letters however she pleased Rodin. She started to send him humorous accounts of her adventures in and around Paris and admitted that, by relating the confused events of her day, she imposed order on them, and order was what she desired. At times these letters read like school essays and even carry headings like 'A Day in the Country', 'A Terrible Adventure' or 'An Incident in my Room', perhaps in obedience to some suggestion by Rodin for improving her French.

There is no doubt that Gwen's French did improve as the letters progressed. There were still occasional Anglicised constructions and there were certain words (such as *minuet* for minute), that she would never spell in any language. But she was now reading a great deal and beginning to use more sophisticated expressions in French than she had ever used in English.

Richardson's *Clarissa*, translated into French, made a deeper impression on her than anything else Rodin ever lent her. Her heart was soon engaged in the story, and when Robert Lovelace finally seduced the virtuous heroine in the penultimate volume she wept at the cruelty of it. It may well be that the book, entirely written in the form of letters, many exchanged between the heroine and her confidante, gave her the idea of Julie.

A large number of the letters Gwen John wrote to Rodin were written in her room in the rue St Placide. The *petit bourgeois* inhabitants of the house are frequently described. There was the mountainous concierge who considered her an angel for keeping herself and her room so nice, only insisting that her son was more important than Gwen's cat (Gwen said they were equal). She used to draw Gwen John into her stuffy lodge and involve her in discussions with the butcher and the carpenter from across the road. With these 'sages of the street corner' Gwen John discussed such subjects as Napoleon's decision to become emperor and exhibition fights between women at fairs. Her husband was less pleasant. He once hurled Tiger across the court for taking a normal interest in dustbins.

Mademoiselle Pelletier, in the room next door, was a laundress, whose lover Jean left her with a maximum amount of noise one night. He was replaced by a succession of men who came up the stairs at odd times. Mlle Pelletier had been kind to Gwen and had offered to do her laundry on one occasion when she was ill but the break with Jean seems to have unhinged her and she stole twenty francs (half a week's wages) from Gwen's wallet. Gwen knew she was guilty because she had seen her enter the room with a key. The concierge insisted that the police must be called to search the house, and to avoid this Gwen went to the restaurant where

Mlle Pelletier, in a white silk blouse and pearls, was lunching in gay company, on Gwen's wages. Gwen confronted her and the money was returned.

Gwen John was perhaps fortunate to meet Rilke while he was Rodin's secretary, for Rodin forbade his secretaries to talk to his models after Eve began to change shape while he was working on her. Gwen John, however, had little to fear from the morbidly sensitive young German poet who now looked on women chiefly as soul-sisters. He had always enjoyed the company of women who were artists. The happiest years of his life had been spent at the artists' commune of Worpswede, on the peat marshes near Bremen. There he had fallen in love with two girls, Clara Westhoff the sculptor (whom he had married and lived with briefly) and Paula Modersohn-Becker the painter, who had married someone else. Paula's death in childbirth affected him deeply and increased his morbid obsession with virginity and death. Like Gwen John he enormously admired Rodin (whom he took to be an octogenarian when he met him). He saw him as a man of the people, hardened by a life of poverty and heroic labour.

The summer of 1906 was a lonely one for Gwen John. No sooner had Rodin returned from a long trip to Spain than she received the following letter. 'I have left for Marseille. Write to me, *petite amie*. Eat well because it seems to me you are neglecting yourself. That's what gives you a headache. I'd rest as much as possible.' Rodin had been in pursuit of Moorish architecture in Spain. Now he was pursuing King Sisowath's troupe of Cambodian dancers whose grace he had admired in Paris. The drawings he made of them in a Marseille park are now famous. But Gwen John did not rest. Instead she lost Tiger.

The room at rue St Placide had become intolerably stuffy and she decided to wrap the cat in a shawl and take her to Meudon. Meudon was a small country town built partly on the banks of the Seine and partly on the thickly-wooded hills above. Dominating the town was the recently ruined Château-neuf, its formal park supported by vast retaining walls, its wide avenues (designed by le Nôtre) radiating for miles into the forest.

Rodin had bought the Villa des Brillants at Meudon a year or two before Gwen John met him. It was built in the North Oxford style from variegated red and white brick. Not only was it not a beautiful house, but it was an inconvenient one, having only three bedrooms and a spartan minimum of furniture. But it was well situated amid open pastures with a view over Paris. Rodin had furnished the garden with a care he never lavished on the house, and precious antique statues gleamed among the trees. There was a bench where he often sat with his two dogs at nightfall. From it he could look down on the serpentine Seine and the distant panorama of Paris spread out beneath a net of lights. The whole of this paradise was surrounded by a stout fence. An intruder from the city made her way up the steep rue Paul Bert on 28 June 1906.

She found a 'room' among the bushes outside the fence, unpacked her cat and her sketch-book and started to draw the villa. Tiger was ecstatic. 'It was a pleasure to see the little figure in the country,' she told Rodin, 'beaming with happiness, her tail straight as she ran.' Soon a woman came into the garden, followed by two dogs, and sat on the bench. She was elderly and dressed in grey, and Gwen John felt sure she was Rose Beuret, the peasant woman who had shared Rodin's life and borne him a son, but had never been his wife. To Gwen John she was a friend for while Rodin was at Meudon with the thorny Rose no other woman dared approach him.

When darkness fell Gwen took the tram home. To her horror, when it stopped at St Cloud, Tiger shot from her shawl and out through the door. Some 'red dogs' in the street gave chase and soon the cat had disappeared. Frantically Gwen John ran up and down the village calling her name. She asked everyone she saw, 'Have you seen my cat?' Some of them laughed at her, imitating her pronunciation and several men offered her an arm and said *they* would find her a cat if she would come this way. Three evil-looking girls sitting outside a house with their 'mother' started pretending to see the cat when it wasn't there, and the old woman who called Gwen John a *poupée* turned out to be the owner of the local brothel.

Between the houses and the river there was a piece of waste ground. Frantic to get away from the jeering prostitutes and their patrons, Gwen John wandered there among the clumps of nettles and piles of rubbish. The ground was rough and several times she stumbled into holes. Sometimes she thought she heard the distant cry of a cat, but it was always too far away. She decided to spend what was left of the night on the ground.

For nine days Gwen John went native. 'I am living like Robinson Crusoe under a tree,' she told Rodin. She laid an elaborate grid of meat parcels over the whole area each night and lay down to wait. Her dreams were punctuated by the squeaks of rats and toads, for 'only loathsome creatures inhabit this place'. She woke stiff each morning and found the grass drenched. The meat parcels would be gone, but she knew it was not Tiger who had taken them, for she would have 'unwrapped the paper, not torn it'.

Then she launched a campaign of which a general might have been proud. She offered a reward of twenty francs for the finder of the cat (the money to be paid by Rodin) and she asked Rodin to send her a permit to search every garden in St Cloud and Meudon. This searching of gardens was not popular. One wealthy widow by the river at St Cloud refused to open her premises to a hatless young woman (Gwen John afterwards insisted she was wearing a *small* hat) and promised to investigate the garden herself. Gwen came back that night uninvited and searched it. Once when trespassing at night she was chased by a big dog. Playing for time she threw it the parcel of meat she was carrying and flung herself over the garden fence only to find herself suspended by her skirt on the far side. By undoing the skirt she managed to release herself, but was left standing in the street naked from the waist down.

After six days she lost hope. The men of St Cloud had taxed their brains for original ways for a cat to die and were gratified by the English lady's reactions to their suggestions. *La chatte* might be shut in a house, she might have died of hunger, or boredom, she might have been eaten by a dog, a rabbit or a tramp, she might have eaten a frog, she might have gone down a railway tunnel or down a well. She might even have swum the Seine and got to Boulogne.

Gwen John was by now dishevelled and desperate. She went into Paris to keep a modelling engagement with Constance Lloyd, an old friend from the Slade, but turned white and had to stop after an hour. Worse still, there was an unkind letter from Rodin waiting. He had been angry with her for losing the cat and was angrier with her for sleeping out. After reading the letter she knew that Rodin no longer loved her because she was a stupid person who could not even take care of a cat. 'All is finished for me,' she wrote to him. 'I would like to live longer but I will not be pretty and happy for you without my cat.'

She walked that night by the Seine and sat on the high parapet of the Pont d'Alma. The black water sparkled under the lights of the barges. Suddenly she looked round and saw a crowd behind her. Too embarrassed to move, she looked back at the water and hoped they'd go away. 'Why are you sitting there, young woman?' someone called.

'She's a foreigner.'

'Yes, English.'

'Are you alone in Paris?'

Still Gwen John did not reply.

'She's alone in Paris.'

'Poor thing.'

Now she saw a hand beside her on the parapet. It was a *gendarme*. 'Keen on fishing?' Everyone laughed and Gwen John at last found the courage to escape.

Her room looked forlorn after six days' neglect. Tiger was no longer curled on the wicker chair. She began to prepare the room for death. She did not want Rodin to find anything out of order when she was gone. She dusted and polished and changed the flowers. Perhaps she thought of the death scene in the last chapter of *The Idiot*. And then a message came from

Meudon. A cat that looked white from the front and tabby from the side had been seen near the Villa des Brillants.

Gwen John took the train to Val Fleuri and hurried up the hill to her 'room' among the bushes. Secretly she had always thought Tiger would return to the place where they had spent the day together. Once more she arranged meat on paper plates among the surrounding bushes. A kind peasant woman living with her husband and child near Rodin's villa said, 'As sure as I carry this pot you will see your cat in eight days.' She insisted on making up a bed for Gwen John in her garden but once she was asleep Gwen John slipped away to sleep in her 'room'. The grass rustled, the owls hooted and the mice 'played the flute and the piccolo'. For three days and nights she lay in the undergrowth, naked by day, and turned brown. And then before dawn on the morning of 17 July Tiger came. Gwen John had just risen, stiff from the wet ground, to take a look at a Greek torso. When she returned to the 'room' a white figure was standing there with big unhappy eyes. It was Tiger. In a moment the cat was purring in her owner's arms. Gwen John ran to the peasant's house to proclaim the good news and get food for the famished animal. But it was still only four a.m. and he and his wife were asleep. By climbing on to an outhouse roof Gwen John could see them in bed through the bedroom window. There was nothing to do but settle down once more and wait. The exhausted cat lay quietly across her stomach. When the peasants woke she broke the news. 'How happy we are, Mademoiselle,' they cried. 'How beautiful the little *chatte* is,' although in fact, as Gwen John remarked, she was not beautiful at all but thin and dirty.

Tiger was still stiff and nervous when Gwen John paid a brief visit to Augustus's family at St Honorine des Perthes never Cherbourg. Augustus had rented a small house there. Ida and Dorelia (who was pregnant again) had already been gathered up in a cart from the station at Bayeux. Augustus's mistress, Alick Schepeler, was expected but didn't come. Gwen John arrived with her cat and was introduced to Wyndham Lewis, a young painter whose work she admired. She swam often at Port-en-bessin, where Augustus drew the 'tall and quite prehistoric sea-women' and the boys were encouraged to splash.

Edna Waugh, writing to Ursula Tyrwhitt, described the John boys on holiday a couple of years later, at Dielette. 'The little Johns go where they will, no one worries them with much attention – or often with any. They climb the rocks and race about naked in the pools . . . Dorelia is brown. She wears a velvet frock and necklace of old silver and a scarf round her head. She carries the babes on her shoulder as if they have no weight.'

Ida confessed to not caring for them much. 'David is not very interesting with his silly jokes and noises like engines. Caspar is very fat and solid, dashing in and out of the water. Robin climbs and jumps and Edwin is ugly with tiny blue eyes. We bathe him with seaweed for his red face.' When Gwen John returned to Paris she remarked, perhaps with relief, that her children by Rodin were of bronze, marble and stone.

But if she had no children, Tiger did. In the middle of the night she called and Gwen ran for hot water. All night she sat by the cat, which bit her hand gently. When the first two kittens arrived she drowned them (wrapped in paper) before they could emit their first squeak. She planned to keep the third but there was a long pause and she began to fear she might have acted hastily. At last the kitten appeared and she cut it from its caul with her sewing scissors.

Gwen received no congratulations from Rodin when he returned from Marseille. He had been displeased at the loss of the cat. That his mistress should sleep naked at his gate he regarded as the height of indiscretion. He was far from sure that Gwen had been washing properly either. She admitted that while sleeping out she kept her hair done and did not comb it out at night. He felt a disinclination for love.

For Gwen John love-making was still all-important. A week without love and she froze 'like a stream in winter', she said. And she had been without it for a month. After love she was filled with courage and energy. She drew better, she slept better, she loved everyone, men followed her in the street and her clients said she looked twenty again.

Rodin merely complained that she fell on him when he visited her, greedy only for her own pleasure. 'Immodesty is not charming in a woman,' he said, and his headaches now lasted for days and seriously affected his work. He was also suffering from lumbago. He refused to be alone with Gwen. He even gave the concierge at the studio orders not to admit her unless she was carrying a letter of authorisation from him. Many of his letters to her from this time were no more than permits to visit him at a certain time.

Gwen continued apologetic for her emotional intrusions on her master, vowing as usual not to trespass beyond a kiss, not to spend a whole afternoon with him, not to see him more often than once every other day. And she continued to break these vows. Always she was left with a sense of guilt, a feeling that she was in some way dirty and inferior. Love-making was wrong because it incommoded her lover, so were the substitutes for love because he disapproved of them. Even her profession was one whose name she might not speak. No wonder she told Rodin endlessly that she had just visited the baths in rue d'Odessa, that she had spent two hours burnishing her room and the only unclean thing left in it was a bone the cat was chewing under the bed which she hadn't the heart to take away.

During August 1906 Rodin had been modelling a series of 'tiresome or talkative' celebrities, including George Bernard Shaw (Bernarre Churr to Rodin), whose wife had paid a huge sum of money for the honour. Shaw was often at Meudon and Gwen John once peeped through the hedge just after the two men had gone indoors. She found some comfort in the sight of Rodin's coat still hung over a chair. There was also Eve Fairfax, a society beauty Rodin had met in England in the spring (he complained of her flat breasts, 'the planes and the bony structure of these English women!'). Gwen did not object to being asked to stay away from the studio while people of this sort were being portrayed, but she became angry when it was the turn of the Duchesse de Choiseul to be modelled with her head thrown back in a fit of laughter.

Perhaps to placate Gwen Rodin now set to work on her head. For a short time the happy afternoons in the studio recommenced. If Rodin no longer worked with Gwen's head between his knees, as he had with Choiseul,[12] he at least worked with his arm round her shoulders. But he dismissed her as soon as work was over. The bust that resulted was exhibited in white marble in the Salon of 1906 where Ida and Dorelia admired it. In its veiled, questing calm it contrasts with the Duchess's head. Rodin was usually more reserved in portraying women's faces than their bodies. 'Their nature is not ours,' he once said. 'We must be circumspect in unveiling their tender and delicate mystery.' In white marble Gwen John's flesh appears soft and translucent, the bones of the brow and the cheeks so delicate that they are almost liquid.

While the head was so quickly translated into marble, the body remained armless in plaster. Four years later the International Society sent a lady from London to enquire about Whistler's Muse. 'I am working on it,' Rodin assured her. 'It *will* be done . . . Please understand that I cannot work quickly, that I must work when I feel I can, and that it often happens that I must turn from the work. But England shall have the statue.' England did not have the statue, because the arms were never made. In many of Rodin's pieces, as in the antique, limbs and even heads were deliberately omitted to the alarm, according to Rilke, 'of narrow-minded pedants'. But it is almost certain Rodin never intended this to be so with the Muse, since his drawing of her at the Musée shows her sketching on a pad supported by her knee. Eventually the Society decided they didn't want the statue. The little Muse was left forgotten in a shed in Paris and not finally cast until recently.

12 It was during this session that the Duchess's hair is said to have fallen off and proved to be a wig.

7

Rodin II

1907

Gwen John spent Christmas 1906 with Augustus and Ida at the garden studio they had rented at 77 rue Dareau. Dorelia and her children had moved away but they attended the celebration and so did Wyndham Lewis. They ate a traditional turkey dinner and drank kirsch punch while *le père Noël* distributed presents. The six boys wore Russian blouses and knee-length trousers and their hair came down to their shoulders. Ida was pregnant for the fifth time.

Rodin had chosen to spend February in England, adding a degree at Oxford to his mounting honours. Unable to stay in her room, Gwen John hurried to the studio to kiss him goodbye, which she later admitted was 'not respectable'. For her penance Rodin gave her a letter from England to translate while she waited. He was not pleased with the result. When he got into the car to go to the Gare du Nord she did not follow but lunched at the restaurant opposite the studio, as he had ordered. As he had not given orders about where she was to spend the afternoon, she spent it there, writing a letter.

She was full of good resolutions. While Rodin travelled she would draw. She would convert her thoughts of love into drawings and meditations. But she did not keep her resolutions. There was no fire in her room and she soon ceased to draw. After a month without Rodin she lay in bed, her limbs frozen with longing for him. She no longer cleaned her room or dressed herself prettily. Only with the prospect of his return did she take down her dresses from the wardrobe to wash and brush them. She spent hours in joyous anticipation, wondering whether he would bring her a book or a flower.

He arrived home with a cold and lumbago and retired to bed at Meudon with a nightcap and a steam kettle, fearing his usual bronchitis. Gwen John's letters were filled with good advice. He had bought an ancient horse called Rataplan to which, like all animals, he was greatly attached, but Gwen advised that his morning drives with Rose should not be too extensive or they would tire his eyes and brain. Raw horse-flesh, she added, was a strengthening addition to the diet. Miss O'Donnell's friend, the actress Miss Horden, had told her so. Perhaps Rodin tried it. Certainly when he recovered he paid Gwen John a highly satisfactory visit.

She now decided that the room on the court in the rue St Placide lacked light and air although it had been chosen for both. In winter there was no sun at all and even in summer flowers died for lack of light. Furthermore the court had proved a failure as an exercise area for Tiger. Gwen had not forgotten the time her beloved had been propelled through the air by the concierge's husband's boot.

Other distressing things connected with cats happened in the court. One night Gwen John was woken by what seemed to be the cries of a human baby. ('Surely they *are* children,' she said to Rodin.) Down in the court she saw the glowing eyes of the local charcoal burner's cat that was almost all eyes. Unable to bear listening to its coughing she gave it half of Tiger's meat. The coughing stopped but Tiger was furious.

Something worse happened to a dog in the court next door. It began to scream every morning because they were doing something to it that Gwen John could not bear to name. All the women at St Placide were shocked but it was Gwen John who went to the *Société Protectrice*. There they assured her that the criminal would be imprisoned for eight years if he didn't heed their warning, but they must have his name.

The dog beater lived at the hotel next door.

'Who has a dog here?' enquired Gwen John of the fat woman at the desk.

'We do. Two little ones,' said the fat woman.

'Could I have your name please?'

'Why do you want it?'

'You have been brutalising a dog.'

At this pandemonium broke out. A maid who was also fat rushed forward and pushed her red face into Gwen John's. She shouted that they adored their dogs, that they fed them with a silver spoon and gave them satin cushions to sleep on. A tall man who stood in the background swore that Gwen John must have heard another dog out in the street, but she knew from his guilty face that he was the culprit. In the end Gwen John's plea succeeded, a letter, according to her, was sent by the Society to the Secretary of State and there were no more cries. But for some days Gwen John was chased and mocked in the rue St Placide by the fat maids from the hotel.

Miss O'Donnell, the sculptor, was instructed by Rodin to help in the search for a room that was just right and at the same time cheap. Gwen

John had little faith in her taste. She always chose 'square rooms'. St Placide had been too square. It was a depressing business, viewing the succession of 'horrible rooms' in the rue du Maine. Either the concierges were rude or their husbands lewd or there were single men among the *locataires*. There was one in the rue Madame for 600 hundred francs but the mansard windows were too narrow, though the sloping ceiling was attractive. In despair Gwen John even strayed beyond the Eiffel Tower in her search. In the end she settled for 87 rue Cherche-Midi, round the corner from rue St Placide in a street that was slightly wider and busier. Her room was the first on the left on the fourth floor.

The last few weeks at rue St Placide had been embarrassing. The concierge could not understand why Gwen John was leaving the room. Her husband insisted that, far from being stuffy, it was so draughty that he always contracted toothache when he went up there. He now made a point of showing prospective *locataires* round himself. He would hammer on the door shouting, 'Open up! I want to show people round.' Having entered he would tell the visitors how to arrange their furniture, pointing to Gwen's furniture item by item. 'Here you can place your bed, your mirror, your night table, your work table, your bookshelf, your armchair, your dressing-table, your wardrobe.' Then he would walk over to the window and fling it open saying, 'Air! Sun!'. When Gwen John in the background said quietly, 'No, no sun!' he pretended not to hear.

Gwen's wardrobe was to cause trouble when the day of the move came. It was a precious possession, for not only was it a gift from Rodin but Gwen John drew her self-portraits in it. It was very large. She hired two colossal men with a horse and cart to do the move. They arrived an hour late, at seven p.m., drunk and with cigarettes hanging out of their mouths. They could not get the wardrobe through the door and decided it must be lowered from the window on ropes. The wardrobe was half way down when the fiercer of the two men refused to continue with the job unless Gwen gave them fifty centimes for an immediate drink. It was, he assured her, 'the custom'.

At last, all was on the cart except the pictures and the hats which Gwen carried. Then the men lost their way although it was only a journey of a few hundred metres. By the time they arrived at the rue Cherche-Midi they had drunk more and even the gentler of the two had become very fierce. Needless to say, the wardrobe stuck again and the men threatened to fight each other. Soon the *locataires* from the other rooms gathered on the landing to give advice. There was a strange man in her room on all fours putting up her bed, another was negotiating a price with the removal men and a third, a bald man, was attempting to translate what they were saying into English for her. The only phrase Gwen could

extract from the argument was the constantly repeated '*Je regrette infini-
ment mais* . . .' In the end the drunkards, who had hoped for thirty-one
francs, slunk off with only twenty-one.

It is hard to associate the uproar of Gwen John's arrival at the rue
Cherche-Midi room with the calm she imposed upon it in what is surely
her most frequently reproduced painting.[1] 'A corner of the artist's room
in Paris' was painted soon after she moved there in March 1907, in order
to convey the feeling she had about the room to Rodin. She had woken
one morning at dawn, she told him, and seen it different, mysterious and
beautiful, with everything in order. In her attempt to convey this
mystery, she painted an interior that has a powerful effect on all who
see it. She presented a room that is practically unfurnished, devoid of
carpets, curtains and ornaments. A cheap table and a wicker chair stand
on bare tiles. The only decoration is a bunch of primroses on the table.
Yet these objects are transformed by the diffused light from a French
window hung with muslin. The chair and table each assume a compel-
ling and expectant stillness. Somebody or something is in the room.

Gwen John was never more enchanted by a room than she was by the
one in Cherche-Midi. 'It is the prettiest ever,' she declared. The large
window flooded it with sunlight. At midday the houses opposite stood
quiet and still in the spring sunshine, casting great shadows. At midnight
there was the mystery of a sky filled with stars. She would stand by the
window in her nightdress and listen to a nightingale who was, perhaps,
distantly related to the myriad voices in the woods at Meudon. She was
constantly making changes to the room. A coat of rose-coloured paint on
the hexagonal tiles, a mat beside the bed, a water-loving fern at the
window. She rejoiced in an entrance hall that was not much more than
the space between two doors, and in her first kitchen which, to the
distress of the artistic ladies who employed her, appeared to contain
nothing but a tea kettle. Tiger settled in at once and sharpened her claws
on the arms of the wicker chair to show her satisfaction.

The household seemed almost as 'heavenly' as the room. The concierge, who called Gwen John 'Mademoiselle Miss', loved cats and had a
fifteen-year-old one herself. The bald man who had talked English
during the move turned out to be an Englishman called George. He was
married to a Frenchwoman and had lived in Paris so long that he had
almost forgotten his own language. His wife, who was kindness itself,
embroidered church vestments from five in the morning until dark and
did not even have time to keep their room clean. To console himself
George 'surprised' the ladies of 87 rue Cherche-Midi on the stairs.

Gwen John dreaded invitations to visit George and his wife. She was

[1] Now at Sheffield Art Gallery.

afraid she would laugh at the wrong moment. 'Little George' was continually being sent into the kitchen as a punishment for spitting out of the window, for sighing and yawning, for suggesting that the Salon was nothing but a collection of 'bare bottoms'. 'If she knew what he was unbuttoning all the time under the table!' Gwen confided to Julie. 'Perhaps this *is* an earthly habitation after all.'

If little George and his wife amused her, the Hugels next door puzzled her. 'How could they stay well? They had only one bed and so must sleep together each night. What do they do? Not much I'm sure or they'd be dead long ago. But how can they resist doing much? Perhaps they did too much at the beginning and now they are tired and sleep each on his side.'

But all these people were kind. When Gwen John was ill George's wife brought her meals and when the cat got locked in an empty room by mistake the concierge revived her (the cat) with rum and hot milk and gave her a hot water bottle. Gwen was considerate in her turn. When she gave Madame Hugel a plant for New Year the lady let out such a scream of amazement that Gwen John thought she had committed a *gaffe*. Her rescue of the baby canary that flew out of the window was more successful. Gwen assured Rodin that the bird was restored to its grateful mother and that she climbed the window-sill both ways without showing an inch of leg.

After a gap of three years, Rodin once more summoned Gwen John to model nude for him. He was creating a group of which Gwen was to be a member. Saturday mornings were again passed blissfully behind the screen, for when Rodin saw Gwen John's nakedness he could not resist an embrace. Rodin's interest in her nakedness aroused her own. She started to draw her nude reflection in the wardrobe mirror once more. The preparations for these sessions were arduous, for buckets of coal had first to be heaved up the stairs. Even so the room could not be kept warm for more than an hour or two.

At this time Rodin's interest in drawing also increased. He had always made drawings, not as sketches for his sculpture but as part of a continuous reassessment of his work, and to help the engravers who illustrated his sculpture catalogues. But he never regarded his own drawings as having importance in themselves until people started to praise those which he did of Cambodian dancers at Marseille. These he exhibited this year with great success.

Lover and beloved now indulged in mutual drawing sessions in the room at Cherche-Midi. While Rodin drew the slight oval-faced girl she portrayed the man with the craggy brow, the jutting nose and the luxuriant beard. Her drawings of Rodin are lost. Perhaps they are masquerading as Rodin's among his vast collection at the Musée Rodin. The drawings he gave her have also vanished. Yet Rodin's constant encouragement was essential to her art. If he neglected her, she despaired. She could not force herself to work and sometimes, when she could not draw, she would be seized with a fit of terrible impatience. During these moments she found it best to 'concentrate on a flower and wait for the mood to pass'.

But in her heart she knew that something strong was growing in her, something the world could not touch. She saw herself as a flower, a blue flower, growing high in the Alps with deep strong roots. 'There is something beautiful in me, not to be cut and left to die. This flower, with all my thoughts however silly, belongs to Rodin. He will await its flowering.'

She preferred to draw in her room in the mornings. As the weather improved she sketched out of doors, for she had never lost her childhood habit of carrying a sketch-book. She drew classical statues in the Luxembourg gardens and Rodin's statues in the Luxembourg museum. She drew the concierge's old cat and also a pair of omnibus horses standing outside a café, a drawing which was never finished, for she was extremely shy of amateur critics. This particular specimen of the breed suggested, just as she was drawing in the horses' ears, that she should have given asses' ears to the conductor. This made her laugh but it sent her home. She found there were worse problems if she drew people. Indeed, she became so embarrassed when sketching one morning on the boat to St Cloud that she decided to try and memorise the faces of the peop e she saw and draw them afterwards. The experiment was not a success and from this period there exist few drawings of strangers.

She was convinced, like Rodin, that Nature was the artist's true inspiration. There was poetry, she told him, in the faithful depiction of natural objects, 'in an attic, a family group, a basket of kittens, an ant hill'. So too was there poetry in landscape. A landscape was a living body. Woods and hills were haunted by their own familiar spirits. She painted a fountain with great cumulus clouds piling up round it. To her the clouds were prayers. The style of Gwen John's drawings at this time became increasingly simple and severe. She admired the clean lines of some Japanese drawings she saw in a shop window near the Luxembourg gardens and persuaded Rodin to bring others from Meudon. These were to influence her work profoundly.

But there was still time in her life for some frivolity. Her interest in dress revived with Rodin's interest in her. He seldom failed to comment on her appearance. With the help of her client, Miss Bowser, she managed to part with one hundred and fifty francs in a day at the Bon Marché. Miss Bowser had a knowledge of the mode and that, as Gwen John pointed out to Rodin, was always expensive. A fine ensemble was amassed which was topped by a grey ostrich feather (Gwen wanted vermilion).

She spent much time sewing in her new room. Some cerise coloured faille caught her eye at a sale at the Bon Marché and she bought it although she 'did not really need it'. When she wore the dress she had made from it for the first time she felt as nervous as if she were exhibiting a picture, for it was on the 'arty' side. She tried it out in the street on the way to the studio. Fortunately the men at the café tables shouted *jolie fille* and *belle femme* as she passed. Rodin also had some charming things to say.

Dorelia was responsible for Gwen John's new interest in dressmaking. Now that she had moved to the rue du Château with Pyramus and Romilly, in order to get away from Augustus, Gwen John saw more of her and less of Ida. Tiger's kitten now went to Dorelia. But Ida, back in the rue Dareau, was alone. 'I am alone again. Alone and alone.' Without Dorelia Paris was solemn and silent. Her marriage to Augustus was a failure and she had no woman friends. 'As to a woman, I know only one, and that is Gwen John,' she wrote. But now she never saw Gwen. Life seemed dreary and pointless. 'There is always death, isn't there?' she said. And then, quite suddenly she died.

In the first week in March Ida had walked round to the Hôpital de la Maternité in Boulevard du Port Royal. A boy (Henry) was born without difficulty on 9 March. Complications set in immediately afterwards. Ida was feverish and in pain, and her mother, who was in Paris on business, arranged that she should be transferred to another hospital, the Maison de Santé, for a small operation on an abscess 'which will clear things up in forty-eight hours'.

The Maison de Santé in the Boulevard Arago was light and cheerful and the nursing was done by nuns. For a few hours everyone's hopes were high, but after the operation it became clear that Ida was unlikely to survive. She was suffering not only from puerperal fever but also from peritonitis. Only a powerful will to live could pull her through, and she had no desire to live. Ida slept neither day nor night. She kept Mrs Nettleship in a turmoil, demanding 'all sorts of things that are not good for her'. Augustus could refuse her nothing. She made him ransack Paris for a particular beef lozenge, for violets, a flask of scent. Finally she sent him to have a bath.

On the night of 13 March there was a violent storm and she became delirious. Augustus would not leave her side and she spoke all night of the wind and the stars and of a land of miraculous caves. She pulled Augustus's beard about and he tickled her feet. 'Ida felt lovely, she was so gay and *spiritual*, she had such charming visions and made such amusing jokes.' In the morning she roused herself and proposed a toast to

Augustus in Vichy water. 'Here's to love!' she said and relapsed into unconsciousness. She died at three thirty that afternoon. 'She has gone very far away now,' said Augustus. 'She has rejoined the spiritual lover who was my most serious rival in the old days.' He went out and got very drunk.

Gwen John's reaction to Ida's death was similar. She wrote to tell Rodin not to bother with condolences but to save his strength for what he would give her at the studio on Saturday morning when she enjoyed her weekly ration of his love. Ida was cremated at the Père Lachaise cemetery. Gwen John was the only person Augustus could bear to visit when he surfaced from his three day bender. Letters of condolence from England irritated him and made him 'long to outrage everybody'. Sympathetic friends were strongly encouraged to stay at home. Worst of all was William Rothenstein, who would never forgive himself for not having gone out to Paris, and wrote Uriah Heep-like letters in expiation imploring Augustus not to give way to remorse. Gwen stayed with him for several days at his studio in the cour de Rohan. He declared that she was one of those who *knew* Ida, who understood that she was one of the most utterly truthful souls in the world.

There was a memorial service in Henry Lamb's room. Henry Lamb was a handsome ex-medical student who had studied at Augustus's Chelsea Art School and now regarded himself as Augustus's chief apprentice. If Gwen John attended this memorial service she saw Ambrose McEvoy again. He had arrived too late for the cremation and 'had the delicacy to keep drunk all the time and was perfectly charming'. He had come for the day, intending to go back to London the same night, but was incapable of going anywhere for a week.

Gwen returned as soon as she could to her room at the rue Cherche-Midi. As it grew dark she lit a fire and gazed at the photograph of Rodin, the one with eyes that changed expression. She sipped tea and hoped that this would not make her resemble the loveless women for whom she worked. Ida's fate had given her little cause to envy the loved ones.

Gwen John was now seeing a lot of Miss O'Donnell who was carving Rodin's group in marble. She constantly required Gwen to take the pose. She also called in Rodin's disciple, Bourdelle, to view Gwen and compare her with the statue. He reported favourably on her beauty but what he said about the statue is unknown. Praise for others never pleased O'Donnell. She was jealous of all the English ladies for whom Gwen John worked, and knew a great deal about Rodin's love affairs. When Gwen refused to take an interest in gossip she accused her of being mentally fourteen and only interested in her looks. Sometimes Gwen complained that she treated her like a servant. When Gwen John said timidly 'I draw too', Miss O'Donnell brusquely told her to stick to modelling. And always she nagged her for unpunctuality, swinging her little ornamental watch in Gwen's face when she arrived at the studio to model and telling her it had been set by the clock at Montparnasse Station that very morning, which, Gwen commented, was impossible. Modelling sessions were not deemed to have started until Gwen's clothes were off, and she was on the stand.

Miss O'Donnell was a lonely woman, in spite of the fact that she shared her apartment with Miss Horden and a cat. She constantly kept Gwen talking for an extra hour after work, for which Gwen secretly considered she ought to be paid, since it was a great deal more boring than the hours spent on the stand. Innumerable mediocre drawings were leafed through or, worse still, the grey dress with the fur-trimmed décolletage was donned and out came the silver coffee set and the assorted liqueurs. Gwen John dreaded these evenings in the studio decorated in the Persian style, with Miss O'Donnell presiding at her overloaded coffee table and confiding her greatest fear, that Rodin would cease to send her work and she would die of starvation within a year or two.

The crisis came over a bottle of medicine. Gwen John had developed a cough while she was room-hunting and Miss Horden recommended a bottle of her own favourite chest remedy which cost Gwen John six francs eighty centimes and, like most substances, made her ill. Gwen John gave the remainder of the bottle to O'Donnell who offered her five francs for it. And then Gwen John exploded. How dare O'Donnell pay her. She didn't run a chemist's shop, Miss O'Donnell might buy her services but she could not buy her soul. She rushed out of the studio and took a tram to the country. But beside the river at St Cloud the vision of the evil O'Donnell stayed in her head. To forget her she called on two peasant women who had helped her in the search for Tiger the year before. Their earthy conversation was more to her liking than O'Donnell's bourgeois affectations. They told her of lost fortunes and of a child who had died young. She specially liked the story of the child. There was a letter of dismissal from Miss O'Donnell waiting when she got back to the room at Cherche-Midi.

But there were other artists willing to employ her, for her circle of clients was widening. Miss Bowser, who had helped refurbish her wardrobe, was already booking any part of the day left vacant by O'Donnell. She was a good painter and a kind woman, concerned for Gwen John's welfare. She quickly took the deplorable kitchen at Cherche-Midi in hand, supplying it with a frying-pan, a saucepan and something called a 'devil'.

Another contributor to Gwen John's kitchen was the gruff Miss Hart, who had recently had a severe shock and decided to abandon Paris, leaving Gwen a complete (and unwanted) *batterie de cuisine*. After Gwen had left Boulevard Edgar Quinet Miss Hart had rented a studio nearby. All went well until *la vie de bohème* started up in the studio next door. Two Finnish painters took to sharing a prostitute every night. Gwen John suspected that Miss Hart must have spent *her* nights with her ear on the partition for she was able to relate every detail of the trio's relationship including the fact that each Finn paid five francs for his privileges and all three fitted into one bed all night. After a few weeks of this Miss Hart finished the torso she was doing of Gwen John and left 'filthy' Paris never to return.

Constance Lloyd, like Miss Bowser, became a friend. When her sister, the other Miss Lloyd, was in Paris Gwen John agreed to entertain her for a day. She took her on a boat to Meudon and showed her the Villa des Brillants without telling her who lived there. When the sister became ill Gwen John visited her in the hospital where she was being nursed. For the first time she saw nuns close to and was enchanted by the beauty of their black and white habits.

Another client was the German painter, Miss Roderstein, 'who wore a collar and tie, had a male corporation and barked masculine enquiries like "Hope you're not too cold, my dear!"'. She was too mean to light her studio stove and often embarrassed Gwen John by making her do exercises on the model stand when she turned blue. In spite of incessant effort she was a poor painter. Gwen John, watching her in the mirror, would see her brush poised with a load of paint of a colour that would certainly unbalance her picture. A moment too late Miss Roderstein would see it too and let out a howl of agony. 'I *must* do better,' she would cry, beating her head. On leaving Paris Miss Roderstein introduced Gwen John to some of her German friends. They invited her to meet others at their studio. When she arrived there were German cakes and many Germans. Going to the point, Gwen John asked one of them: 'Will you want me to pose nude?'

'Yes.'

'How do you know I'm not hunchbacked?'

'Why don't you show us?'

There and then, among the little cakes, Gwen let her clothes fall to the floor. There were many favourable verdicts, she told Rodin.

The artist from Russia was more cautious. She sent a socialist friend ahead of her to vet Gwen John. The friend was fat and spoke poor English. She arrived late at night and admired the room (which was perfect except for 'a vest drying over a chair'). As she left she said, 'I shall expect to see your soul next time.' Gwen John concluded this was a socialist form of farewell. When the painter herself arrived she was frighteningly intelligent. She invited Gwen to dinner at her studio and then was too lost in her books to prepare it. It was Gwen John who bought the cold veal, buttered the bread and made the tea. When the Russian left for Berlin in December she sent Gwen a book about Michelangelo, which pleased her.

More prolonged and less pleasant was Gwen John's relationship with another Russian, Miss Gerhardi. Miss Gerhardi was in love with Rodin. She also fell heavily for Gwen John and constantly invited her to her studio, entertaining her with her favourite pastries and showing her desirable books and prints. It was Miss Gerhardi who actually succeeded in taking Gwen John to a theatre, unlike O'Donnell who was always promising to. The theatre was a music-hall, the Gaieté Montparnasse. The jokes were incomprehensible to Gwen John, though not to Miss Gerhardi. But the effect of the plump belly-wriggling chorus although shocking was exciting. Gwen John confided to Julie that she longed to embrace the actors. But she did not long to embrace Gerhardi.

Gerhardi became increasingly repugnant to her. She disliked Gerhardi's attempts to kiss her and her constant references to her naked body. She also began to despise Gerhardi as a painter, deciding that her talents, which she spoke of incessantly, were slight. She was 'frivolous and lazy and thought only of appearances'. She was also mean about money. Although she constantly told Gwen John to take care of herself she was the only one of her clients who dared offer her a mere franc an hour for posing. Gwen began to refer to her in her letters as an insect, even an earthworm.

That Gwen John was attractive to women is certain. They even stopped her in the street and made suggestions to her. There was a peculiarly evil specimen, fat with straw-yellow hair, who haunted the rue St Placide where Gwen did her shopping. When they met at the *crémerie* she would touch Gwen and rub herself against the wall so that her fat calves became visible beneath the hem of her long dress. She once insisted that Gwen come to a restaurant with her. When Gwen John refused she said she could always see her naked at Rodin's studio.

Rodin was angry when he heard about Gwen John's impertinence to Miss O'Donnell over the cough mixture. He deplored the explosions of anger to which the normally submissive Gwen was prone. He insisted on an apology and Gwen, with characteristic courage, made it in the presence of Miss Horden. It was well that she did, for Miss O'Donnell now had the use of a house in the country. It was the property of Miss Brown, an American painter. Here Gwen John was to spend several weeks during the spring of 1907 and on later occasions. Monneville, in the department of Oise, was some way from Paris, in what Gwen John called 'the real country'. On the seven franc journey from the Gare St Lazare the train crossed the Seine four times. From Villetêtue, the last four kilometres had to be done by cart. Gwen John was pleased by the drive across the plain, by the vertical lines of shimmering poplars and the horizontal lines of men sowing seeds from baskets on their hips. Early orchids were already in flower by the roadside. The driver of the cart, like everyone in Monneville, proved to be animal mad. His black three-legged dog could ride on his lap if it chose or run behind. Once it fell so far behind that it was only a black dot on the plain. Then its master pulled up the horse and waited while it caught up.

Outside the little house in Monneville Miss Brown was waiting with Armandine, the fat and friendly housekeeper. On seeing Tiger, Armandine made a gesture of despair. Miss Brown's cat, Marjorie Lane, had just had kittens. With much effort the kittens were transferred to the house which Armandine shared with her husband Clovis next door. But Marjorie Lane was not to be fobbed off so easily and she stole into Gwen John's room that night and pounced on Tiger. The ensuing battle was terrifying and all the lady painters, Miss O'Donnell and Miss Brown, and also Miss Ludlow and Miss Wolff, were roused. Marjorie Lane was secured by Gwen John and carried back to Armandine's house but it was tightly shut. Armandine was obviously in bed with Clovis. 'Who knows what they might not have been doing together!' commented Gwen John, though she did not communicate this idea to her companions, for she felt sure 'they would not know what she was talking about'. In the morning it was Tiger's turn to escape. She sat all day on a beam in the barn and would not be dislodged by the most tempting offers of raw liver from Clovis. Clovis claimed to be the greatest animal lover in a village of animal lovers. When Miss Brown was in town he sent her tufts of Marjorie Lane's fur tied with blue ribbon. (Gwen found this silly.)

The fortnight at Monneville passed pleasantly. On fine mornings the ladies drew in the garden and Gwen, if she was not required as a model, joined them. She usually drew flowers – on one occasion a clump of pansies. Then Armandine brought out an excellent picnic of brown bread, cheese, radishes and rhubarb, all home produced. In the afternoon the ladies walked, or rather strode, pinning up Gwen John's skirts so that she could keep up. Miss Brown and Miss O'Donnell seemed to know everyone and they called on the local charcoal burner, ostensibly to buy coal, but really to see the eyes of his ne'er-do-well son burn with desire from the depths of the room. Miss Ludlow told Gwen that he had proposed to all four of them in turn. On a farm Gwen John admired the beauty of a farmer's daughter, a beauty, she thought, that could only be produced by country air. In the evening they sat down to Armandine's delicious roast lamb, served with home grown vegetables.

It is a strange fact that the only two occasions when Gwen John speaks favourably of food in her many letters are when she is speaking of meals prepared by Armandine, both of them on this day in the spring of 1907.

She rarely spoke of food at all, and if she did it is usually with disgust. But she was obviously fond of Armandine, who was just the sort of simple peasant woman who attracted her.

Perhaps she was feeling a need for security for she was short of money for the first time since she had met Rodin. Rodin, who had always been over-generous, had decided that too much did her harm and made her lazy. There were now times when she was down to her last sou. Once she arrived at Roderstein's without breakfast only to be told that she was not booked. Roderstein often made mistakes about bookings and, driven by hunger, Gwen John insisted that she should pay two francs of some money she was owed even if she was not wanted. Roderstein parted regretfully with the money and Gwen John went to a restaurant and spent all but the last two sous on luncheon and two glasses of wine. As she sat alone at the table she was surprised to find strength flowing back into her limbs. By the evening the smells of her neighbours' cooking reminded her that she was hungry again. She went to bed to try to forget about food.

Ursula Tyrwhitt now arrived in Paris on a long visit, determined to become a sculptor and study under Rodin. As usual there were diffi-culties in finding a room up to her standard. Eventually one was found and she set to work on a ten-inch head of Gwen John in terracotta,[2] who sat to her three times a week. She also insisted on meeting Rodin. The visit to the studio in the rue d l'Université was not a success. Rodin was civil enough to Ursula but he afterwards berated Gwen John for intrud-ing on his time. Ursula remained undismayed and requested that the master give an opinion on her head. He made the one comment, '*Con-tinuez*.' It was not his custom to waste words when acting as a critic. As Gwen John explained to Ursula Tyrwhitt, in an instant he would make you *feel* how good or bad your work was, and he would never bore you by telling you about the Old Masters and all that.

After Ursula Tyrwhitt had returned to England she was still un-satisfied. She wrote to Gwen John asking her to write down some of Rodin's maxims. Gwen wrote that he was above all in love with Nature, that he worked with patience and humility. He advised his followers to imitate not the appearance but the spirit of his work. If they were doing an arm, for instance, they should simply portray it. They should not consult theories or maxims. They should just observe the grace, the life of the thing. They should make it boldly, not being preoccupied by details but not leaving gaps either.

As always, Gwen John writes to Ursula Tyrwhitt as a fellow profes-

[2] The head with the questing nose turned upwards and the long girlish hair, is not without charm. It was Ursula Tyrwhitt's only sculpture, and is now in the Ashmolean.

sional. She once told her that she belonged to that quiet part of her mind where her love of Art was, a part which was undisturbed by the events and difficulties of life. Ursula Tyrwhitt in turn had a strong influence on Gwen John. She was becoming seriously interested in exhibiting and selling and, now that Rodin was less generous with his money, Gwen also began to find the idea of selling attractive. But she still retained her horror of hurrying to finish a picture for an exhibition and said it was best to have one or two canvases always in reserve, 'and for that it is necessary . . . to disappear for a few years!'

Ellen Boughton Leigh and her sister Maude were also in Paris at this time. Like Ursula Tyrwhitt they had been at the Slade, but seven years before. They were the daughters of Edward Ward Boughton Leigh of Brownsover Hall, Warwickshire. Maude,[3] who loved cats, was already a friend of Gwen John's but it was Ellen, known as Chloë, who required her services as a model. She made life studies of Gwen John over a period of several weeks, but while these no longer exist, the portrait in oils which Gwen John made of Miss Leigh now hangs at the Tate. It is unusually large for a Gwen John (twenty-three inches by fifteen inches), almost twice the size of 'A lady reading', perhaps at the suggestion of the sitter. An extra piece of wood has been tacked on at the bottom of the canvas to lengthen it by an inch. It represents a three-quarter length figure of a woman almost full face with long fair hair tied back and a fringe, wearing a blue and white check dress. She holds a letter on her lap and her prominent eyes have a sad, empty expression suggesting that the letter brought bad news.

Another scorching summer now had Paris in its power and Gwen John was out early to buy her supply of food before the sun was high. She sported bare forearms that year which caused Little George to forget himself not only on the stairs but also in the *crémerie*. The effect of the short sleeves on a priest on top of a tram was almost equally devastating. While making polite conversation to Gwen John he let the coat he was carrying fall across her lap and under its cover proceeded to massage her forearm. The lady in black who accompanied him went on making conversation quite unaware of what was happening.

Gwen John continued to have trouble with *rôdeurs*. Men followed her in the street, they sat next to her in cafés, they frightened her in forests, they suggested lifelong friendship on river steamers. Sometimes she did not seem to try too hard to throw them off; sometimes she tried so hard that her efforts verged on criminal assault. There was the occasion of the Terrible Adventure when she went to sketch Rodin's house and museum from the hill above. She found a little clearing among the bushes and

[3] Her work can be seen at the Tate.

settled down with her pencil and pad when something like a great snake moved out from under a bush. It was a hideously fat man, a veritable ogre, running with sweat, and leering horribly. Instantly Gwen John's French deserted her and the only insult she could come out with was, 'How ugly you are!' Upon this the man raised himself to his full height revealing even greater ugliness in the form of disarranged nether garments. Gwen John bolted from her lair and started to search the ground for ammunition. A sardine tin made little impression, but as soon as she lifted a stone 'as big as a hat' she made a very big impression, although, as she pointed out, she couldn't have thrown it if she had wanted to. It was the ogre's turn to bolt now, to the police station where he accused Gwen John of being a 'bad girl'. Luckily she was able to get a curé and three young girls on her side. All insisted that it was the man who was bad, and the policeman agreed.

The season was approaching when Gwen John usually lost her cat, and again she did. She was deeply embarrassed. When a man on the boat asked if it was not she who had lost a cat the year before she denied it for fear people would think she had a mania for cat-losing. Tiger, once more near St Cloud, had wandered away among the trees of a plantation as soon as Gwen John released her from her shawl. She had returned once to show her white face in the distance and then had turned without a word and vanished from Gwen John's life. Gwen John was instantly desperate. Once more she put up a 'Lost' poster and, forgetting her shyness, organised a line of beaters to walk the plantation from end to end. She asked everyone she met, 'Have you seen a cat that looks white from the front and tabby from the back?'

As before she was mocked and sent to search for her cat in impossible places. Obscenities were scrawled on her poster, like 'What a shame that young girls lose their *chattes*.' When she approached a man who was patrolling an overgrown castle and asked if he would trail her cat with his dogs he said he would do anything for her, including kiss her eyes. Nevertheless, with him and his guard dogs she covered many miles, while he told her improbable stories about his employer, the countess who lived in the castle. Gwen John once caught sight of the countess getting into a car with two female friends. She was a large woman who wore ringlets. According to the gamekeeper she liked to dress up as Napoleon and then do something with her Alsatian that he could only tell Gwen John when he knew her better. Almost immediately he decided that he *did* know her better.

Even the local policeman, a handsome man with a grey moustache, seemed more interested in appraising her figure than in finding her cat. At the Hôtel St Cloud he made an apache-like lunge at her. He said he had seen Tiger in wild hill country when riding a tram. He had stopped the tram and gone to investigate. Sure enough he had seen a cat that was surely Tiger. He imitated the way she turned her head from side to side when emerging from a bush. Not surprisingly the cat had vanished on his approach.

These suitors would no doubt have grown more frustrated if they had known that Gwen John was again, as the year before, spending the idle hours of the day, brown as a wood nymph, in Tiger's plantation near the Villa des Brillants. Like a cat, she could be still. Sometimes she spent a whole hour watching the activities of ants. Nature was her mother, she said, and she feared her father. Despair was once more in her heart. She was convinced that Rodin could no longer love her without her cat.

On those August nights the golden sky turned black and then the .moon rose slowly between the trees. The land was enveloped in a calm mystery. A twig moved somewhere on the edge of the plantation. She kept very still, so still that she could hear the tweet of mice and the rustle of dead leaves like a skirt passing over the ground. And then she thought about her visitor.

> My visitor calls me
> His name is solitude
> He comes constantly in life
> I love him though he is cold.
> He'll follow me till the last day
> But I know him well
> I don't fear him.

Death was a friend of solitude, almost as welcome. To die in Rodin's arms would be bliss, she said, for in dying she could prove her love, which she never could in words. And Rodin would love her when she was dead, just as she now loved Ida so much more than she ever had in life.

For Rodin was again angry. Gwen John was once more wandering round St Cloud spending the little she earned on meat for stray cats. She was eating less and less. She had promised to dine daily at the hotel at St Cloud, but now she said the smell of cooking made her feel sick and she preferred to take food back to the plantation. When she returned to Paris to keep a modelling engagement Miss Roderstein said there was nothing of her, no stomach, nothing. At Miss Lloyd's (who, with her sister, had come to help hunt the cat) a grey mist came down over her eyes and she only just managed to reach an armchair before she fainted. At Miss Gerhardi's she fell asleep. She ate only to please Rodin, and to preserve a body for him to love. If he ceased to love her she threatened that she would cease to eat.

At last she had to give up the search. When she returned to Paris it seemed for the first time hostile. The 'city of stone mountains' as Rilke called it, had something hard in its air. Perhaps because Rodin was still distant at night she pulled the covers over her head but could not shut out the vision of a soaked and freezing Tiger in the wilderness. Sometimes she could swear the voice of a stray outside was that of her own cat. As the nights grew colder she comforted herself with the thought that Tiger's coat must surely be growing.

The memory of the cross little queen filled her with sadness. Tiger, it was true, had been an embarrassment at times. She had once flown at the kindly Miss Lloyd like a chained dog and had driven her downstairs and out into the street. Even her kittens were fierce. One had, understandably, attacked Miss Hart, when she sat on the bed. But the cat had loved Gwen John in her fashion and had talked to her in a special voice which was different from the one she used to her kittens. When they were in the bed together she would warn Gwen John if she was about to lie on the kitten. When it was tucked up in its box at night she would jump on to the bed and creep purring into Gwen John's arms so that she should not be lonely. Gwen John described her feelings about the cat in a letter to Rodin. 'I know all her thoughts and needs, she tries to understand me, she understands what I say but she never obeys even when she wants to.'

She became more than ever convinced that her hold on Rodin was tenuous in the extreme. She described herself as being in a continual state of distress for him. The fear that he had ceased to love her was like a hand squeezing her heart. She hung with aching fingers over the precipice of rejection. She was a mere glove crumpled in the fist of the great artist. At any moment he might let her fall.

She dreamed that she was in his studio and he was wiping the tears from her eyes. She went to the Salon and felt a little comforted in the presence of the busts he had made. She vowed to be obedient and strong and go to the country to draw something for him. But instead she went back to her empty room. She had eaten nothing all day. If only Rodin was behind her, telling her what to eat and drink. 'I'm not going to cry tonight,' she told him, 'I am going to buy two eggs.' But she did not buy two eggs. She stayed at the table by the window with the letter before her. Later she wrote, 'It is almost dawn at my table. Oh! I don't like to be left alone.'

With Rodin and Tiger both estranged, life suddenly seemed meaningless. There was nothing to it but the twice-weekly visit to the market, the daily meal, the nightly bed. And once she was in bed she could not sleep. Either she abandoned the day at nine p.m. and lay awake till two a.m., or she woke at four a.m. and waited for the dreadful day. When it came she would be so exhausted that she could not go to work. Sometimes she get up only to go back to bed for the rest of the day because her brain would not function.

One Sunday evening sadness fell on her 'with all its weight' and drove her into the Boulevard Montparnasse in search of any familiar face. But all she found was the inevitable *rôdeur*, whom she quickly outpaced for if he found out she was a model he would treat her like a prostitute. In desperation she called at O'Donnell's studio and found her at home. She poured out her troubles to her. She told her that she had given up hope of finding Tiger, that Rodin had gone away and left her without money, that she could neither sleep nor eat and that a client had sent her home for being too pale and drawn to pose. She felt she would soon be beaten and the end was near. She spoke of suicide. Miss O'Donnell, who could be so cruel, gave her tea and sympathy. She also gave her some money.

It was at this time that Gwen John started to complain of headaches which sound very like migraines. While she was at Monneville she had had one which lasted three days and was accompanied by vomiting. The ladies had been sympathetic and had given her cups of tea and put hot water bottles behind her head. On another occasion at home she had been so weak that she could not lift a damp towel to her forehead. She was aware that the complaints from which she suffered were probably psychosomatic. She once said that she was always well when she was happy. She envied the plump sales ladies at the Samaritaine and swore they must make love daily to stay that way. Certainly she used her illness as a weapon. When Rodin refused to see her she wrote, 'I'll be ill in my room soon.' Yet even love, the universal panacea, was proving less efficacious. She, like Rodin, began to complain of post-coital headaches and of an embarrassing pallor that Miss O'Donnell invariably remarked upon. Her body, she said, now folded up with exhaustion after love.

Gradually she was beginning to feel the need of a comforter who was even greater than Rodin. At one time she had only to raise her eyes to his and read in them the message 'Come close in your great sorrow'. Now she began to desire Him who called, 'Come unto me all ye that are weary and heavy laden'. Rodin knew this God. He had even entered a monastery for a time. He still came into Paris for High Mass at Notre Dame every Sunday. Gwen John began to attend the same Mass. While the music of the organ echoed among the dim vaults she sought the figures of her master and his mistress.

Religion would give a reason for her sufferings. Life was a bed of thorns smothered in flowers. As life proceeded the petals dropped and only the thorns remained. Yet these thorns were for our good. By bearing our sufferings and conquering our faults we came nearer to another country.

At last Gwen John felt she had found a source of help in her perpetual effort to conquer the desires that would not let her rest. She took to saying prayers before she went to sleep and found they calmed her. Although she made no effort to enter the Church at this time she had a strange vision of it one day when standing in the concierge's little lodge. The concierge's husband, a bejewelled dandy, had made some disparaging comment on the Church. 'You must *know* about the Church before you speak against Her,' Gwen John said. At that moment she saw the Church, a cathedral, misty against the sea, set in a deep valley with woods. Black birds crowded the towers and inside there were endless and frescoed vistas where music sounded like the wind in a forest. And then in Gwen John's mind the cathedral was multiplied and she saw thousands of cathedrals and in them ant-like legions of scholars in whose souls were elevated mountains to science, history and literature. The cathedral was no doubt St David's.

Gwen John's own devotion to literature was increasing at this time. Miss O'Donnell had lent her a biography of Rodin from which she learnt for the first time facts that everyone else had known for years: that he was descended from Norman peasants, that his father had worked for the railways, and that he had had an older sister, Marie, who died young. About the same time Gwen did something she rarely did and bought a book, though admittedly with money Rodin had given her. The book was Shakespeare in French. She found this enormously impressive and as usual copied out fragments for Rodin. She also began to keep a journal. It was largely filled with her thoughts on religion and she apologised to Rodin for it being dull and heavy.

Perhaps it was because of these alternative outlets that the letters to Julie ceased about this time. Gwen John had always been embarrassed about relating the humble events of her day to Rodin and was far more inclined to use the Julie letters as an alternative channel through which to convey her love. When she ended the letter describe Mme Pelletier's theft of twenty francs she commented that it was repugnant to her. Now she told Rodin that the Julie deception was too hard to maintain.

Most of all, she still longed to write poems. A love poem to Rodin bringing in a whole ornithology of birds was not a success. A poem to Tiger in French worked better.

Oh mon petit chat
Sauvage dans le bois
As-tu donc tout oublié
Ta vie d'autrefois?

Peut-être que tu es
Fâché avec moi
Mais j'ai tâché de comprendre
Ton tout petit coeur

Je me sentais jamais
Ton supérieur
Petite âme mysterieuse
Dans le corps d'un chat!

J'ai eu tant de chagrin
De ne pas te voir
Que j'ai pensé de m'en auer
Dans le pays des morts

Mais je serai ici
Si tu reviens un jour
Car j'ai été confortée
Par le dieu d'Amour.

8

Conversion

1908–13

The affair with Rodin took five years out of Gwen John's painting life. During that period she concentrated entirely on drawing. It was shortage of money, combined with encouragement from Ursula Tyrwhitt, that induced Gwen John to send the original version of 'A lady reading' and the portrait of Chloë in a blue check dress to the N.E.A.C. Exhibition of 1908.

Her anxieties about the exhibition were hydra-headed. She confided them to Ursula. 'I didn't tell Mr Robertson there was no glass on them. I do hope they hang us together, I shall be lonely on my own. I must tell Mr Chapman not to put the "M" on my name.[1] Send me a card if our pictures are accepted. And tell me how they look there.'

In the event the pictures arrived safely and were accepted and hung. Augustus, as usual, was delighted with them and declared his sister far outstripped her contemporaries. 'Gwen's pictures are simply staggering,' he told Dorelia. 'I have put up the price to £50.[2] They will surely sell.'

There were letters from others, including Will Rothenstein, 'filled with promises that took my breath away', and some lines from Alice 'asking me to *stay* with them!' Gwen John told Ursula Tyrwhitt. But the pictures didn't sell. Chloë bought her own portrait, but £50 was considered too much for 'A lady reading'. Mr Winter, who was in charge of the exhibition, had the effrontery to offer it at £10 ('not even guineas!' Gwen John exclaimed). In the end it fetched £30. Ursula Tyrwhitt was even less fortunate. She ended up by giving her picture to Edna Clarke

[1] Her full name was Gwendolen Mary John.
[2] It is a measure of Augustus's enthusiasm for his sister's work that two years later his own paintings were fetching between £40 and £70, and it was 1912 before her American patron, John Quinn, reckoned a new Gwen John was worth £50.

Ursula Tyrwhitt's head of
Gwen John, 1907

Rodin's 'Muse' photographed in
his studio

Auguste Rodin, around 1900

Véra Oumançoff

'The student'

'Girl in profile'

'Mère Poussepin'

'Two women seated in church'

'The convalescent'

'Green leaves in a white jug'

'Interior, rue Terre Neuve'

Hall. To console her, Gwen John fired her terracotta head and bought her some dress material.

During the next two years Gwen John was to do several drawings of Chloë Boughton Leigh and also some of a handsome woman who has not been identified, probably an English friend. In all her portraits this woman wears her dark hair piled on top of her head, a white blouse and a high black scarf.

At this time Rilke discovered an enchanted palace in a secret garden in the heart of Paris. It was the eighteenth-century Hôtel Biron,[3] magnificent former home of an aristocratic family at 77 rue de Varenne, near the Invalides. Although it was a town house it had the air of a château. For a time the nuns of the Sacred Heart had run a school there, adding the gothic chapel and removing most of the panelling, but they left when the property was sequestered in 1904. Since then the State had let out its draughty rooms at low rents to artists like Isadora Duncan, Cocteau and Matisse.

Rodin at once rented the ground floor with the three tall windows opening on to the garden at the back. Through them he could see the tangled thickets where rabbits lived and the mossy glades where they played. Luckily 'Le Biron' as it was known, was not far from the old studio in the rue de l'Université and some of his favourite sculptures were transferred there. He hung the walls with canvases by his old friend Carrière and also with a Van Gogh, a Renoir and a number of his own watercolours. There was practically no furniture.

Gwen John was slow to appreciate what she called 'that château'. She preferred the intimacy of the rue de l'Université to 'the beautiful rooms'. Perhaps the windows made her feel undefended. According to a visitor they distracted Rodin from his work. Again he was failing to keep appointments in Gwen John's room. Once he kept her waiting three days, and she was obliged to put off a modelling engagement with Miss Roderstein. When he did appear she didn't spare him. She told him he was 'impolite' and that he was so rushed off his feet (*bousculé par le monde*), that he would pass by a dying dog. Apparently he was adorably penitent ('like a poor little punished child') and Gwen John resolved that in future she must scold him more.

As a result of Rodin's move to the Hôtel Biron Gwen John again met Rilke, who she referred to simply as 'a German poet' in her letters. He lent her *The Love Letters of a Portuguese Nun*, and wrote her some letters of his own which, like Rodin's, were chiefly concerned with her continued self-neglect.

Another book which made a profound impression on her at this time

---

[3] Built 1731, now the Musée Rodin.

was an Edgar Allen Poe Ursula Tyrwhitt had given her while she was in Paris. She read it all through a Saturday night and the insupportable Sunday that followed was made supportable by it. She found herself led, refreshed, into 'a new phase of life, very mysterious, which still savours of him'.

Late one night when Gwen John was going to bed, Miss Roderstein, the man-woman, arrived carrying a big bunch of flowers in one hand, a hideous bronze in the other and five francs in her bag. She said she was on her way back to Germany and had come to apologise for cancelling a two-week block booking. She also wanted to know if the bronze was by Rodin. The next day Gwen John took it to Rodin who glanced at it in horror but would not give his opinion till Roderstein had paid the five francs a sitting that she owed Gwen John.

There were other clients to replace Miss Roderstein. Monsieur Jacques S. employed Gwen John again and proved still to have the disadvantage of being male. He asked her to take an excruciating pose and as usual filled her brain with a flurry of vacuity. Three lady portraitists with hard expressionless faces weren't much better. They did not speak to her, only discussed her. There was a table of cream cakes in a corner of the studio to which they constantly had recourse. Gwen John was not invited to join them at it. They *were* American, she pointed out.

She was now beginning to experiment with gouaches. The first mention of these efforts was in a letter to Ursula Tyrwhitt on 30 July in which she said she was drawing, or rather painting herself in the nude in the mirror, using watercolour mixed with Chinese white. Six months later she had produced a number of outline drawings in pencil on brown paper[4] with the room in the rue Cherche-Midi for a setting. The table at the window is clearly recognisable in the background and there is a bed on the right. These identical drawings were produced by holding two sheets of paper against the window and tracing. Gwen John explained her gouache method to Ursula Tyrwhitt.

> It is like painting in oils only quicker. I have begun five. I first decide absolutely on the tones, then try and make them in colour (i.e. on the palette) and put them in. I have finished one, it was rather bad because of the difficulty of settling the exact tones in colour and not knowing much about watercolour. I want my drawings to be definite and clean like Japanese drawings. I think, even if I don't do a good one, the work of deciding on the exact tones and colour and seeing so many pictures and the practice of putting things down with decision ought to help me when I do a painting in oils – in fact I think all is there except the modelling of the flesh perhaps.

[4] Eight of these can be seen at the National Museum of Wales, Cardiff.

Looking into the same glass in the same room Gwen John painted a self-portrait in oils, seated and a little disconsolate in a check skirt.[5]

She had promised to visit Ursula Tyrwhitt in London in the summer, declaring that it would be amusing and 'so different'. But she did not and Ursula Tyrwhitt, having failed to sell her pictures at the N.E.A.C., could not afford to leave her father's west country vicarage and visit Gwen John. Instead there were frequent expeditions to St Cloud in search of Tiger. 'My sweet little outcast was so hungry last night,' she told Ursula Tyrwhitt. 'The moon is full, I'm going to be out all night. When the cats make love I run to see if my sweet is one of them.' Yet, as always, the lost cat was a source of guilt. Not now because Rodin would be angry, but because cats were becoming too important to her. When Ursula Tyrwhitt enquired about Tiger, she was sharply rebuked. 'You are always proving how wonderful you are, a fact I know already, so why insist? The last unnecessary demonstration is the mention of my *petite chatte*. Yes, she is very important, perhaps the most important thing. But that ought not to be so, *nespas*?' In another letter she wrote, 'Don't bring me a kitten. I don't want to get attached to a little beast again as I did before, it was too dreadful when I lost her. If I did not live alone so much I could take one and be reasonable now I think I should put all that energy of loving into my drawing, don't you?'

In the end Gwen John compromised by giving a temporary home to an unwanted grey cat. It was with this cat that she travelled to Monneville in the spring of 1908. But somehow this year Monneville was not so idyllic. For one thing Miss Brown didn't send the cart to Villetêtue for her and she had to walk four kilometres lugging a suitcase, a cat basket and an umbrella. Once again she was aware of her inferior status as a model. She felt it again when she trailed behind the ladies on walks, or sat alone in the breakfast room because she was late for the *petit déjeuner*, or mended Miss Brown's stockings in the evenings (a job which she had volunteered to do).

The lack of privacy at Monneville was also trying. When some 'aristocrats' from the next village arrived she crept up to her room and sat there trying to recover her peace of mind. The noise the frogs made, like drops of water, as they fell into the garden pool below her window, comforted her. There were also swallows' nests under the eaves and it may have been here that she wrote her poem about swallows, 'Who fly from Memphis in the spring and fill the old nest with eager youngsters.' In this poem, entitled *Arondelle* (sic), she compared the hungry nestlings with her own hungry heart.

[5] 'The artist in her room in Paris', no. 12, 1968 Arts Council Exhibition. Private Collection, Paris.

Also the loveless state of the virgins of Monneville was oppressive. While thoughts of an artist filled Gwen John's head, they thought only of Art. Although surrounded by dogs and insects who were 'doing it all the time', they paid no attention, and in Gwen John's opinion never would until a man had seen the thing they had under their dresses. And no man ever would. In time, she prophesied to Rodin only too truly, they would be obliged, like all spinsters, to turn their love upon objects, such as flowers.

During the summer Gwen John continued to take the river steamers to Meudon and St Cloud where she walked by the river or in the meadows. She watched a water rat 'with a large family to see to' and she met a horse. He was standing at the side of the field where she was picnicking and ran up to see what she was and take the cake she was eating. Alarmed, she ran away, leaving him to examine the other cakes which were spread on a napkin on the ground. Luckily they were so small that he could not get his lips round them and went and stood disconsolately at a distance. During the course of the hot afternoon he made several approaches, smelling her and looking at her with gentle eyes. By the time she left it seemed to her that they were friends.

Men were more alarming. This was the period of the great *apache* scare in Paris when tales of heartless murder were rife and even Rodin had taken on a third dog, a friendly Alsatian called Flora. Mademoiselle Gerhardi, the mischief maker, had terrified Gwen John with horrid stories and when Gwen John saw a coatless giant skulking beside a forest ride at Clamart she knew instinctively that this was an ambush. She proceeded at a steady pace, reading her book, knowing he would attack at once if she ran. Sure enough the man came out from between the trees as she passed and fell in step, first behind and then beside her. She looked down at his hands which were big enough to fell her at a blow. When he told her that he was a thief her blood ran cold. But she could not help observing that the look in his eye was amorous rather than aggressive. Eventually she signalled to a passing cart to stop. The driver offered her a seat and she decided it was wiser to accept although he was going in the wrong direction. In the event the driver proved more amorous than the thief.

In September the stalls in the Edgar Quinet market were loaded with fruit, but Gwen John had fruit that was more precious than any they could offer. Rodin had brought her a basket of plums from Meudon. To make them last she spread them on the floor of the little kitchen and cooked herself six each evening. Yet Rodin was not always kind. Once more he stood at the table by the window and laughed because she said she was unhappy. If he did that often, she told him, she might hide herself away for ever.

Her desire to hide was becoming more pronounced. She was beginning to avoid even her neighbours, people like little George and his wife. She explained that when she was unhappy she didn't feel like saying 'Turned out warm again' to them on the stairs and when she was happy she didn't either and 'I am always one or the other'. Once Madame Hugel next door knocked for half an hour without receiving a reply. Gwen John was furious because she then entered. In the summer of 1909 the concierge announced that her husband was ill and needed to move into an airier room. Gwen John's, alas, was the only one suitable.

In many ways the move to 6 rue de l'Ouest[6] was disastrous. As she refused to give anyone her new address she became more isolated than ever. The rue de l'Ouest was a narrow street in the heart of old Montparnasse. The room was on the first floor, approached by a dark corridor, unlit by gas. (Gwen John used to light a paraffin lamp when she was expecting Rodin.) Worst of all, it faced what the horrified Ursula Tyrwhitt insisted on calling 'the Wall' although it was in fact the house opposite. As a result it was dark and dreary and although Gwen John lived there at least five years she never spoke of it with affection. She merely insisted it was all she could afford, or was likely to be able to afford. 'There are reasons,' she explained to Ursula Tyrwhitt, 'which make this possible to live in. It is quiet and the concierge is nice and the other people in the house don't trouble me.' Smaller neighbours were dealt with by fumigation before Gwen John moved in.

Yet it was here that she painted one of her most luminous portraits, that of the blue-eyed Fenella wearing a white dress against a green background. Many have admired this frail beauty with the sloping shoulders, the small drooping mouth and the great eyes moist with melancholy. Gwen John too was enchanted by the pretty little face of the model who had been passed on by Rodin. It was rare, almost unheard of, for Gwen John to employ a professional model but she spent fifteen pounds on sittings with Fenella and took her out to dinner twice. For a time she was in love with her beauty, but then, as so often, the base personality began to show through. She caught her first glimpse of it on a walk in the Luxembourg gardens when Fenella insisted on saying insulting things about her lover in a loud voice all afternoon while Gwen John thought that she would have been glad of a kind look from hers. A visit to the Bois de Clamart was worse. It was Fenella's custom to pose as a gypsy, and for this purpose she wore gypsy clothes and had assumed the name of Lovell.[7] When the *rôdeurs* of the Bois de Clamart saw her she was

[6] On the corner of the rue Vercingétorix. Now destroyed.
[7] The Lovells were a well-known Romany tribe who travelled mainly in Cambridge-shire, central England and occasionally Wales.

practically mobbed. Edwardian men were quickly excited by the sight of a bare foot in a sandal and some of the remarks passed were, to say the least, familiar.

Fenella's reception by Gwen John's artist friends was more to her liking. She squatted in their midst like a *romanchiel*[8] as Gwen put it, and told their fortunes with cards. But to Gwen she was by now no more than 'that dreadful little creature'. She was a fake 'old-fashioned girl' without character, or rather with 'a horrid character'. Gwen John worked hard at the portrait simply to get its subject out of her studio.

And yet she knew the painting was good, and she insisted that the reason it was good was because it hadn't been intended for exhibition. The N.E.A.C.'s dreaded show was once more looming, but Gwen John insisted that 'no one would want her portrait. It will be good because I have not thought about it being seen by anybody.' In spite of her complaints about Fenella she continued to paint her. She executed the famous companion portrait of her naked, which now hangs at the Tate, the expression subtly changed by awareness of nudity. One day perhaps the twin pictures will hang side by side, like those of Goya's Maja, no longer separated by the Atlantic.

The summer with Fenella slid into a winter of deeper discontent. Gwen John was extraordinarily sensitive to climatic change. Like a cat she was always depressed by rain, whereas the first hint of spring made her dream of primroses and the country. In the summer she took to the woods and the fields like a wild animal.

The first winter at the rue de l'Ouest was worse than usual. For several weeks the stove would not work and she was too miserable to get it mended. She had a bad cough which made her unable to hold her poses and kept her awake, so that the nights seemed as long as the days. Too nervous to stay at home, she went out with her sketch-book, for she needed to draw something well in order to calm her spirit. She went to the Gare Montparnasse and drew people while she shivered. Here her loneliness became acute. In all that crowd not one person spoke to her. Of all those footsteps not one stopped to say a kind word.

At home it was the same. On the dark wooden stairs there were only the heavy footsteps of working people, never the tread of the person she longed to see. He had shut her out in the cold. She was at his knees demanding happiness. She was not a hysteric but she had only him in the world. When he neglected her she would not eat. The food went back untasted into the cupboard. Once she had been beautiful and he had made her take poses in her room, turning her slowly to admire her. Now she was thin and no longer beautiful and he left her alone.

[8] Romany.

Gwen John's attitude to food was becoming increasingly complicated. She undoubtedly used semi-starvation as a weapon against Rodin. She often refused to eat at home because the smell of cooking was disagreeable, but she seldom ate in restaurants. She often implied that food she was given in other people's houses was poison. Her diet at this time seems to have been reduced to chestnuts boiled in milk which she commended because it was easy to prepare. People began to notice how ill she looked. The faithful Miss Bowser, who was now employing her almost exclusively, said she was becoming too thin to draw and Miss Brown (the American lady), who met her in the street, hardly knew her. It was agreed that she must have a winter holiday at Monneville.

At Monneville she suffered as usual from lack of solitude although everyone was kind. She helped in the house and pleased everybody although she was not deemed strong enough for two modelling sessions a day. Instead she was sent for solitary country walks in the short December afternoons. The best times were the evenings when she sewed and either Miss O'Donnell or Miss Brown read aloud. She was able for the first time in weeks to sleep at night.

'In or about December 1910 human character changed,' wrote Virginia Woolf. In that year Roger Fry astounded the British public with his exhibition, *Manet and the Post-Impressionists*. Over the Channel advanced movements had been afoot for a decade. In 1905 the beasts in the *cage des fauves* had been let loose in the Grand Palais, in 1906 Matisse had presented his show at the Druet Gallery and in 1907 Picasso confronted Parisians with *Les Demoiselles d'Avignon*.

Gwen John, like other English painters born in the 1870s, had to face the challenge of great stylistic changes when she was already thirty-five. She had always avoided the anecdotal realism of Ricketts and Shannon, considering herself more a disciple of Sickert. Comments she made on the Italian Futurists, Balla and Severini, when she visited their exhibition at Bernheim Jeune a few years later,[9] show that her attitude was far from rigidly conservative. 'They are very amusing and have great talent, I think,' she told Ursula Tyrwhitt. 'I don't know whether it is art. The school of Matisse is far far behind and most academic and conventional beside them.' But there was never any sudden change in her vision, only a gradual development.

The N.E.A.C. was becoming increasingly stuffy (several of its exhibitors had recently been transferred without pain to the Royal Academy, including Orpen). In London at this time (1910) the Camden Town Group was formed in opposition to the N.E.A.C. by painters like Gilman, Ginner and J. B. Manson, so-called because its members were

[9] *Peintres Futuristes Italiens*, February 1912.

also disciples of Sickert, who had painted the streets of Camden Town, and it was for this reason that Wendy Baron included Gwen John among them in her recent book.[10] Certainly Gwen John was not aware of being a member of any group.

There was however a brief flirtation with Picasso. Augustus had met him and admired the work of his Blue Period[11] when he was living in Paris with Ida in 1907. He was attracted by the remote antiquity of Picasso's figures and by their resemblance to those solitary people of Pierre Puvis de Chavannes (1824–98) who stood in empty landscapes half a century earlier. In 1910 Gwen John painted a modified Blue Period Picasso called 'Woman sewing'.[12] An angular woman with cropped hair is threading a needle at a round table (the round table in the room at Cherche-Midi). Her face is illuminated by a table lamp in the manner of 'Dorelia by lamplight'. Like Picasso, Gwen John has chosen a mono-chrome scheme, yellow in this case, but the reposed concentration and introspection of the face could only be the work of Gwen John.

More important than this temporary deviation was a permanent change in technique at this time, demonstrated in a portrait of Chloë Boughton Leigh in oils.[13] The picture was painted under difficult circumstances, for Chloë had only three weeks to spend in Paris and Maude insisted that Gwen should hurry in order to finish it. As a result Gwen became so exhausted that she had to give up before the end and, to the fury of both ladies, refused to send the picture to the N.E.A.C. Yet the resulting portrait is a lovely thing, full of calm. The rather vacant face of the earlier portrait has developed a contemplative cast (Chloë was now forty-two). The fussy blue and white dress has given way to a dark grey one which emphasises the sitter's sloping shoulders and gives a triangular and monumental character to the figure. The hands are coarsely painted and clasped. The whole pose is typical of future portraits. By 1910 it was evident that Gwen John had defined her aims as a portraitist and only minor changes were to follow.

But although the style was fixed the technique was still in a state of transition, and indeed in this painting Gwen John employed two differ-ent methods, the old and the new. Whereas she painted the figure in her usual manner, using fluid layers of semi-transparent paint, she painted the background in a different one, putting the paint on thick and chalky and using a quick-drying medium. From this time Gwen John began to produce many canvases of the same subject, never working over one

[10] *Camden Town Group* by Wendy Baron. Scolar, 1979.
[11] Picasso once called Augustus John 'the best bad painter in Britain'.
[12] Collection of Mrs Robert Henriques.
[13] 'Chloë Boughton Leigh', no. 16, 1968 Arts Council Exhibition. Leeds City Art Galleries.

twice and never allowing herself more than one sitting, or at the most two. 'One must paint a lot of canvases and probably waste them,' she was later to tell Ursula Tyrwhitt. Increasingly small patterned strokes on a thinly primed canvas produced a dry fresco-like effect similar to Puvis de Chavannes, 'Surely the greatest painter of the century.'

In drawing too she changed her medium, and although she never abandoned pencil she often preferred to use charcoal which produced a firmer and more varied line and discouraged the introduction of detail. She also began to experiment with ink and wash.

On 4 February 1910 Gwen John wrote to Ursula on the ornately headed notepaper of the Taverne de La Brasserie Dumesnil Frères in the Boulevard Montparnasse. It was of key importance because in it Gwen John made a statement of her artistic position in 1910. For the first time she knew that she had a vision that was 'important to the world', that her work had a distinct personality. 'I have only to fix something in painting . . . to be sure and certain for ever of some ideas of painting, that have half shown themselves in the last two days,' she wrote. Her experience with Fenella had convinced her that she must not dissipate her energies in painting 'vague things and people. That kind of painting, and only that kind, depresses me,' she said.

Gwen John's handwriting was very uncertain in the Dumesnil letter and she appears to have been suffering from a mysterious illness. She complained of migraines in the letter and, in the autumn of 1910, was taken seriously ill with an unspecific complaint which left her with a fear of light and of people. This illness, and those that followed in the next few years, she placed firmly at Rodin's door. 'Love is my illness,' she wrote, 'and there is no cure till you come.' But Rodin, alas, was more deeply involved than ever with the dreadful Duchess.

Meanwhile Gwen John insisted more than ever on the necessity of solitude for her work. She complained of the intolerably strong impression that people made on her which she could not shake off and declared that she wanted to see *nobody*. She longed to imitate a girl painter who had gone to Mexico to find peace of mind. 'I think I shall do something good soon,' she confided to Ursula Tyrwhitt, 'If I'm left to myself and not absolutely destroyed.'

In fact 1910 was one of her most productive years. She painted a 'good watercolour head of myself nicely framed' for the N.E.A.C. spring show and added some cats. She also started on the second version of 'A lady reading', for John Quinn, entitled 'Girl reading at the window.'

John Quinn was a Wall Street lawyer who was beginning to take Rodin's place in Gwen John's life as a patron. He collected modern paintings because, as he frankly admitted, he could not afford Old

Masters. Augustus had met him when Quinn was exploring his Irish origins in Dublin and had passed him on to Gwen John with strict instructions that she was not to offend him. Augustus then proceeded to exhibit a portrait of Quinn at the N.E.A.C. spring show, showing an elongated triangle of a body surmounted by 'a head as round and unexpressive as a billiard ball. I howled out loud with glee,' said Quinn. But he was not amused.

On 30 July 1909 John Quinn wrote to Gwen John offering her thirty pounds for any painting she cared to send him and she characteristically replied to Mr Quinn (it was always 'Mr Quinn') that she had spent a long time deciding whether to send a certain painting to him and had decided not to send it. 'People say it is so ugly and I'm sure it is,' she added. The letter was addressed to 31 Nassau Street, New York, L'Amérique (she usually got addresses wrong), and was the first of many excusing the unfinished state of paintings on the grounds of the inadequacy of the picture itself or of her own ill health.

John Quinn was not a man to be easily discouraged. In July 1910 he wrote again informing Gwen John that a five hundred franc advance on a future painting (any painting) awaited her at Brentano's bookshop (he assumed she had no bank account) and that she might ship the painting when finished to the Chenil Galleries, London. By putting Gwen John under an obligation Quinn showed some cunning. With her delicate conscience she would never rest until she had earned her salary. Quinn was virtually the only collector who ever succeeded in buying anything from her directly. As a result of his badgering she moved gradually into her most productive phase which reached its peak in 1924.

In 1910 Gwen John also experimented with etching for the first time. She executed two portraits, taking the plates 'when bitten' to a printer. Apparently they were successful and she declared herself very interested but, unlike Augustus, did not repeat the experiment. She also told Rodin she had started a self-portrait in oils. At the end of the year an unfinished portrait of Fenella came back to haunt her, conveyed by her older brother Thornton who was on a visit to Europe. She stacked it with its face to the wall, feeling sure it was dreadful.

Despite her new and more professional attitude to painting Gwen John continued to model, although she was becoming increasingly convinced that too much modelling made her stupid. She worked once more for Rodin's assistants, Soudbinine and Jacques S. (who did a bad statue of her) and for a lady who left her posed while she went into an adjoining room to make love. As usual she found talking to her clients more trying than modelling for them. After tea with a group of artists she was unable to sleep because there was 'no charity in their hearts'. She told Rodin she preferred to talk to workmen who did not deal in sentiments. In the night an angel told her she need not bother about society. This was a great relief to her.

Miss Bowser was an exception. She was a conscientious painter who found Gwen John beautiful as an angel and often employed her in nude poses. She knew about her affair with Rodin. She had even visited Rodin's studio. But she was never an intimate friend. Gwen John once carried a frame to her fifth floor apartment from a shop in the Boulevard Montparnasse. The rain started just as she was leaving but she would not stay until it passed. She preferred to walk out into a cloudburst and rejoiced to feel the rain pass through her hat and her cotton dress and run down her back. She was free.

Miss Bowser tried not to be impatient with Gwen John's increasing illnesses, her fits of coughing and faintness and her failure to keep appointments. Gwen had to put up with Miss Bowser's little vanities. She prayed constantly not to lose her temper. About this time Miss Bowser invited her to stay for two days at her house up near the Observatory at Meudon. Gwen as usual was a perfect but unhappy guest, helping with the housework and longing to be at home. But she met a painter who shared the house with Miss Bowser who was to play an important part in her life. Her name was Ruth Manson and she had a child and was very poor because her husband had abandoned her and gone to Italy. The two women however did not become intimate for some years to come.

It may have been on this visit to Meudon that Gwen John found a home for herself there. To reach the church and the shops from the Observatory she would certainly have passed down the rue Terre Neuve. It was near the top of this winding street, tucked under the retaining walls of the terrace, that she found number 29 (now destroyed), an old rooming house with a crumbling yellow facade and three vacant attics. 'Now I am going to tell you my little joy,' she wrote to Ursula Tyrwhitt. 'It has three rooms and a little kitchen and heaps of cupboards and a *grenier*. When you come you shall have a lovely bedroom with the sun coming in early and no street noises.'

Gwen John was becoming increasingly fond of Ursula Tyrwhitt. In 1910 she wrote her nine long letters, more than she had ever written in a single year. Ursula Tyrwhitt, like Gwen, was reaching a crisis in her life. She too was thirty-five and still living at home. She longed for independence and found the constraints of the vicarage at Easton-in-Gordano well nigh intolerable. Like Gwen John, she needed solitude for her work and sometimes encouraged her mother's callers to leave by going round the house slamming doors. Occasionally she resorted to standing in the middle of a field and screaming. Her flower paintings were now attracting favourable notice. She would soon be able to support herself. Why should she not move to Paris and live with Gwen?

Gwen was enthusiastic about the plan. They would share expenses and save money by using each other as models. 'It must happen within a year at least,' said Gwen John. Meanwhile the affair with Rodin continued to cool. Only four of Gwen John's letters to him survive from 1910, but one was a touching one in which she acknowledged greetings on her *fête*, 15 August, the Feast of the Assumption of the Virgin. 'I didn't know I had my own *fête*,'[14] she wrote. 'We don't in England because of the religion.' She would wait for him in her room, wearing her new silk dress.

A much less welcome visitor than Ursula was her father, Edwin John. In the fifteen years since Gwen John had left home he had done nothing very much with his life except move into the house round the corner. He still dressed himself in his dark suit, his black hat, his wing collar and his spats each morning. He still took his morning stroll along the promenade at Tenby. He still played the organ at Gumfreston on Sundays and occasionally proposed marriage to a young woman. His letters to Gwen were mostly about the weather or enquired about her health and usually remained unanswered. She used the backs of some for writing to other people on. Now she was condemned to abandon her easel and escort the man who paid little towards her upkeep, round Notre Dame, the Louvre and the Eiffel Tower. 'I wouldn't mind if he did it for love of me,' she told Ursula Tyrwhitt, 'but he only does it because it's the thing to do.' More and more she was feeling the necessity of freedom from relations. 'We don't go to Heaven in families any more,' she said.

At Christmas Augustus searched for her in the rain (she had not given him her address in the rue de l'Ouest). He was unaccustomed to such treatment, for he was now at the height of his powers as a painter. His fifty almost visionary oil sketches of the lake at Martigues showed for the first time that he had a gift for colour. And he was making money. He could exhibit whenever he liked at the Chenil Galleries and his canvases fetched forty pounds each and sometimes changed hands for seventy pounds.

In the late autumn of 1910 he had come to Paris in search of distraction. He spent his time whoring in Montparnasse 'like a tourist' with Fabian de Castro, a gypsy guitarist who had recently escaped from a Spanish gaol. Augustus clowned in an embarrassing manner. At one point he underwent a fake appendix operation in order to avoid the embraces of an Austrian 'tiger woman', and at another he threatened to elope to Marseille with a Miss George who may have been the Teresa George whom he and Gwen John had known as children at Broad Haven. In the event he returned to London taking a number of his disreputable friends with him and leaving Gwen in peace.

[14] Rodin usually called Gwen John Marie.

In the New Year Gwen John evaded more unwanted visitors to Paris. Dorelia and Henry Lamb passed through in January, accompanied by Pyramus and driven by a rich American called Mrs Chadbourne. Dorelia had left home again because de Castro spat in the bathroom of the house in Church Street, Chelsea. With Henry Lamb she saw the city in all 'its glamour of history and romance'. But she did not see Gwen.

A more serious threat appeared over the western horizon in the summer, nothing less than John Quinn, 'eager to give myself the pleasure of calling on you if you would let me'. Worse still, he was to be accompanied by Augustus. Gwen John hastily arranged a month in the country but as her letter was misdirected it did not reach Quinn in time. Augustus had already made a fruitless visit to Meudon before it reached them. Augustus and Quinn now borrowed a seventy-five horse power Mercedes from a copper king, Thomas Fortune Ryan, and set off on a tour of the south with Marseille as its objective. Within a week they 'did' (Quinn's expression), Tours, Montélimar, Le Puy, Avignon, Aix and Martigues. Quinn shocked John by donning a slate-grey cap as soon as they left Paris, saying that Chartres was too good to be used as a cathedral and complaining that the hotels in the south were not as good as the Ritz. Worst of all, he proved to be a coward, as Augustus related in his autobiography. 'One night, when the car was creeping at a snail's pace on an unknown road through a dense fog in the Cevennes, the attorney suddenly gave vent to a despairing cry and in one masterly leap precipitated himself clean through the open window to land handsomely by the roadside!'

Gwen John's health continued to deteriorate. The psychological illness of 1910 was followed by a severe *grippe*, an attack of flu verging on pneumonia, in the spring of 1911. These *grippes* were to become a regular occurrence in the later winter and early spring. She had only to be caught in a shower of rain, the rain she had once revelled in, to start to shiver with fever and know that weeks of illness lay ahead. Now she lay in the dark little room in the rue de l'Ouest 'too weak to think and too sad to go out'. She saw the April sunshine make cloud shadows on the house opposite. For the first time in her life she did not want the spring.

In religion alone she could find consolation, a consolation which she confided to Rodin. She told him, in the only letter to him preserved from that year, that if she lay in the dark with her hands joined and thought of God she could feel a presence surrounding her. For a few moments at least she knew happiness. To her notebook she confided her morning thoughts. 'I will trust in God. I will keep near to Him. I will abandon myself to his kindness.'

Meanwhile she laboured on 'Girl reading at the window' which the politely impatient John Quinn had paid for two years earlier. It is typical of Gwen John's diffidence about her work that she should paint Quinn a version of something she had done three years earlier. Perhaps she felt that, because the original had eventually found a buyer a near replica was more likely to please him.[15] When she sent the new painting to the autumn N.E.A.C. exhibition of 1911 she was still far from sure it would be liked. 'When you see it you will allow me to send another,' she wrote to Quinn. To Ursula Tyrwhitt she added, 'Do give me a critical opinion of this picture. Mr Quinn doesn't know anything about painting.'

It was Quinn's custom to use the painters he patronised as unpaid talent scouts, since he himself was often too busy to visit Europe for years at a time or preferred to take health cures with his sister in the Pennsylvania hills. Augustus had turned to the work willingly, commending his friends, but it was little to Gwen John's liking. A bombardment of questions like, 'Do you like Renoir?' 'Would you like an introduction to James Durand-Ruel?' 'Have you visited the Galerie Volland?' and 'Do you know the work of Maurice Denis?' went unanswered. But she did make one sally into the world of art dealing on Quinn's behalf. On 22 August 1911 she wrote a letter to him drawing his attention to Rousseau, a painter who came to mean a great deal to him. She had seen some of his posthumous work (Rousseau died in 1910) at the Indépendants and explained '. . . he was a *douanier* and at fifty years old he felt he must paint and so he painted, not knowing at all how to paint. His pictures are very remarkable works as you can imagine, but they are works of art.'

Meanwhile Gwen John was beginning to live at the flat in Meudon. She had spent three days cleaning it and now she only went into Paris to work. She continued to urge Ursula Tyrwhitt to join her there, or at least to pay a visit and paint something for the N.E.A.C. exhibition. 'People who think are of the opinion that anything good must be done *dans l'austère silence*. I have lately read that. You need only see me *au petit déjeuner et pour souper* as I shall be coming to Paris to work,' she wrote. But still Ursula did not come.

Quinn was back in Paris in the summer of 1912 and Gwen John was conveniently ill, thus missing him for the third time. Quinn also was ill. 'Paris is like women, I suppose,' he wrote. 'Sometimes it appeals to one and sometimes it does not. This time it was hateful to me and everything in it.' The weather was wet during the week he was there and on several occasions the indefatigable seeker after art retired to bed half way through the afternoon. On his way back through London he stopped at the Chenil Galleries to see, for the first time, his purchase, Gwen John's

[15] 'A lady reading' was in fact to have a considerable success. Its anonymous owner presented it to the Contemporary Art Society in 1911 and by 1914 it had been exhibited in Manchester, Newcastle and Belfast. It was also exhibited twice in London during these years, once under the name 'Interior'. In 1917 the C.A.S. donated it to the Tate.

'Girl reading at the window', where it was now being exhibited. He was enchanted and described it as 'a little gem that will have a place of honour in my small collection'. Later he wrote, 'the charmingly Vermeer-like pose is invariably picked out in my apartment and immensely admired.'

In fact Quinn's collection was far from small and was soon to become one of the most important collections of twentieth-century French painting in the United States. Although he was rather shy of the Post-Impressionists to start with he ended up as the owner of Matisse's 'Blue nude', Picasso's 'Three musicians', Rousseau's 'Sleeping gypsy' and many other works that now draw crowds in American national galleries. His ability to tell a good picture from a bad appeared instinctive, for he seldom made an intelligent comment on a painting. Gwen John herself sought advice from him in vain. 'I can only say the picture is very nice and I like it,' he would say. Having amassed his treasure he had nowhere to display it. He was a bachelor living in an apartment. At 79 Central Park West hundreds of canvases were stacked against the walls. Dust covers disguised stone heads by Modigliani and bronze heads by Brancusi. If a visitor mentioned Braque, twelve canvases would be instantly paraded for him and they would all be good ones. Quinn insisted on the best examples of an artist's work and on a quality he called 'acid' or 'pain and struggle'.

Gwen John's postal friendship with Quinn was one of the strangest in her life, for at first sight she would appear to have nothing in common with this son of a baker from Fostoria, Ohio, apart from their interest in painting. He was conceited and humourless and often displayed a startling lack of taste in the matter of frames. Gwen John never liked Quinn's choice of frames. Her canvases were invariably small (often no more than a foot high) and he tried to increase their impact with impressive surrounds. When he suggested replacing the original frame of 'Girl reading' she wrote politely, 'I think it had better be kept in it, it is a shabby little old frame but I tried it in new ones . . . and bright yellow gilt made the picture look out of tone.' Quinn hastily agreed, adding that although the frame was little and not expensive the dull red did indeed show through the gilt and went well with the picture. Gwen John was always deeply concerned about frames and trudged many miles through Montparnasse seeking out old ones in shops she knew, both for herself and for her friends. But she was not always satisfied with them and after a fruitless search once declared, 'My pictures look much better *without* frames,' a statement which horrified poor Quinn.

The management of this minor disagreement between the patron and the artist shows with what forbearance each treated the other. Quinn, who made history in Wall Street by sacking five partners from his law firm in a year, showed the patience of Job in easing pictures out of the shy lady of Meudon. When she failed to send a picture promised for an exhibition he forgave her at once. When she spent two years doing a painting for a nun which he considered he had paid for, he merely bought the picture from the convent, thus paying twice over. When three greatly desired oils were recalled to Meudon on the day they were due at the shipper he simply sent words of commiseration.

The humble tone of Gwen John's letters, combined with their innocence, began to appeal to the man who had never met her but who was beginning to suspect that she was a true 'lady'. Quinn liked ladies. He had met some in Ireland. Quickly his letters ceased to be concerned solely with sums of money and instead began to deal with the more interesting subject of his health. Quinn was obsessed with his bodily functions. He once devoted a long paragraph of a letter to Gwen John to a minute description of a blister he had contracted on the twelfth day of a walking holiday in the Adirondacks: how it had grown, how he had pricked it, how fluid had exuded, how it had started to spread up the inside of his foot, how, worse still, while sitting in a room having it attended to he had had the misfortune to be in a draught which had given him a stiff back which at first he had taken for a kidney infection. And so on. For the sake of his health he boiled himself in springs, wore rubber-heeled shoes (Gwen John agreed that they produced a floating sensation) and rode a horse every morning in Central Park until it fell on him and made him rather ill.

He was equally concerned about Gwen John's health and always enquired about what he called her 'grips' and her teeth, agreeing that there is nothing like a cough to knock you out. He once sent a fifty-word Western Union cable advising her to see a doctor, having already written a long letter. In the same letter he advised her that next time she felt a cough coming she should take a dose of castor-oil to expel the poisons in the system that had accumulated through improper food or lack of exercise. Most people, he warned, turned their stomachs into distilleries by eating:

> Pork, pickles, pastries, pies,
> Fish, fritters, fats and fries.

Quinn's letters to Gwen John were always longer than her letters to him, in spite of the fact that he carried on a vast correspondence with artists and men of letters in both France and England. This may well account for the fact that he often felt 'very very horribly horribly terribly driven'. On Sunday mornings a boy from the office brought 'the bag' to the apartment at Central Park West and three typists sat round the dining-room table and took down letters while Quinn dictated to them in turns. Sometimes he would announce a paragraph that was suitable for inclusion in all the letters and the typewriters clacked in unison. The letters that resulted were verbose and not always grammatical. But one letter written on 1 November 1912 brought good news to Gwen John. He was so pleased with 'Girl reading' that he was proposing to make her an allowance of a hundred and twenty pounds per annum to be paid quarterly in return for two or three paintings a year, and would also be happy to accept drawings. He told her he now considered her paintings were worth fifty pounds each. Gwen John replied, 'I find it difficult to thank you as I wish to for your offer to buy my pictures and to send me the money regularly. It would be very good for me to have money regularly and to be able to have models but I'm not sure at this moment whether my pictures will be good.'

In fact Gwen John was already employing models. In 1912 she worked on several portraits including 'Woman in a red shawl'.[16] She also produced gouaches. She offered all or any of these to Quinn but assured him he could have a *genre* painting instead if he preferred. When the first quarterly cheque arrived she confessed it made her 'rather breathless'.

The sting in the tail of Quinn's generosity was not long in showing itself. In January 1913 he wished to contribute to the great Post-Impressionist exhibition at the New York Armory. He sent Gwen John an urgent request for pictures and a sample of the cable he expected from her by return. It was to run:

QUINNEX N.Y.
FOUR (OR THREE)
GWEN JOHN

In reply Gwen John cabled:

QUINNEX N.Y.
ONE
GWEN JOHN

In fact even that one portrait did not materialise for Gwen John was dissatisfied with the face. Nevertheless Quinn declared that the two pictures of hers that *were* exhibited, 'Girl reading at the window' and 'Woman in a red shawl', were among the 'quiet successes' of a show that was far from quiet. Augustus had no less than twenty paintings in the exhibition. New York society raised a cheer for him. His prices were still rising.

[16] Collection of the Duke of Devonshire.

With money to spend Augustus was at last able to move to the country house that Dorelia longed for. As soon as they were established at Alderney Manor, near Poole, Augustus conceived a fearful desire to entertain his sister. Gwen refused emphatically. She saw no reason for going. 'Why should I stay with a man who is not sympathetic?' she asked Ursula Tyrwhitt. 'Unless one had no nerves it is a waste of time.' There was only one person in England she wished to visit and it was too late to visit her now. Ursula Tyrwhitt had married her second cousin, Walter Tyrwhitt, a man older than herself and like her a painter. The couple moved into Orchard House at 225 Iffley Road which Walter had built in 1900, a typical 'architect's house' surrounded by a brick wall. Walter had a studio upstairs where he painted watercolours with elaborate frames (which Ursula hated). They were to travel a good deal during their married life and lived in Sicily for a while. Before she married, Ursula Tyrwhitt visited Gwen John once more in Paris.

Her visit was not entirely a success because Gwen was unwell. She woke every morning with a headache which lasted all day and made her 'feel strange'. She was unable to paint and she slept badly. No doubt the two women visited galleries and dress shops as they always did but for some reason they were not together for the last evening of Ursula's visit. While Gwen John was out Ursula delivered an assortment of presents which included a rose tree, a chinese plate and a tie to wear with her turn-down collars. Perhaps these objects were intended as an apology for the fact that the two women would now never share a home.

Rodin was at last free of the Duchess. The scales had fallen from his eyes and he saw her for the horror she was. But Gwen John's relationship with him could never return to what it had been. Rodin was over seventy now and though he was still amazingly strong his first stroke was not far off. His bouts of bronchitis were increasingly frequent and he often needed the full-time nursing of Judith Cladel at Le Biron and of Rose Beuret at Les Brillants. Judith Cladel was his secretary during the last years of his life and afterwards his biographer. She was one of the few women connected with him for whom Gwen John felt no jealousy, perhaps because, by her devoted labour, she saved Le Biron from demolition and secured it as a museum where Rodin's work would be preserved for posterity.

Gwen John and Rodin continued to meet. Rodin was now too old to walk far and a car used to fetch him from the studio. Occasionally Gwen John would ride in it with him and draw a little pleasure from a lingering exchange of glances in the back seat. But there were more hours than ever apart. One night she went to Meudon in the rain and prowled the familiar terrain below the villa. The windows on the ground floor were open and she could see the lights in the dining-room and even thought she could see Rodin and Rose at dinner. Someone else was prowling nearby. It was Camille Claudel, sister of the novelist Paul Claudel, the brilliant sculptor who Rodin had first instructed and then seduced thirteen years earlier. She too had modelled for Rodin and read Shakespeare to him. She too had loved Rodin passionately and exclusively for nine years. Now she was an emaciated hag who only crept out of her shuttered room at dusk to haunt her master's boundaries. A few months later she ceased to come out and the hospital attendants found her, crouching in her studio like a beast at bay, surrounded by dried up clay figures. Hanging on the walls were the Stations of the Cross cut from a newspaper.

Gwen John now also turned to religion. She was attracted towards Catholicism because Rodin was a Catholic and because his religion could at once give a purpose to suffering and at the same time alleviate it. For some years now she had been attending Mass at Notre Dame, partly to catch a glimpse of Rodin but partly because she found consolation in the magnificent building and music. Now she started to attend Mass at the parish church in the main street of Meudon, just at the bottom of the rue Terre Neuve.

It was in this church that she finally found the courage to approach the curé and ask for instruction. There is little record of her transactions with him, but a letter survives written on 10 October 1912, excusing herself for not having attended instruction. And on 12 February she noted that she would receive the sacrament for the fifth time. Presumably she made her First Confession and Communion around the beginning of February 1913. In her notes she wrote, 'I have chosen to be God's spiritual child. I will ask God to make me faithful to the life I have chosen. Each day is for work.'

Gwen John was never a conventional Catholic although she was always an ardent one. She resented rules imposed from above by a hierarchy whom she considered less well informed than herself. She was disgusted by the hypocrisy of many of her fellow Catholics. 'Their frequentation of the sacraments, their church going, their alms giving,' she wrote in a note, 'contrast strangely with their anxiety to get into society and their . . . almost gross respect for those who are very much richer than themselves.' She attended Mass daily (except when she was at work on a picture) but, for her, private meditation was always more important than public devotion. It was however in the church at Meudon that Gwen John met a nun who was to have a profound influence on her.

In the chairs in front of her during Mass she admired the costumes of the Sisters of Charity (of the Dominican Order of the Presentation of the Holy Virgin at Tours), who ran an orphanage at Meudon. Like all the nuns in that order they wore the black aprons of domestic workers, for their work was to give practical help to the poor. St Vincent, who had founded the order, was said to have designed their head-dress from a starched napkin. It extended like a pair of wings on either side of their head. Gwen John found the costume of their charges equally beautiful. Rows of girls in black dresses with white collars kneeled at the prie-dieu in front of her. They wore wide-brimmed hats with white ribbons round them.

One day Gwen John must have followed the demure crocodile home. It had turned right on leaving the church and walked only a hundred yards before reaching the convent, which was on the other side of the road facing the picturesque village wash-house. An elegant house stood behind a high wall,[17] formerly the house of the notorious courtesan Madame de Verne. Just inside the gate a neo-Gothic chapel made it clear that the house had now been put to a respectable use. In the dusty courtyard the girls played.

How Gwen John got past the guardian of the lodge is not known. All that is known is that the meeting with the Mother Superior, in the musty visitors' parlour, was a success. Mère Armand was a woman of great simplicity and wisdom, lacking intellectual pretensions. In her Gwen John found a spiritual mother to whom she could confide more intimate problems than she could to her spiritual father, the curé at Meudon. So enthusiastic was she for this new friend that she promised her she would paint a picture of the foundress of the order, the highly regarded Mère Poussepin (1653–1744). Indeed, she promised to paint several pictures of the mother foundress, one for every room.

Gwen John started to paint her portrait from a prayer-book engraving, which showed the foundress in the seventeenth-century version of the order's habit, the wings of the coif being turned down like a bonnet and the black apron rising to a bib in front. She made little progress at first and told Quinn on 26 July 1915, 'I am troubled just now by a picture I promised two years ago to a convent.' She told Ursula Tyrwhitt too that she was tired and depressed with the *bonne soeur*. 'I should have done some nice things in all the time I have taken with her,' she wrote. Meanwhile, charmed by the face of a young nun at the convent, she did an oil sketch of her in Poussepin's costume and pose, which probably did not please the Mother Superior.[18] Some time later she wrote, 'The nuns have suddenly lost patience. They don't understand why it is not done. It has been quite a trouble but I think it will soon be over.' In the end the picture took six years to paint.

---

[17] The house still stands and the nuns still inhabit it.
[18] 'Study of a nun'. Private collection.

9

War

1914–18

On 23 August 1914 the Germans invaded France. Memories of the war of 1870 were still vivid at Meudon, where the famous Château-neuf had been razed to the ground. The people there now felt perilously close to the Marne line and terrified crowds looked down on 'the chase of the aryplanes' when the enemy dropped bombs on Paris in the early days. In Paris itself many shops were shut and the traffic decreased dramatically. Soldiers marched in the streets and crowds gathered round the wounded men limping along the pavements. To Gwen John the saddest sight was that of blind men in a line behind a sighted one, each with his hand on the shoulder of the man in front. Soldiers who were in a healthier state did not make life easier for single women. On her way back from a modelling engagement she would often have to run to escape an eager private. As she crossed the bridge over the Seine, she told Rodin, she often looked down longingly into the black water as she had eight years ago when she first lost Tiger.

Almost all the foreign residents were leaving Paris and for a time Gwen John thought she would. There was a possibility that the mayor would evacuate Meudon. But she hung on, pointing out to Augustus that she had her room in Paris to withdraw to. She still visited it every day to finish work she had on hand. It was as a result of these visits to Paris that she decided to stay in France. After seeing the Gare Montparnasse crammed with 'luggage and cattle trains loaded with frightened people I felt more and more disinclined to go,' she told Ursula Tyrwhitt. She was well aware of the danger. She knew that the enemy soldiers were 'brutes and vandals' and that the French and English were locked in a desperate struggle for 'everything we are interested in', but she put her faith in the three girdles of forts round Paris, and assured Quinn that there would be no food shortage and prices would not rise.

She suffered the usual humiliations of foreigners in time of war, being obliged to register herself as an alien with the police. One day, although still weak from her spring attack of flu, she queued for five hours until the Montparnasse office closed. She was then sent to another one which sent her back to the first. Once her papers had been stamped she became a temporary prisoner in the Paris region, but her loyalty to France did not waver. In August she told Quinn that she was safer in France than in England, but, she added, 'I am so relieved the English are going to come up to the mark.'

Alone and defenceless in a country at war, she amassed her 'fragments': passages copied from the books she read. Her mind increasingly craved the calming effect of philosophy even when she could not understand it. She took to borrowing books from the library in the rue St Placide for sixty centimes a week. Once she brought home two volumes of Taine's *Intelligence* and read them till her eyes ached. She declared to Rodin that she found them hard to understand but felt they 'must have done her good'. Novels she now despised, saying they left her with a feeling of emptiness. When Quinn, who knew Conrad and owned most of his manuscripts, sent *The Arrow of Gold* he went unthanked. Like Lacordaire, Gwen John considered, 'when one can read Augustine, Teresa, Bossuet and Pascal it is a sin to spend one's time in salons'.

And it was increasingly works of devotion and the lives of the saints which began to absorb her. She was attracted by saints like Francis who had led humble obscure lives and had mortified the flesh. She copied out the whole of a brief biography of his disciple, St Margaret of Cortona, who abandoned her wealthy lover and starved to death at an early age. Among religious writers she preferred the Victorian poet and mystic, Father Faber, to whom her father had introduced her. Edwin read him every day of his life. She described him to Rodin as, 'an Englishman who wrote many books about the interior life. Some of them have been translated into French.' She proceeded to send him so many passages from Faber that it was not necessary for him to read him.

Frederick Faber was indeed an extraordinary man. At Oxford he had been a lively effeminate youth with an ambition to become a poet. He had then obtained a living in the Lake District. With Newman's publication of Tract 90 he became a Catholic and founded the order of Wilfridians at Elton. Later, as the leader of the London branch of the Oratorians, he built the famous basilica in the Italian style opposite Harrods and filled it with effigies, candles, holy water stoups and other objects delightful to the 'invalid souls' of his 'poor Belgravians'.

At the age of fifty Father Faber had grown corpulent and ill. He now devoted his time to writing the seven books by which, apart from some rather bad hymns, he is today remembered. In *The Creator and the Creature*, one of the last and the best of them, appalling lapses of taste alternate with passages of great beauty. The book was Gwen John's favourite, for it constantly spoke of the theme which was dearest to her, that of a universal and all-embracing Divine Love. She wrote out a passage for Rodin in the year of her conversion, 1913. 'We are in the midst of Him as fishes in the sea . . . His ear is on our lips . . . We sigh into it even when we are asleep or dream.' Another passage must have reminded her of the view over Paris from Meudon.

> Let us sit upon the top of this fair hill . . . Beneath us is that rolling plain, with its dark masses of summer foliage sleeping in the sun . . . There is the gigantic city, gleaming with an ivory whiteness beneath its uplifted but perpetual canopy of smoke. The villa-spotted hills behind it, its almost countless spires, its huge many-steepled palace, and its solemn presiding dome . . . Close around us the air is filled with the songs of rejoicing birds, or the pleasing hum of the insects that are drinking the sunbeams, and blowing the tiny trumpets as they weave and unweave their mazy dance. The flowers breathe sweetly, and the leaves of the glossy shrubs are spotted with bright creatures in painted surcoats.

In Father Faber's grand scheme even the insects blowing their tiny trumpets had a place, and this added to the charm of his writing for Gwen John who spent many hours watching ants. Indeed at this time she copied out several passages from a very different Faber, J. H. Fabre, the famous entomologist. These fragments and many more were despatched to Rodin to help him pass the time when in boring company. And he was in boring company, for he had escaped to England. When his secretary, Judith Cladel, decided to go there in the spring he accompanied her with Rose Beuret, who, from this time, hardly left his side. He stayed for six months at a private hotel in Cheltenham, where, accompanied by elderly ladies, he descended regularly for breakfast, lunch and tea, preserving the silence that was expected. Silence was in fact obligatory to him for he was becoming a child again, although still able to work and make impressive, if silent, public appearances. He would not visit the exhibition of his work at Grosvenor House, organised by the Duke of Westminster, because he was afraid that he might make a fool of himself if he tried to pronounce English names. He did not even see The Burghers of Calais installed on St Stephen's Green.

For Gwen John Rodin never grew old. She wrote him passionate love letters all through his stay in Cheltenham and when she heard that he planned to return to France in October she bought a new outfit (to last for many a season) and told him that she was still ready to model for the arms of his statue. She had been a Catholic for a year now, but made it clear that she expected to continue their former relationship.

As a result of the war Gwen John continued to see the curé regularly after her period of instruction was over. Many wounded were coming to Meudon and it was his job to billet them. He had asked her to hear the confession of any dying Englishmen who might arrive, but, to her relief, none did. She did, however, make a point of talking to any English soldiers she met. 'They are so pleased to be spoken to and I find them so charming. They all have something young in their faces like boys of 14, even the old men.'

Gwen John used also to share her copy of *The Times* with the curé; that is to say she interpreted selected passages for his benefit, for he confessed to finding the full sixteen pages 'a little frightening'. It was Ursula Tyrwhitt who had taken to sending her the paper. She had been in the habit of reading *Paris Midi* but now found it little more than a network of blanks from which the news of French casualties had been excised. She confessed she came to *The Times* like a stranger. 'England has become quite a foreign country to me,' she told Ursula Tyrwhitt. But there was comfort in the dyke of solid facts it erected against a sea of gossip.

In December she read news of the massacre at Ypres and understood for the first time 'the awful cost of trench warfare'. 'How dreadful if the Germans won after all,' she wrote to Ursula Tyrwhitt. Alone at 29 rue Terre Neuve one stormy winter night she trembled to think of ships engulfed in the black waters of the Channel. 'Perhaps it is safe on the lines that passenger steamers come by,' she wrote. Augustus took the risk and crossed, convinced that she was likely to suffer real hardship if she remained in France.

He strode up the rue Terre Neuve, tall and broad-shouldered, wearing a loose tweed suit with a brightly coloured bandana round his neck. Gwen John did not accept his invitation to stay at Alderney Manor although she was no doubt aware that one more eccentric guest would make little difference. She had a home and she would not leave it now.

Things were not easy in France that first winter of the war. At the first hint of war all the foreign ladies who had paid to paint her vanished like a flock of homing pigeons. Miss Flodin, Miss Gerhardi, Miss Roderstein, Miss Wolff, Miss O'Donnell, Miss Brown, Miss Ludlow, Miss Bowser, Miss Lloyd and the Russian had all gone. It seemed unlikely that Quinn's money would get through. Severe economies were necessary and, as Gwen John lived practically without food already and supplemented her meagre coal allowance with firewood from the forest, it was only on clothes that she could economise.

Here the faithful Ursula Tyrwhitt came to the rescue with parcels of second-hand dresses, which Gwen John never despised. Her taste was similar to Ursula's and indeed she had chosen the stuffs of many of the dresses herself. She thanked for them carefully, item by item. During the bitter December of 1914 she wrote, 'I am wearing your brown coat and skirt. It is nice to wear another colour than blue and it is warm. A woman in the house, a dressmaker, took out some of the stuff in the coat and skirt and it is *à la mode* too.' *A la mode* it may have been in Gwen John's eyes, but from now on her style of dress was to be neat rather than fashionable by French standards.

Meanwhile in the United States Quinn waited for pictures. In March he had been told to expect nothing because of bad health and 'beginning too many things'. There were several unfinished canvases at the rue de l'Ouest including a painting of a woman in a blue dress knitting, which Gwen John mentioned to Ursula Tyrwhitt but not to Quinn, as was often the case.

Then in August 'Study of a woman' arrived and Quinn was ecstatic. The figure was a three-quarter length one with hands clasped, large by Gwen John's standards. Quinn declared it was better than Whistler. Gwen John asked as usual for criticism but he could only 'admire and appreciate'. She was relieved because the picture was 'so different from the others. I see by his letter he likes it much better than the other', she told Ursula Tyrwhitt. Gwen John now felt that her new style of painting had received the official approval of her patron. A drawing accompanied the painting. It was by another woman, Ruth Manson. When Quinn asked to what address he should send Ruth Manson's money, he was told by Gwen John 'this one'.

Gwen John's friendship with Ruth Manson is one of the most mysterious in her life. They had first met in 1911. She was the painter with a child who had been abandoned by her Italian lover and was living with Miss Bowser at Meudon. The process by which she and her daughter left Miss Bowser's house and came to live in Gwen John's is unknown, but it may have had something to do with the war. There is, however, one letter to Rodin, possibly written at an earlier period, which suggests that the two women had known each other before. In it Gwen John told Rodin she was in Finistère[1] for the month of April modelling for a Madame Manson. As usual, when staying away, she does not appear to have been enjoying herself. She told him the sessions at the dinner-table were more boring than the modelling sessions and the books in the house were worse.

In the summer of 1915 Gwen John went to Brittany with Ruth Manson and her ten-year-old daughter Rosamund. Gwen had not been well, and Ruth Manson wanted to get Rosamund further from the fighting. This time they did not go as far west as Finistère, but stayed at Pléneuf, near St Malo, adjoining the resort of Val André.

---

[1] Her address was: Au Grand Moulin, Point l'Abbé, Finistère, Brittany.

Pléneuf was a remote Breton village in those days, where the old customs survived. Visitors from Paris took the train from Montparnasse and alighted at the market town of Lamballe in the interior. The *diligence* to the coast cost two francs and ran twice a day between lush pastures and oak copses. The village was of granite set amid green hills. Streets of austere terrace houses radiated from the market square where the church stood. Between Pléneuf and the fishermen's beach (the Grève des Vallées – not to be confused with the Val André beach with its grand hotels) was a hamlet of fishermen's cottages called La Ville Pichard.[2] Here, in Madame Cahier's house at 3 rue des Pêcheurs, Gwen John and Ruth Manson rented an attic.

The Breton coastline was similar to that of Tenby. Val André's beach met the beach of the Grève des Vallées at a headland with an island off it which could be reached at low tide. (At Tenby, North and South Sands met at Castle Rock in much the same way). On the beach at St Pabu, beyond the Grève des Vallées, great outcrops of rock vanished regularly at high tide as they did at Manorbier. Even in August the waves would fall crashing and swirling on the shore as they had at Giltar Point. But on other August nights the moonlight was reflected in the wet sand and the air was mild.

Here the childhood love of swimming that Gwen John had shared with Augustus, revived. The recluse of Paris, who would spend days shut in her room and shocked even the laziest of her friends by taking no exercise, now bathed daily. The invalid who feared even a shower of rain plunged into the breakers on days when no one else would swim. At low tide she walked for miles along the 'wonderful bay' where the low cliffs were not 'spoilt by houses'.

Even her work was now out of doors. Gwen John started to draw the children of La Ville Pichard in Monsieur Litalien's home pasture. Litalien was the farmer who lived across the road and it was his two daughters, Odette and Simone, who were Gwen John's models. She, or more probably Rosamund Manson, made friends with them when they brought the milk each morning. Odette and Simone still live at La Ville Pichard and remember *Mee Jaune*. Odette (now Madame Cardin) showed me the remains of the fields where Gwen John used to draw and from which, before the houses were built, you could see across the dunes to the breakers. The children used to pose in their school pinafores with their hair in plaits. Odette was Gwen John's favourite because she could keep still. Simone (now Madame Basset), could not. She was only eight and the tomboy of the family. She couldn't help giggling at 'Mee Joan's' extraordinary gestures as she perched on the stool behind the easel. She

---

[2] A local corruption of *Pêcheur*.

would stick her finger in the air to measure with, and say '*Ne bougez pas*'. The forty-five minute sessions seemed, to Simone, to last for ever but the gift of the only doll she ever possessed, a Paris doll with a china head, made it worth while.

Another child neighbour, Marie Hamonet (now Madame Ferrec) says she used to fall asleep posing on a hot day. Her father was a poor fisherman and she was working in a shop by the time she was ten so she was often tired. She is now a chic widow who has retired to La Ville Pichard from Paris and lives in the original Litalien farm house which she has decorated with her own paintings. Two other models, Louise Gautier and Marie Chantoiselle, also daughters of fishermen, died young.

From these three women it is possible to construct a picture of Gwen John at the middle point of her life. Odette remembers her as a thin woman, friendly but not talkative. Simone insists that she was neither shy nor lacking in humour when she was with people she knew. But she did not mix with the English in Val André. Both agree that she was definitely a lady, but not, definitely not, chic. For Odette and Simone the most interesting member of the trio was Rosamund,[3] who was always accompanied by a most delightful black poodle called Pluton and who could 'speak French, English and Italian'. (A tear still comes to Simone's eyes when she remembers the death of Pluton.) Perhaps because she was half-Italian, Rosamund was dark. She was also big, jolly and adventurous. The Litalien sisters shake with laughter when they remember going to their first cinema, the Flora[4] at Val André, with Rosamund, and Odette falling off the bike Rosamund had hired.

With Odette and Simone as her models Gwen John entered her most brilliant period as a draughtsman. The drawings of the girls were executed either with charcoal or with the point of the brush without correction. The children were portrayed with a tenderness that never lapsed into sentimentality. Their features were at times only hinted at or even omitted, but the personality was always there. Gwen John considered her drawing just as important as her painting, an opinion Quinn obstinately refused to share. 'Your paintings are more *serious* than your drawings,' he kept repeating. Gwen John merely informed Ursula Tyrwhitt that they were just as serious and that she knew how good or bad they were. She even suggested to her, at this time, that they should have a joint exhibition, each contributing about twenty drawings. She sent some of hers for Ursula to comment on, saying, 'I haven't had an

[3] Rosamund, who married Louis Lucas, was living at 2 Boulevard Henry IV, Paris IV in 1930. She cannot now be traced.
[4] The Flora still stands in the rue Kennedy.

opinion from an artist for a very long time,' and adding character-istically, 'You may not like them at all and then you would not like to have an exhibition with me.' For Gwen John to suggest an exhibition was rare indeed.

Canvases also were now being rapidly covered in the studio at the rue de l'Ouest, and equally rapidly discarded, for the theory formulated in 1910 about painting the same subject many times was being ruthlessly applied. 'I think there will come a time when we will never paint for a few hours without doing something – a picture for every sitting,' she told Ursula Tyrwhitt.

She was using two models. They were of strongly contrasting types. One was the refined young girl with the pale oval face and the long dark hair who later sat for 'The convalescent'. Gwen John made several rapid oil sketches of her head[5] and proceeded to a more finished three-quarter length portrait entitled 'Girl in a blue dress'. This is greatly admired by David Fraser Jenkins, till recently the curator of paintings at the National Museum of Wales, where it hangs. 'This tiny portrait is a perfect example of the best of Gwen John's painting. Its serenity is achieved partly by the choice of colour and the placing of the figure and partly by the extra-ordinary technique. The paint is so dry and applied so evenly that the figure and the background have exactly the same texture and the girl seems to be absorbed into the surface of the painting.'

The other model Gwen John used at this time had coarse Slavonic features and a black fringe. She may well have been the concierge at the rue de l'Ouest. Certainly Gwen John painted her over that title. She also painted her, many times, as 'Young woman in a mulberry dress' and 'Girl with a blue scarf'. The nature of the girl, that of a frightened animal, is sensitively portrayed in these pictures. Her dark eyes are wary and she backs against the wall. Her hands are curled in front of her almost like the claws of a rodent. In her portraits of both these sitters, 'The convalescent' and 'The concierge', Gwen John was now settling down to a fairly uniform treatment of her almost invariably female sitters. Cecily Lang-dale, the New York art historian, has described it well. 'In almost every picture the three-quarter length figure nearly fills the canvas; the impas-sive sitter, who is placed before the simple background, faces the viewer almost directly. Attention is focused on the head and outsize hands, the latter often rather tensely clasped. These hands, often intentionally inaccurate, are always tensely expressive.'

During the next five years Gwen John also painted 'Girl in rose', 'Woman with hands clasped', 'Seated nude', (a portrait of an oriental

[5] Private collection.

woman, semi-draped) and 'La petite modèle',[6] a portrait of a child with long straight hair and a fringe surmounted by a bow. In this portrait the sitter looks directly at the viewer, which rarely occurs except in Gwen John's child portraits. And she continued to work on 'Mère Poussepin'.

This sudden fecundity between the years 1915 and 1925 is hard to explain. For years Gwen John had painted very little, complaining 'There must be so much weakness in me doing so little work and never exhibiting.' Now that there was a war on and Rodin had all but vanished from her life she started to produce. There are two possible reasons for the change. The distraction of her love affair with Rodin was declining, and with Quinn's support she was no longer obliged to spend many hours a day modelling for other artists. To Ursula Tyrwhitt she summed it up in a few simple words: 'I had a tiring life for some years and so seem only now to begin to paint.'

There was a third incentive to work and that was her religion. Gwen John's religion was always closely associated with her art. In her studio notes, admonitions to work hard and pray hard went side by side. 'I must work every day and each day. Each day is for work. Abandon yourself to God's kindness. But you must work with fervour.' Increasingly the emphasis was on fervour. 'Don't be vague or wavering. Impose your style. Let it be simple and strong. The short strong stalks of flowers. Don't be afraid of falling into mediocrity. You would never.'

It is a strange fact that the year that marked the start of Gwen John's best decade as a painter marked the end of Augustus's. From 1915 Augustus, although still Britain's best-known artist and able to clear five thousand pounds from an exhibition, began to decline into something not much better than a portraitist of 'fat women and other horrors' (his own expression). Already he was a man with a past rather than a future. The future lay with the Vorticists and the Futurists. There was a hollowness at the heart of his pictures, picked out by a critic of his exhibition at the Alpine Club in November 1917. 'He seems to have, with the artistic gifts of a man, the mind of a child . . . Life to him is very simple, it consists of objects that arouse in him a naive childish curiosity and delight, but he had been artistically educated in a modern, very unchildish world, and has learnt very easily all the technical lessons that the world has to teach.' As the quality of Augustus's work decreased its quantity increased. His output was prodigious. He held shows almost every year at the Chenil Galleries, sometimes covered whole walls at the N.E.A.C., worked on his private commissions and regularly sent work to the Society of Twelve and to the National Portrait Society, of which, in

[6] 'Girl in rose', 'Seated nude' and 'La petite modèle' are in the collection of Thomas F. Conroy, California. 'Woman with hands crossed' is in a private collection in America.

February 1914, he had been elected the president, to the amused delight of his sister.

Rodin had now been abroad for almost a year. He had followed his long absence in England with an equally long one in Rome in 1915. He probably knew that this would be his last visit to the city that had given him Michelangelo. Here he started work on a bust of Pope Benedict XV, which would probably have been more successful if the subject had sat still and if the artist had kept quiet. As it was he told His Holiness which side the Vatican should have taken in the war, and after four sessions was dismissed.

Rodin's more habitual silence now was noted by his Roman host, Albert Besnard, director of the Villa Medici, who mourned the passing of the man who had said such beautiful things about Art and Nature. 'I think he feels that people are paying too much attention to the war and too little to him,' he said. Rodin was equally taciturn towards Gwen John who felt him moving inexorably away from her into old age. For three months she implored him for a letter, saying that she was sad and unable to work. The amorous reunion she had hoped for on his return from Cheltenham had not occurred. He had visited her room, but had not even kissed her. He had only growled about its untidiness. 'If I was loved my faults would be excused,' she wrote sadly in 1914. The little consolations of home were not enough. 'I was born to love,' she lamented. And so once more she turned to the one who would not grow old and concluded a letter to Rodin with a statement of her almost childlike faith. 'I am a suffering little creature but my room is tidy and I say my prayers. The stars in the sky and the leaves of the plants on my terrace console me in the night. They are presents from God and tell me that He loves me.'

The winter of 1915 was one of the hardest of the war. Food was rationed, prices had catapulted, but worst of all, coal was practically unobtainable. Even wealthy families felt themselves lucky to lug home a bag of coal dust with which to bank the stove. Poor families (and that surely included Gwen John) sat around in overcoats.

Gwen John had however made a new acquaintance. Maude Gonne, known in Dublin as Ireland's Joan of Arc, and in England as 'that murderess', was a colonel's daughter from Aldershot. She was six feet high, thin and awe-inspiringly beautiful. She had stood on street corners in Dublin and preached independence. W. B. Yeats loved her and wooed her unsuccessfully with poems. When war was declared she sped to France, eager to embrace a new cause; not the cause of the British of course, for she always insisted they had engineered the war to fill their tills, but the cause of the wounded.

Quinn had met Maude Gonne in Dublin, where she had conceived a great admiration not only for him but for Augustus's disastrous portrait of him, declaring that it expressed a strength and determination which made her furious that he did not belong to Ireland *entirely*. In January 1915 Quinn commended her to Gwen John, adding somewhat ungallantly that she had once been a great beauty (Maude Gonne was now fifty). It was not till April that Gwen John summoned the courage to make the visit to the flat in Passy where Maude was staying. The two women declared themselves delighted with each other. Gwen John said that Maude Gonne was 'very beautiful' and Maude Gonne said that Gwen John had 'a quiet sincere way of looking at things that I like very much'. For a moment Quinn was tempted to join them and at the same time kidnap 'Mère Poussepin' (which he was now convinced was an altarpiece) from 'those dear nuns',[7] but wiser counsels prevailed in view of the unhealthy state of France.

It was from Maude Gonne that Gwen John received her most vivid impressions of the 'bloody, wasteful mess' of war, impressions that she could hardly bear. Maude had been working at an eleven-hundred-bed Red Cross hospital in the Pas de Calais. She spoke of 'patching up the poor mangled creatures in order that they may be sent back to the slaughter' and declared that 'the young art and intellect of France is being killed in the trenches'. Gwen John was always anxious for accurate information about the war. The French public was still being deluded about the true numbers of the dead and the trains bringing the wounded to Paris arrived at night.

She visited Maude Gonne again in July and saw her young son, Sean, briefly when he came in from doing lessons in another room. He was in Paris with his older sister Iseult. Maude was educating them by her own method to have 'a great sense of justice'. The girl was so beautiful that in Dublin old women were said to kneel in the street as she passed. Gwen John makes no mention of Iseult, but told Quinn that some of the mother's drawings were good and she would visit her again when she was less worried about 'Mère Poussepin'.

In January 1916 Rodin had a stroke and Gwen John was plunged into a state of profound grief and dread from which Ruth Manson could do little to rescue her. For several weeks he lay motionless, but gradually he rallied and started to sit in an old upholstered chair, the only one at the Villa des Brillants. Judith Cladel, his secretary, noticed that his eyes were no longer screwed up with the effort to see as they had been all his life. His mind was gone. Wartime shortages combined with family problems made life almost unbearable at his home. The house, on its exposed hill, was bitterly cold. Even when fuel could be found for the antiquated

---

[7] Quinn had a sister who was a nun, and once remarked that they did not always keep their promises.

heating system, the boiler in the basement could make little use of it. The drains did not work and the servants had been called up. Rodin's son, Auguste Beuret, who had moved into a house in the grounds, was an additional hindrance. He had married the alcoholic widow of a rag picker who made appalling scenes, complaining nightly that she had to sleep with a dog on top of her because the cottage was so damp.

In search of peace Rodin, frail though he was, began once more to make his daily journey to the Hôtel Biron. Here confusion reigned, for Judith Cladel had not yet wrested the building from the City of Paris and it was virtually unguarded. A steady stream of pictures and small bronzes were said to be leaving the building, and ex-mistresses jostled each other for the privilege of supporting the beshawled old man round the garden and persuading him to make wills in their favour. Similar scenes were being enacted even under Rose's nose at Meudon, where a sculptress threw her rival's bust of Rodin out of his bedroom window while he lay helpless. Meanwhile the faithful Mademoiselle Cladel attempted to catalogue three thousand drawings in the studio there. On 15 May 1916 Gwen John wrote her last preserved letter to Rodin.[8] It was addressed as usual to the Hôtel Biron but was not delivered by hand. It told him that she was quelling her passionate desire for him by copying photographs of six French war leaders for 'the American'.

Regrettably, this occupation did indeed keep Gwen John occupied during part of 1916, but Quinn was not responsible for it. Gwen John was hard up. She told Quinn that she could not even afford the six francs necessary for a *certificat d'artiste* to accompany a picture she had despatched to him, let alone the fifteen francs necessary for works valued over five hundred francs. Finally the curé, horrified by Gwen John's poverty, had suggested that patriotic citizens might like to possess the likenesses of the great wartime leaders of France.

A stranger subject for Gwen John's pencil could hardly be imagined, since she seldom drew men. Yet with professional determination she set about producing portraits in charcoal and ink wash of Generals Pétain, Mangin, Gouraud and Serrail, Admiral Boué and Venizelos, making five copies of each. The results were the works of Gwen John which an admirer would surely least like to own. Certainly Quinn found them hard to sell. He ended by giving them to his friends for Christmas. Gwen John herself confessed to Ursula Tyrwhitt, 'one ought not to do such stuff. Of course one could, with much talent, make a work of art from a photo but after doing one, the others are too mechanical and a waste of time.' To Quinn she added, 'In a day or two I shall begin to paint what I like.'

---

[8] An envelope remains of a letter posted on 18 August, but the letter is lost.

Meanwhile an unnamed interior, and 'La petite modèle', accompanied by nine gouaches, had gone to Pottier's shop in Paris (Quinn employed Charles Pottier as an agent for shipping his art purchases to the United States) and thence on board ship. The pictures were accompanied as usual by a note to say that if Quinn did not like them Gwen John would 'be pleased to do another in their place'. There was an agonising pause during which she became convinced that they had gone to the bottom of the Atlantic. Then Quinn wrote to say that he liked them and would pay seventeen pounds for the interior, thirty pounds for 'La petite modèle', and two pounds each for the gouaches. He also suggested it was time she invited Maude Gonne to visit her. By the time Gwen John sent the invitation Maude Gonne was in Normandy growing potatoes for the troops.

Meanwhile Gwen John continued to share the attics of the house in the rue Terre Neuve with Ruth Manson, Rosamund and the dog Pluton. One result of this cohabitation was that ten-year-old girls began to appear in Gwen John's Meudon drawings as well as in her Pléneuf ones. These were Rosamund's middle-class school friends, very different from the peasants of Brittany. There were the round-faced Villecoque sisters who sat for a rare double portrait, 'Two little girls with bobbed hair',[9] and there was the lanky Elisabeth de Willman Grabowska, the child of a Polish woman professor of anthropology living at Meudon. Gwen was attracted by her long hair and her thoughtful deepset eyes. She drew her many times in charcoal and wash, often with a doll laid awkwardly across her knees.[10] No doubt 'La petite modèle' was a friend of Rosamund's too. In the portrait she was shown three-quarter length. She is almost the only child Gwen John portrayed in oils. She painted her twice, the second time omitting the smile, the bow on top of her head and the background.[11]

For the summer holidays Gwen John and Ruth Manson once more rented the attic at 3 rue des Pêcheurs. Rosamund renewed her friendship with Odette and Simone. But this year Gwen John and Ruth Manson did not limit themselves to the north coast of Brittany, but also went to South Finistère, the part of Brittany they had first visited together. In September they spent several weeks with a friend, probably a painter called Mlle Stephan, who lived in the quayside rue de la Gale at Loctudy. Loctudy was a small fishing port at the mouth of the Quimper estuary overlooking a group of islands. It was almost too small to rate as a resort in those days but boasted and still boasts the finest Romanesque church in Brittany.

[9] The Carter Burden Collection, New York.
[10] 'Figure study', the Tate.
[11] Collection of Mrs Robert Henriques.

The winter of 1917 was the worst of the war. In January coal was rationed. To the misery of empty grates was added the misery of long and often fruitless queues for a *carte de charbon*. Gwen John's annual *grippe* returned leaving her 'deathly tired'. She found she coughed every time she went to Paris and so she almost ceased to visit the rue de l'Ouest during the winter months. But with the spring her spirits as usual revived and she wrote to Ursula Tyrwhitt assuring her that letters were getting through. She told Ursula that after the arrival of her latest clothes parcel she felt like a butterfly coming out of a chrysalis. 'The grey silk blouse and the coat and skirt gave me new energy and courage. I'd be letting myself go otherwise. What a wonderful influence on the mind new clothes have. I have had to buy only a hat this spring. Black. And I have put a green ribbon I had round it. Spending so little on clothes lets me have some money in hand so I am spared anxiety about paying for food.'

She also gave her opinion of the Royal Academy. 'I should have forgotten what sort of a thing it was but that I read a long criticism of the R.A. and all that strange plastering of canvases that I used to see passed in procession before my mind. It seems nothing has changed in the R.A. All other human institutions have some movement. The R.A. is superior and alone.' She received with hilarity Ursula Tyrwhitt's news that McEvoy had had no less than ten pictures in the Royal Portrait Society's spring exhibition. Since his marriage to Mary Edwards, McEvoy had deteriorated from a serious painter into a fashionable portraitist, delineating duchesses in showers of pastel sparks, or materialising, ghostlike, out of murky backgrounds. Augustus described him as being in a state of 'exultation bordering on hysteria' as a result of so much well-born patronage, and certainly he was over-excited about the amount of money he was making.

Letters from Quinn were also getting through, although opened by the censor. In his efficient way he sent back copies of those of her letters which reached New York. She congratulated Quinn's fellow countrymen on taking up arms against the Germans and said that their arrival had done much to persuade people that the war might yet end one day. She added, 'It is true I speak to very few people, so I know very little. How dreadful it is the destruction of the castles and the beautiful villas and the woods!' Again she made excuses for not seeing Maude Gonne, who, very much against her will, was still in France. She had packed up her flat in Passy with a view to returning to Dublin only to discover that the British authorities insisted she must either go to London or stay where she was. She was now inhabiting a small attic which she had originally rented for storage. Socially indefatigable, she still wanted Gwen John to come and meet some people. Gwen John did not go. 'I don't like meeting people,' she told Quinn.

Instead she departed for her last joint holiday with Ruth Manson at the
Ville Pichard. When she returned to Meudon, the news of Rodin was
very bad. Sensing that his end was near, he had finally married Rose
Beuret so that she would be able to inherit. As the wedding ceremony
took place, Big Bertha, the German long range gun, boomed to such
effect that Rose almost died of a heart attack before she could become a
wife. Added to that there followed two gigantic explosions as the muni-
tions factory at Puteaux blew up. As Rodin slipped the ring on Rose's
finger the heating system of the villa exploded.

Rose died of bronchitis a month later, in an icy room. Rodin stayed on
almost alone, watching his statues being removed by lorry to the Hôtel
Biron. The state had finally accepted the gift of his life work. He longed
to draw but was not allowed pencil and paper for fear he should make a
new will. His hands groped for imaginary clay, but that too, for unknown reasons, was withheld. His visits to Le Biron were limited to one
a fortnight, and then under escort.

On 12 November he developed a high fever and lay inert with the
breath whistling in his throat. He became unconscious and his breathing
grew deep and heavy, interrupted by an occasional gasp which seemed to
fill the house. The breathing stopped at four a.m. on 17 November 1917.
The shock must have been very terrible to Gwen John. For fifteen years
she had regarded herself as Rodin's 'true wife'. She had met him when
she was twenty-seven and now she was forty-one. He had been a lover,
he had been a father, he had been the great artist who had encouraged her.
Although she had seen little enough of him in recent years, the letters had
never ceased and there was always the boundary of the villa to haunt with
the knowledge that he was inside.

Now the old man at the villa lay as white and still as one of his statues,
his white beard spread over his white working smock. 'I don't know
what I am going to do,' she wrote to Ursula Tyrwhitt. Her writing was
at its worst, almost illegible. She thought she was going mad. 'One must
be unwelcome when one isn't normal,' she wrote. She was ill for many
months during that terrible winter and remarked, 'When one gets tired
one loses something which one never gets back.'

But she brought herself to execute a copy of a photograph of Pope
Benedict XV at this time, using the method she had used for the French
generals. The cover of the New York Times Mid-Week Pictorial for 23
August 1917, squared in ink, is still preserved at the museum at Cardiff.
So is the squared ink drawing she made from it and the final wash
drawing of the bespectacled pontiff with his hat and cloak and jewelled
cross. It is not easy to discover Gwen John's motives for executing this
chore. She had already discovered that copies of photographs were
tedious to make, and she had no particular admiration for members of the

ecclesiastical hierarchy. When Pius XI died some years later she shocked her neighbour at Meudon by her lack of concern. 'What do you expect me to do?' she said, and burst out laughing. 'I am a million times more concerned about old Mme M. dying even though she was disagreeable. I knew her. I passed her door every day. But the Pope! There'll be another, so what?' It is possible that Gwen John made the drawing for the curé to hang in his study. It was he who had suggested the drawings of the French generals after all.

Gwen John was still in the depths of grief in mid-December when Augustus arrived in fancy dress driving a motor-car. He was wearing the uniform of a Canadian major, an immaculate greatcoat and leather gloves. He was in France as a war artist under the auspices of Beaverbrook and had made an impressive figure patrolling the Vimy front with his batman, heedless of the gunfire (which he was fortunately too deaf to hear). Many of the soldiers took him for King George V, who was the only other officer allowed to wear a beard.

Brother and sister described the meeting differently. Augustus claimed that he called three times during the day without success. Finally he found Gwen, looking alarmingly ill and obviously not eating. In Paris at that time it was hard enough to eat properly if one put one's mind to it, almost impossible if one didn't. Augustus once more suggested Alderney Manor but this was turned down. Gwen John did however agree to return to Brittany where food had been plentiful all through the war, and where Augustus hoped the rest and the change of air would do her good. (Ursula Tyrwhitt had also been anxious that Gwen should go to Brittany at this difficult time.) 'Perhaps one might send her some photographs,' Augustus wrote to Dorelia. 'And perhaps a Jaeger blanket as she admits the cold keeps her awake at night. The Lord only knows how she passes her days.'

Gwen gave a more cheerful account of the meeting. Rather surprisingly, she had enjoyed Augustus's company. He had given her dinner at the Café de Versailles in Montparnasse (paid for out of a fiver he borrowed from her) and it had been 'nice hearing about his life and things'. The 'things' were presumably Dorelia and the children. Two little girls, Poppet and Vivien, had recently joined the row of boys. Dorelia now lived exclusively in the country. Augustus sometimes joined her there. Brother and sister also talked about art, his art. He showed her the current issue of the magazine *Colour* which contained two colour reproductions of his portraits. She admired the quality of the reproduction rather than of the pictures, writing to Ursula Tyrwhitt, 'They want something which perhaps will come soon.' But she added that they stood out by comparison with everything else reproduced in the magazine which was dreadful. 'I don't want to see any English pictures again except the work of two or three artists,' she declared. They also discussed John Quinn, and Gwen told Augustus that he had recently been operated on for cancer. Augustus complained that the American took no more interest in his work. Quinn had recently remarked in a letter to Conrad that John was 'entirely facile. There is no harshness, no acid, no pain in his work. Fine draughtsmanship is not enough.' From this time the relationship between John Quinn and Augustus declined from bad to very bad. The reduction of the price of Augustus's portrait of Arthur Symons from £500 to £400 and the deduction of £283 and 16 shillings from that amount to cover an advance already paid were merely the opening shots in a war that was to produce many casualties.

As Augustus John's standing with Quinn decreased Gwen John's improved. He wrote to Arthur Symons declaring his preference for the sister's work, and boasting that he now owned four important oils by her and twenty drawings.

Gwen John discovered that her meeting with Augustus had provided a distraction which was surprisingly welcome. But her thoughts were still with what lay in a box under the statue of 'The Thinker' at the Villa des Brillants. Augustus, returning to the luxurious rooms supplied for him at the Palais d'Orsay, had not much more cause to be happy. Melancholy was becoming habitual with him. Beaverbrook's lush entertainments only increased his sadness. There was a dinner party in a suite at the Hôtel Bristol one night. Half way through the evening a bevy of young women arrived in evening clothes and placed themselves in the empty chairs between the guests. These girls, the pick of the local emporium, came strongly recommended for their dexterity: one or two of them were even said to be able to 'bring the dead to life'. The gentlemen, however, were sadly embarrassed by their presence. Beaverbrook disappeared as soon as they arrived, followed by William Orpen. The remaining diners drank a great deal of champagne and Augustus managed to muster enough 'compulsory conviviality' to raise his girl to the level of the table and effect 'a successful *retroussage*', in spite of her struggles.[12] At the end of March he was hurried back to England 'in a state of utter mental confusion', having knocked out a Captain Wright who, he claimed, had insulted him.

Augustus may have had other reasons for leaving Paris in a hurry. At the beginning of 1918 the Germans launched their final offensive in an attempt to capture Paris before the arrival of the Americans. Paris was now close to the front line and on 9 March 1918 Gwen John told Ursula Tyrwhitt of bombardment both from the air and from Big Bertha. 'Balls of fire' were falling from aeroplanes all round her and when she went to

[12] *Finishing Touches*, Augustus John. The chapter 'Lord Beaverbrook Entertains' was omitted from the first edition for fear of libel.

the Edgar Quinet market she heard them falling in the Avenue du Maine, the rue de Rennes and at the Gare Montparnasse. By May the dreadful 'Gottas with torpillos' were going over. It was at this time that she finally abandoned the room in the rue de l'Ouest. One at a time, she moved her possessions to Meudon. A thin woman in a hat clutching a complete Shakespeare in French, a statuette of The Thinker, a potted fern or a kitchen devil became a familiar sight on the Meudon train that year.

At 29 rue Terre Neuve a common danger brought the *locataires* together in the cellar at night. The air raid warning was three cannon shots from Paris; the all clear was a siren and church bells. During the raid the worst part was the noise made by the anti-aircraft gun placed at Meudon and trained on enemy aircraft returning over Versailles. But for Gwen John, a greater penance was putting up with the company of the other people in the cellar. 'It is so tiring to listen to uneducated talk and nonsense,' she said to Ursula Tyrwhitt. She preferred to get out of bed as soon as she heard the three guns and run down several streets to the house of 'a man and wife'[13] she knew who were 'rather old and good'. The journey was frightening. The leafy rue des Clos Moreaux seemed to hide sinister *rôdeurs* in the shadow of its bushes. In a dream she fancied that she was chased by 'the Boches' and tried to hide in the hedge but it was never thick enough. If there was a second alert she ignored it, unless the noise became intolerable.

Ruth Manson's nerves were also in shreds. She could not sleep through the raids and she was worried about Rosamund. In the end she moved to the country. Gwen John conceded that it was much worse with a child. The friends presumably met again at Pléneuf that summer – certainly Gwen John went there. She wrote Ursula Tyrwhitt the only letter she ever wrote to her from Pléneuf. When she returned to Paris she was able to report three pieces of good news to Quinn. The armistice was about to be signed, a lost trunk containing 'thousands' of her drawings from Pléneuf had turned up, and she had discovered a château for herself at Pléneuf.

To Gwen John, as to so many people, the news of an armistice came so suddenly that she at first refused to believe it and considered that Germany was merely playing for time. She did not know that Germany had been brought to her knees by the allied offensive under Marshal Foch. She believed it when she saw the wild joy in Paris on 11 November and told Quinn that some of the scenes in the streets were touching. He rewarded her with a diatribe against the filthy Germans. He felt more contempt for them than for the filthy Jews; they were loathsome in their shamelessness, vile in their brutality and so on.

[13] Probably M. et Mme Gervais.

One of the minor blessings of peace was that Maude Gonne got herself arrested and it was no longer necessary to ask her to tea. 'Perhaps she didn't mind being arrested,' Gwen John wrote to Quinn. To Ursula Tyrwhitt she added, 'Isn't she silly?'

The saga of the trunk full of drawings at the Gare Montparnasse was a more serious one, because the summer of 1918 in Brittany had been productive. Gwen John was becoming increasingly concerned that her drawings should be hung in groups. On their own, she said, the details could be 'seen too much'. The drawings were becoming so important to her that she was even considering a one-man show of them, first in New York and then in London. She sent some to Quinn and he declared them 'very very charming', and said that the artist Walt Kuhn also said they were very charming and better than the work of Augustus, which 'may not please you'.

But it was the Manoir de Vauxclair that had her heart. Deep in the country, on the other side of Pléneuf from the Ville Pichard, stood a sixteenth-century house in a great neglected garden, formerly the property of Count Danycan de l'Espine, an impoverished landowner. Tall iron gates, painted grey, gave access from the leafy lane in front. A stone-built farmyard flanked the property on one side. A meadow edged with trees protected the other side. 'It is lovely with a stream in it and heaps of flowers. They have hay in it', Gwen wrote.

When she found the house it was empty and its charm was 'a little sad'. She applied to the farm people for a key and found herself, breathless with excitement, wandering through a series of rooms with moulded ceilings and elaborate porcelain stoves. The salon was particularly splendid. Sunlight, strained through the leaves and creepers round the tall windows, produced a green light. 'It is not fine or grand,' she told Ursula Tyrwhitt. 'It has a rather humble beauty.' Most of all she was enchanted by the silence. She discovered that for a few francs she could rent several of the 'beautiful rooms'. 'I think I shall be alone there,' she told Ursula Tyrwhitt. 'I could work.'

Quinn

1919–24

In January 1919 the gossips of Pléneuf reported that an English woman usually dressed in dark clothes was living alone in the Manoir de Vauxclair, accompanied by a large number of cats. Whether she brought the cats with her, or whether they were generated by the presence of a cat-lover is unknown. The cats roamed the empty rooms by day and gathered at night around the stove in the salon which their mistress kept stoked with fallen boughs. The garden they had to share with the chickens from the farm, for there was no wall between the garden and the farmyard.

Mee Jaune soon became a familiar figure to the friendly Hôtelier family who lived at the farm. Her favourite was their twenty-year-old daughter.[1] Every morning, all through the winter, Gwen John walked down to the beach and dived into the crashing breakers of the Grève des Vallées. She was fascinated by the steady succession of those waves and claimed that after nine little ones there always came a big one. In a note found among her papers she declared that her heart also was a sea which had sad little waves, but every ninth one was great and happy.

Bad news came in the spring, just as Vauxclair started to blossom after so many 'dark months'. The place had been sold to a group of cattle merchants who planned to resell it when the railway increased the value of the land. Now the legalised squat must end. But it didn't end. At first Gwen John was to leave in April, then by the end of May. In the end she spent the summer of 1919 at the château, refusing to return to Paris even to sign the 'affidavit' necessary for the export of some drawings to the United States. She pointed out to Quinn that the train journey to Paris would take a day and a night.

There was another reason for avoiding Paris. Augustus was there, this

---

[1] Mlle Hôtelier, now Mme Pottier, is still alive but very old.

time covering the Peace Conference, but still in the uniform of a Canadian major. He was staying in even greater luxury this time, at the Chilean Legation across the river from the conference hall. His host, the opium-eating Gandarrillas, gave fantastic parties under glittering chandeliers. Paris that year was the hub of the social world and Augustus, trumpeting through his beard, was the hub of Paris.

But beneath it all the tide of melancholy rose. His friends in Paris were all gone. Jean Moréas was dead, Maurice Cremnitz was unfriendly and, worse still, Paul Fort had become respectable. Augustus, as so often, turned to a woman for solace, the Duchess of Gramont, whose portrait he was painting. But he only grew more 'helpless and desolate'. Finally, 'nearly dead with depression', he retired to Deauville and Lloyd George.

In November Gwen John received a letter which gave her the courage to face another grim winter. It was from Arthur Symons. Symons was a poet and art critic of the nineties who is little remembered today, but in his own day he had known everybody. His life had been broken in half by an attack of madness in 1908. He came out of an asylum at Crowborough quite changed, no longer eager for 'impreshuns and sensashuns', but frail and retiring. It was probably through Augustus that he saw the work of Gwen John. It could, however, have been through his wife, who was the sister of Isabelle Bowser.

Rhoda Symons was an ambitious woman who considered herself an actress. She made use of her husband's contacts to get parts from the great actor managers, persuading them she needed money to support him. In fact Arthur was usually left alone in the country, writing begging letters for money to pay for his wife's London flat and her car.

In the autumn of 1919 Symons wrote to Gwen John[2] to praise her drawings, and sent her a book of poetry and a book of prose. 'They have been my consolation this dreadful winter,' she told Quinn. Folded into the poetry book was a poem in manuscript entitled *Faces*.

> The pathos of a face behind the glass
> When April brightens in the grass,
> The pathos of a face that like the day,
> Fades to an evening chill and grey,
> Yet has not known the universal boon
> Of springtime at the warmth of noon.

In return she sent Symons three drawings. These he promptly attempted to sell to Quinn, recommending them as vastly superior to the

[2] The letters of Arthur and Rhoda Symons to Gwen John, 1919–21, are in a private collection.

work of Augustus, being 'original and so deeply felt and so emotional'. Quinn wrote back that he had supported the lady for eight years and owned most of her modest output. He declined the offer of the drawings and then, remembering how indiscreet writers could be, wrote a second letter begging Symons never to tell Augustus that he was supporting Gwen John.

Quinn's letters during this winter of 1919–20 showed a growing interest in Vauxclair. So glowing were Gwen John's accounts of the manoir that both Augustus and Quinn considered buying it. The price, however, had doubled since the speculators bought it, and at fifty thousand francs Augustus dropped out of the running. Quinn was more persistent. He had hankered after a large place where he could hang his pictures for some years, and had once even bought a disastrous mansion which he dubbed 'Purchase Street' (because it cost him so much) outside New York. Now, with the example of Mrs Gardener's Boston *palazzo* before him, he pictured himself as the genial host of a residence near Paris, filled with books and pictures, a resort for artists, bibliophiles and connoisseurs. He proposed to install Arthur and Rhoda Symons as concierges.

On 14 February he sent Gwen John a questionnaire. How many rooms were there in the château? Were they comfortable? Did it have any modern fittings in the way of hardwood floors or bathrooms? How was it heated? Was there a cellar under it? How far was it from any town? What neighbours were there? Of what sort was the surrounding country? How much land was there around the place? Was it used for grazing or farming? What sort was the road? And where did the people get their farm produce from? Their butter, eggs, milk, groceries, vegetables, chicken, coffee and sugar?

Gwen John did her best to answer. She enumerated the four bedrooms, the round room in the tower, the attics and the cellars. She said the walk to Pléneuf was rough, passing several hovels and taking about eight minutes. She said Val André was half an hour away on foot and 'not interesting' being 'a fashionable seaside place of hotels and tennis courts'. The letter was the longest Gwen John ever wrote anybody but still Quinn was not satisfied. He sent a 'Kodak' on the grounds that 'snapshotting in the country is rather amusing'. It did not arrive. Then two Kodaks arrived. Gwen John does not appear to have taken any pictures of the manor with either.

Surprisingly enough she did not approve of Quinn's plan to install Arthur and Rhoda Symons as caretakers, although she herself had told Quinn that the place was only suitable for a painter or a poet. 'I don't think it is practical. I have heard it is his great pleasure to spend his time with literary and artistic friends in London. He would be too lonely at

Vauxclair, and his wife would not stay there three days, no, not one. I don't know her but my friend was her sister and so I know what she is like.'

In the summer she met Arthur and Rhoda Symons. They were returning to Paris for the first time after some years. Arthur wanted to relive Baudelaire's life and he dined night after night in the sad hotels where the poet had eaten. Gwen John liked Arthur Symons. Perhaps it was because of his cats. He had a great many. Setebos, Jezebel, Caliban, Beelzebub, Zambo, Tarno, John and Sally, to name only a few. Furthermore both he and she were from the coast of Pembrokeshire. 'I have loved the sea,' Symons once wrote. 'The voice of the wind, the beauty of the night.'

There was nothing in Symons's changed appearance to arouse physical passion. According to Frank Harris, 'the sparse grey hair, the high bony forehead, the sharp ridge of the Roman nose, the fleshless cheeks, the triangular wedge of the face shocks one . . . and the dreadful clawlike fingers of the outstretched hand. A terrible face, ravaged like a battlefield; the eyes like ink pools, the lid hanging across the left eyeball like a broken curtain.' Yet when he spoke all this could be forgotten. 'In descriptive power I have never heard his equal,' wrote Gerald Cumberland. 'He paints picture after picture before your eyes; if he pauses it is only to gather together energy for another geyser-like blossoming of words. As he speaks his eyes glow like jewels in the ivory of his face.'

It is probable that it was while the Symons were visiting Gwen John that they saw her newly painted 'The convalescent' on the easel and bought it. It was the best picture she ever painted in the opinion of Sir Kenneth Clark. A frail girl sits reading in the familiar wicker chair. The familiar brown teapot is on the table beside her. The figure could have been Gwen John herself recovering from her annual *grippe*. Rhoda Symons bequeathed it to the Tate in 1937.

Augustus was also in France, for the third summer in succession, but at last out of uniform. He had decided to have two of his sons, Edwin and Romilly, educated at a school near Rouen. The education of the John boys had never been conventional. Soon after Augustus moved into Alderney Manor he had hired as tutor John Hope Johnstone, a young man with a liking for esoteric knowledge but no knowledge of education. He taught the boys only the rules of Latin gender and part of the book of Job. When Augustus tried to get rid of him by marrying him off to one of his models he fled to Gerald Brennan in Spain.

The first school the John boys attended, and in some cases the only school, was Dane Court, a preparatory school of eleven pupils run by Mr Pooley, who played the flute, and Mrs Pooley, who was Danish and arty. On the first morning three of the John boys arrived in a green governess cart driven by Dorelia. 'Out stepped a lady in a cloak with a large hat and hair cut short. After her three boys tumbled out, their hair cut likewise and they wore coloured tunics. For a moment we thought they were girls. It was soon fixed that the three boys aged eight, nine and ten should come as day boys. When Mrs John was going away she turned at the door and said, "I think there are two more at home, who might as well come."' Those two were Edwin and Romilly who always stuck together although Edwin was Ida's child and Romilly Dorelia's, for they were practically of the same age.

Edwin and Romilly did well at Dane Court until they were above the age limit. Afterwards they hung around at home, as Augustus's children so often did, while he decided what to do with them next. Then he had the inspiration about the Collège de Normandie. It was not a happy one. No one at the school seemed to be expecting the boys except the master in whose house they lived and as he spoke English they learned no French. The classrooms of the school were in buildings scattered over a large park. When they passed a group of boys these would shout '*Oh! Les Jaunes!*' Soon Romilly begged to be sent home. Edwin, though he was fearfully bullied and rolled under the desks, elected to stay, and came, like his aunt, to regard France as a second home.

In August Gwen John returned to Vauxclair's 'atmosphere of beauty and poetry'. Ruth Manson and Madame de Wilman Grabowska joined her with their daughters Rosamund and Elizabeth, but not at the château. They rented a cottage belonging to Monsieur Lesage, a carriage painter from Paris. The Lesages had become friends, perhaps because their house was on the lane leading to Pléneuf, perhaps because they had a daughter of fifteen, Lucienne, who shared secrets with Rosamund and modelled for Gwen John. Lucienne, who is now a stout blond lady married to Monsieur Lejeune, remembers the three women well. The conversation of Madame Manson and Madame Wilma (as she calls her) was very 'educated'.

It was in the Lesage garden that Gwen John did one of her few landscape paintings of Brittany. It shows Ruth and Wilma's cottage standing deep in midsummer foliage, the walls white and shutters blue. Smoke is represented by white paint practically squeezed from the tube on to the canvas. The picture was a gift to Lucienne. It is proudly hung amid her husband's nautical curios (he was a bosun on board the four-masted sailing ships plying to Chile).

John Quinn would no doubt have been extremely angry if he had known that a Gwen John painting had been given to a carriage painter's daughter. He was anyway bothered by the state of his bank balance. Arthur Symons (with his recklessly extravagant wife) was demanding money and so was James Joyce, and Lady Gregory wanted a barrel of apples because the crop had failed at Coole Park. When his eye fell on

Gwen John's account it looked bare. Debit: eight years of financial support. Credit: four paintings.[3] During the war, drawings only. He already suspected she was painting for someone else. 'I should feel *very much hurt* if you part with any oils to anyone else till you send me two or three more,' he wrote in unusually stern tones. Three months later, resolving to use the carrot where the stick had failed, he proposed a new patronage arrangement whereby he would pay her 500 dollars a year in exchange for two paintings, with any additional paintings to be paid for separately. He sent her 3,500 francs immediately as his first half-yearly payment. A month later, on 16 September, he raised his figure to 750 dollars a year and promised to maintain it for at least three years. Translated into francs, the sum seemed astronomical to Gwen John. 'It takes my breath away,' she wrote. And she did not think Quinn should tie himself to her for three years. 'You may not want my work after this year. It may have changed.' She added hastily, 'I know what girl I shall engage for a model tomorrow.'

Meanwhile Quinn insisted that Gwen John should make the acquaintance of his new mistress, a young woman called Mrs Foster, who would arrive in Europe at the beginning of July. Gwen John as usual cringed. 'I am tortured by shyness with strangers,' she pleaded. But Quinn was relentless. Mrs Foster was 'earnest and sincere'. She was a school teacher from the Adirondacks, she had published two books of poems and she was on the staff of *The Review of Reviews* (which Quinn patronised). Gwen John admitted that she felt excited about meeting a poetess. 'I have never met a poetess nor any woman writer,' she wrote.

In the event Gwen John liked Mrs Foster, whose name was Jeanne (although she spoke no French). She was a bronze-haired beauty in her mid-thirties, living with an invalid husband in New York. Quinn had met her when she was modelling for John Yeats (the father of the poet). She had avoided him for many years because of his reputation with ladies but relented when he begged her to nurse him. Augustus made a heavy pass at her when he visited the United States.

In the next three or four years Gwen John was to see more people and pictures than she had done for many years, more indeed than she was to see again. Mrs Foster insisted that she accompany her to galleries. Gwen John admitted that she was stimulated by these visits and told Quinn, 'I am going to see other work more now and be less shy if possible. I like being alone. But I don't pretend to know how to live, and sometimes I think everything I do is wrong.' She took Mrs Foster several times to see her old friend the Mother Superior and to see 'the nun's picture', and Mrs Foster wrote to Quinn about it. He instructed her to make an offer for

[3] 'Girl reading', 1910; 'Woman with hands clasped'; 'Petite modèle'; 'Interior'.

what he always misnamed 'The Mother Superior' and, if necessary, for the altarpiece in which he was convinced it was enshrined.

Thanks to Quinn and Mrs Foster, Gwen John was becoming known to a wider circle of people. Foreign artists and above all writers were flocking to Paris after the war and selected ones were encouraged by Quinn to visit the house in the rue Terre Neuve. He told Lady Gregory of the timid artist who was 'determined to live her own life in her own way . . . certainly the best woman artist who is painting in France today.' Ezra Pound, who fancied himself as an art scout, was told 'confidentially, very confidentially, Augustus has a sister who is an artist of genius, who lives in Paris. She is very shy, almost impossible to help, and lives in the greatest poverty. I know she is a recluse, reads mystical writings and is very shy, scarcely goes out and lives on almost nothing, sometimes on bread and water and even gives what money she has away.'

Through Ezra Pound Gwen John met Ford Madox Ford. His wife painted badly but was convinced she was a Holbein. Gwen John complained that she had wasted four of her afternoons. By way of compensation Ford Madox Ford reproduced several of Gwen John's paintings in the July 1924 issue of *The Transatlantic Review*.

In July Gwen John accepted an invitation to visit Arthur and Rhoda Symons in Kent, perhaps because she had just heard that Quinn was about to descend on Europe. Arthur and Rhoda had lived at Island Cottage, Wittersham since his breakdown. Wittersham was on the marshes near Rye, and like Rye stood on an island surrounded by sheep. Symons led a solitary life on the Isle of Oxney.

The cottage was enchanting and still is.[4] It had long sloping eaves which gave it the air of an inverted boat standing in a large garden. In the sitting-room books and beams fought for space with pictures. Yet this paradise was inhabited by a man who was far from happy, a remnant of the nineties who had forgotten to die, constantly haunted by fearful visions of hell fire. Mrs Druce, who was a maid in the house, still remembers Mrs Symons's alarm when Mr Symons vanished from beside the garden pond. It was instantly assumed that he was at the bottom of it. Arthur Symons was a 'solitary soul in the midst of the world' and did not mix with the village people. He never walked through the village, but would only go across the fields behind the church to visit Sir Lawrence Alma-Tadema. Conrad, Ellen Terry and Henry James also lived not far away. The people in the village regarded Symons as an eccentric, if not mad, because he wore an Inverness cape and a wide-brimmed hat and had gipsies and hop-pickers to tea. Lady Violet Markham declared she

[4] The present owners of the cottage are Admiral and Mrs Sinclair, friends of Admiral Sir Caspar John. See also *Wanderings* by Arthur Symons, 1914.

never knew what he would do (or say) next and the rector knew only too well. Arthur Symons stuck out his tongue at him every time they passed.

Gwen John stayed with Arthur and Rhoda for three weeks and did the series of charcoal pencil drawings of Arthur Symons which were found in her studio after her death. She mostly drew him in profile with his fine-boned hand almost obscuring his face.[5] It is hard to tell whether the visit was a success. Gwen John's correspondence with Symons appears to have ceased about this time and there is no mention of them meeting on his two subsequent visits to Paris in 1924 and 1925, so perhaps it was not. She only described the visit briefly in a letter to Quinn which was mostly taken up with apologising for his wasted journey to Meudon and promising him four more paintings. ('One I think you will like.') She added that Quinn was invited to Island Cottage, but by now Quinn had joined the pack of Rhoda's detractors. 'I hope Mme Rhoda hasn't built a studio on the place,' he wrote to Gwen John, 'the walls panelled with mirrors before which she can admire herself if no one else will.' Quinn hoped in vain. Island Cottage is now dwarfed by a barn transplanted from the marshes at Rhoda's command. Mrs Druce, living on the other side of the road, could hear Rhoda's operatic arias exuding from it.

One thing at Island Cottage did disappoint Gwen John and that was the way her four drawings had been hung. 'My drawings are much better hung in sets,' she told Ursula Tyrwhitt. 'When I saw them hung separately at Symons' I was disappointed.' She did not mention 'The convalescent'.

Gwen John returned to Paris to find she was two days too early. Quinn and Mrs Foster still had a weekend left at the Hôtel d'Iéna. On the Saturday Quinn, accompanied by another man, walked up the five flights of stairs to the attics of 29 rue Terre Neuve to meet 'the greatest woman artist in France or England' for the first time. He declared himself to be delighted with her. Gwen John was also impressed with Quinn. At fifty-one he was a good-looking man, with his regular features, his tall body clothed in gentlemanly tweeds and worsteds. But he never had the confidence of a gentleman, although his whole life had been spent in pursuit of it. Gwen John found him gentler than she had expected. But she also found him acquisitive and domineering. The drawings of the children at Pléneuf, which she declared he had never understood, he now fell upon. She complained that when she was in the bedroom changing to go out, encouraged by 'the other man', he helped himself to the prettiest of her studies of a certain boy. 'He didn't even ask if I wanted to sell it (and I didn't). I was so surprised I couldn't say anything,' she told Ursula Tyrwhitt. 'He has seven of that series and the best. So I will send the little

[5] No. 99, 1968 Arts Council Exhibition, now at Cardiff.

boy to *you* and he shall have yours. I wish you could tell me if I have the right to refuse him my drawings. I owe him a lot of pictures but I said nothing about drawings. He thinks he has the right to all. He bores me.'

The 'other man' was almost certainly Henri-Pierre Roché, who had instituted himself as Quinn's chief adviser in Paris art matters. He was by profession a not very good artist and a not very good journalist who was very good at introducing people. He was tall with red hair and prominent ears and he was to win fame at the age of seventy-five when he wrote *Jules et Jim*. Gwen John does not appear to have liked him.

The visit to the Mother Superior was more successful. Quinn immediately won her heart with a hefty donation to the convent. He knew that a cheque cuts more ice with the head of a needy community than pious words. And he donated an extra five hundred dollars so that the orphans should have jam with their bread in perpetuity. He had been saddened at the sight of the black-overalled girls in the playground eating dry bread. Subsequently, when Mrs Foster asked whether the gift had been put to work, the Mother Superior tearfully confessed that she had used it to repair the leaking roof. She had been praying for money for that purpose and now word went round the community that a miracle had occurred. When Mrs Foster wrote Quinn the story, he said that he was glad to be a principal in a miracle but he still wanted the children to have their jam and sent a second five hundred dollars.

Now at last Quinn was able to take possession of 'Mère Poussepin'. It may well have been the desire to possess this nun that had persuaded him to visit Paris after a nine-year absence. Although the picture was unfinished, it delighted him. It portrays a Sister of Charity seated at the corner of a table with her hands crossed over a book. Her somewhat sharp features wear an enquiring smile. She is painted mostly in chalky greys, but a rose on the table picks out other suggestions of pink in the picture. Quinn declared it 'a beautiful cool thing'. Gwen John also confessed, when she saw it at Pottier, the shipping agents, that she thought it 'the best picture there. But I liked the Seurat landscape.' In the opinion of John Rothenstein Gwen John did nothing better than her portrait of this nun. There were several versions of the portrait. Before the picture left France it was exhibited under a different title. Gwen John did not tell this to the Mother Superior 'because she wants "Mère Poussepin" to be a means of *propaganda* for the order'. To console the nuns Quinn had photos of the picture sent to the mother house in Tours and also to the house on Fall River in the United States.

From the convent Quinn took his party into Paris by car. A day in Paris with Quinn was a formidable occasion. Ezra Pound said, 'To go about Paris with Quinn was to see the doors of palaces, banks, offices fly open as if propelled by gunpowder. Before him even the notaries departed from the routine of their lifetimes.' First he opened a bank account for Gwen John at the Equitable Trust Company of New York, the manager being assured that Gwen John was a true professional although 'painting slowly and exhibiting rarely'. Then they went to Pottier in the rue de Gaillac to see the other paintings that Quinn had bought. Gwen John admired the three Picassos there although she considered they 'lacked charm'. They consisted of a canvas of monumental nudes inspired by the antique, a smaller abstract and a watercolour. Gwen John and Mrs Foster met Picasso at Paul Rosenberg's studio after Quinn had sailed for the United States. Unfortunately there was no Boswell present to record this meeting.

Another portrait by Gwen John, besides that of 'Mère Poussepin', awaited shipment at Pottier's. She always referred to it as 'The blue picture'[6] but its correct title was 'Girl in blue'. It represents a girl of about fifteen, probably another of Rosamund's friends, with her hair done in plaits. She is shown three-quarter length, three-quarters facing the viewer. The attic window of 29 rue Terre Neuve can be seen in the background. The seven drawings of the little boy from Pléneuf were there too. Gwen John asked Pottier to postpone shipment until she had completed a flower painting and put some finishing touches to her nun.

Quinn's last day in Paris, 14 August, was a peaceful one. No doubt at Gwen John's suggestion, they lunched in the woods at Meudon, walked round Versailles, then dined at a restaurant called the Pavillon Bleu. Quinn sailed the next day, declaring he had 'never hated so much leaving anywhere'. Mrs Foster and Roché saw him off but Gwen John did not. It was the feast of the Assumption and perhaps she was recalling that it was nearly twenty years since Rodin had first told her that this was her feast, the feast of Mary. It was four years since anyone had called her Marie.

Mrs Foster remained in Paris because Quinn wanted Gwen John to paint her portrait, declaring, 'I'm sure you will make a beautiful and very distinguished and very noble thing of your picture.' Gwen John, however, was not a portraitist whose services could be hired, and although preliminary sketches were made, the painting was never finished. 'If there had only been more time,' Mrs Foster said kindly. Derain eventually undertook the commission, but when Quinn saw the first version he did not like it, complaining it was too sensual. 'I know Quinn's trouble,' Derain said. 'He doesn't want a portrait, he wants a Derain.' He painted him a Derain and Quinn was satisfied.

While she was in Gwen John's flat Mrs Foster made an interesting discovery. In the leaking room that Gwen John always referred to as the

---

[6] Collection of Thomas F. Conroy, California. Not to be confused with 'Girl in a blue dress' at Cardiff.

grenier she found countless canvases rotting. Some, she told Quinn, were excellent, all, Gwen John had told her, were the property of Quinn, but she could not bring herself to send them to him. Mrs Foster sailed finally on the *Berengaria* on 17 October, suffering from an intestinal complaint. Vauxclair was threatened. Eager to get the house off their hands, the cattlemen wanted to add to the number of windows in front, but Gwen John persuaded them that this would take away the 'antique character' of the house. She objected also to white paint which they insisted would be '*très chic*' on the gates and to electricity and bathrooms. She conceded that a wall to keep the farm animals out was necessary. In the autumn the house was sold to the father of the man who now lives there, and the Manoir de Vauxclair became the trim country residence it is today with bright flower-beds edged with box and thoroughbreds grazing in the meadow. A dream had vanished and Gwen John never returned to Brittany.

An unusual note of optimism crept into Gwen John's letters on her return to Paris in the autumn of 1921. She was working hard. 'One of the things that gives me most pleasure is the crowing of the cock here,' she wrote to Ursula Tyrwhitt from Meudon. 'It tells me of long quiet days of work.' She remained well and able to work all through the winter though the 'acanthus leaves of the frost' stayed on the window of her room even after the fire was lit. She had sent Ursula Tyrwhitt's winter coat away to be trimmed with fur and was still wearing 'an elegant summer costume'. On 22 March she told Quinn, 'I am quite in my work now and think of nothing else. I paint till it is dark (the days are longer now and lighter) and then I have supper and then I read about an hour and think of my painting and then I go to bed. Every day is the same. I like this life very much.'

Quinn, meanwhile, was involved in three exhibitions of modern art, an English, a French and an American one at the Sculptors' Gallery, New York. In the English exhibition there was sculpture by Epstein and Gaudier-Brzeska on show and paintings by both the Johns. All five of Quinn's Gwen John oils were displayed, but 'Mère Poussepin' had not yet arrived. There were also her gouaches (including one of two little girls) and her drawings.

But Quinn's opinion of his English pictures was fast declining, and it was as well that, in his heart, he classed Gwen John as French. 'I would be willing to part with all of them at about 25 cents in the dollar what I paid for them,' he told Roché. In particular, he had turned against Augustus, declaring that 'the Café Royal and drink and women' had utterly ruined him as an artist and that he had squandered his talent in riotous painting (Arthur Symons's epigram). He planned to sell sixty-five Augustus Johns (his entire collection save four) and all his drawings, having first erased 'To Quinn' where it appeared over the signature. In all the English accounts of the London sale Quinn was described, to his fury, as a 'Tammany Hall Lawyer' who had arranged the sale without the artists' permission, and as a result glutted the market.

John behaved with remarkable equanimity. He travelled to New York and asked to see Quinn. The two men had not met for ten years. He dined at the flat, drank a quart of Bourbon, drew Quinn and his seventeen-year-old niece Mary and ogled Mrs Foster prodigiously. He then went off to Buffalo to empty General Conger Goodyear's 'hooch locker' and paint a portrait of his mother. Mrs Foster assured Gwen John that 'all the newspapers reproduced photographs of him'.

Gwen John spent the summer of 1922 at home, although at times she found Meudon 'hot and noisy', and must have longed for the rolling breakers of the Grève des Vallées. 'I didn't want to go away this summer,' she told Quinn. Why Gwen John abandoned Pléneuf after seven summers, four at the Ville Pichard and three at Vauxclair will probably never be known. The loss of Vauxclair alone would not appear sufficient reason. Perhaps, with the end of the war, she no longer felt the need for a retreat. Perhaps the children who had been her models had grown up. Perhaps she was losing touch with Ruth Manson. The transport of half a dozen cats and their kittens must have been exhausting.

1922 was probably Gwen John's most active year as a painter. She had worked undisturbed by illness, holidays or visitors all through the winter and all through the summer. A small group of models sat to her regularly.

Both the 'Girl in a blue dress' and the 'Girl in a green dress' were painted this year.[7] They typify Gwen John's fully developed style as a painter. In the words of Cecily Langdale's catalogue to the 1975 New York exhibition, 'The artist has abandoned her interest in portraiture as such and is concerned with formal problems. The static, monumental figures seem . . . flattened and pyramidal in shape.' David Fraser-Jenkins, curator of the Cardiff paintings until recently, adds that Gwen John began to apply her paint in increasingly small, more patterned strokes. The tonal qualities were drawing closer together, so that some of these paintings of the early twenties are virtually studies in greys. The lovely 'Girl in profile' at Cardiff is one of these studies. The aloof and rather pert pose of the sitter, with her tilted nose and pale mane of hair, is unusual, but the ashen colours are typical. A cloak on one shoulder divides the figure into two shades of grey; flesh and even hair are lighter shades of grey and the background is cream, applied so hastily that the priming underneath shows through. The whole gives the impression of having

[7] Nos. 8 and 10, 1976 Exhibition, Cardiff. Now in National Museum of Wales, Cardiff.

been dusted with wood ash. The only point of colour in the painting, a purple ribbon, was scraped out afterwards.[8]

And then the *grippe* hit the household at 29 rue Terre Neuve like a plague. Gwen John gave Quinn the satisfaction of a full account. She had woken feeling weak and could hardly bring herself to dress and rouse the girl in the house who helped her in the studio. The girl went for the milk but was almost as ill as Gwen John and soon it appeared that everyone in the house was in bed. An evil air seemed to have blown through the building and they were all too ill to look after each other. The others, according to Gwen John, saw the doctor 'a lot of times and took a lot of medicine' but she saw no one and got well first. She just cured herself by sleeping.

Quinn wrote back in horror, saying it was dangerous not to call in a doctor and the landlord should install central heating. He meanwhile had been feasting on the fearful tale of the decline of Marie Laurençin. Although he no longer considered her worthy of 'booming' on account of her 'monotonous use of colour', he followed accounts of her illness with sympathy. She was gradually being bereft of all the organs of her abdominal cavity (though she lived on until 1956). Although Gwen John's illness was less serious it was a good enough reason for delaying the export of pictures to America[9] and none were despatched during the year. At Christmas Gwen John strained her right hand and was unable to send any Christmas letters or, of course, paint any pictures, until the spring.

In September 1923 Quinn was back in Paris for the last time. He came on business, for he was acting for the New York art dealer Demotte who was suing Duveen. He had also come to rescue Ford Madox Ford's *Transatlantic Review* from ruin. He was in a state of considerable nervous tension from overwork. In photographs taken in Pound's garden studio with James Joyce and Ford Madox Ford he looked pale and ill, his face closed and stony. He was living largely on prunes, sieved for him by the faithful Mrs Foster. Yet after his business affairs were settled he was able to relax with his artist friends for a week. With Roché and Mrs Foster he visited Rouault at the Musée Gustave Moreau, and Braque, Picasso, Brancusi, de Segonzac and Derain at their studios. He called on Gwen John several times and together they had a friendly visit to the Mother Superior and to her elderly friends the Gervais. Quinn declared that she was looking well and she declared that he was 'a charming boy at my side'. He even persuaded her to attend a dinner party with him and Mrs

[8] One of the few poster reproductions of Gwen John's work was made from this painting at Cardiff.
[9] 'Girl in blue' and seven drawings reached New York in April but they had been sold to Quinn the previous year.

Foster at La Pereuse, which he afterwards declared 'a most distinguished thing'. The fourth diner was the etcher and illustrator de Segonzac. After dinner they went to a party in the studio of Brancusi. Gwen John had probably met the Rumanian sculptor in Rodin's studio in 1903 when he was a student there. That was before he started to produce the simple polished shapes for which he had become famous. After the party at Brancusi's Gwen John insisted on going home. 'I am not accustomed to parties. I liked other things we did better,' she said afterwards. Quinn, however, had developed an improbable taste for champagne and continued his revels the following night. With Mrs Foster and Roché he trooped up the seven flights of stairs to Derain's studio by the light of a match. After champagne with Derain he lighted his way down, crossed the courtyard to de Segonzac's studio and repeated the ritual of the climb, before departing finally for his hotel at two thirty in the morning. 'I hope you will keep up with Brancusi and de Segonzac,' he wrote to Gwen John. She did not.

Meanwhile Quinn departed by train to Venice, Rome, Bologna, Florence and the hill towns of Tuscany. It was Quinn's first visit to the cradle of the Renaissance, but he was irritable, bored and contemptuous. Back in Paris he wrote to Poincaré demanding an interview about German war reparations. He would probably have been granted the interview if his letter had not miscarried, for he had been created a chevalier of the Légion d'Honneur in 1920, in recognition of his financial contribution to the French war effort.

On 21 October he boarded the *Berengaria* but even here there was no rest, for the women were ugly and the men were Jews. He had the comfort, however, of knowing that a Cézanne, an El Greco, a Matisse, a Rousseau, a Picasso and two Braques awaited shipment at Pottier's. Also four pieces by Brancusi, including a small highly polished fish which he planned to use as a paper knife. Gwen John was instructed to go to Pottier's and see these. She picked out Cézanne's gigantic crudely outlined portrait of his father and the two Braque drawings. There were three of her own paintings with them. When the trio arrived in New York it was praised by Captain Longton Douglas, ex-director of the National Gallery of Ireland. Gwen John had already exhibited the three pictures at the Salon.

After a long lapse during the war years she had started to show her pictures again, but this time in France. She sent several still-lifes of dolls both to the Salon and to the Salon des Tuileries at this time. In one of these pictures a Japanese doll is propped against an open workbox on the round table in her room in the rue Terre Neuve. In another, two rag dolls in print frocks sit side by side.[10] (The dolls are called Dodo and Dorothy,

[10] National Museum of Wales, Cardiff.

both versions of Dorelia's name.) Gwen John shared this liking for dolls with Rilke. A few years earlier he had written a strange essay about them.[11] He spoke of the life in death he had led with these 'soulless travesties of reality' as a child, a life which was to shadow his adult inability to relate to real people. To Gwen John also these silent presences were substitutes for friends and children. They may even have betrayed a longing to be a child herself.

The brown teapot took the place of the dolls in three more still-lifes, one entitled 'The brown teapot'.[12] The rue Terre Neuve was again the setting; a heavy fireplace surmounted by a white earthenware jar of paintbrushes formed the background in one, in another the deep-set attic window. This last picture now bears the words 'Interior: Meudon nr. Paris' on the stretcher, in Charles Rutherston's hand. This brother of William Rothenstein was in Paris in 1923 and bought it at the Salon des Tuileries.

Another visitor in 1923 was Ursula Tyrwhitt, who does not appear to have seen Gwen John since her marriage. The visit was not entirely a success, as was usually the case. Gwen John's friendship with Ursula Tyrwhitt, like that with Arthur Symons, seems to have been conducted more smoothly by letter. Ursula now came encumbered by her husband and stayed in a hotel. The two women could only snatch the odd hour alone together and one of those hours was lost through a misunderstanding. Ursula waited for Gwen John at the Bernheim Jeune Gallery while Gwen John waited for Ursula at home. Ursula was concerned that Gwen John had not had a holiday and suggested she could come and see the Giottos at Assisi. Gwen John's reaction was indignant. 'You *know* I can *never* go to Assisi or anywhere else because there is nobody to feed the cats.' Ursula left Paris without saying goodbye.

That year someone else left without a farewell. Quinn wrote his last letter in March. It was a long one that conveyed both his respect for Gwen John and his affection. For the first time he dropped the 'Dear Miss John'. He spoke warmly of the three portraits which had just arrived along with Derain's portrait of Mrs Foster. Gwen John had been afraid they would be too like the three previous ones she had sent him, but Quinn praised them, especially the 'Study of a young woman in grey'.[13] Five drawings were also acknowledged. Of these a child drawing and a nude had been given to Mrs Foster at Gwen John's suggestion. But still Quinn was not satisfied. He had received six paintings in six months, as many as he had received in the previous fifteen years, but Mrs Foster had told him about the canvases in 'the granier' as he called it. He wanted

[11] *Puppen*, Rainer Maria Rilke.
[12] Private collection.
[13] The collection of Amanda Burden.

three of them and was enclosing 10,735 francs. He also wanted to know how the flower piece Mrs Foster had seen in the studio was progressing.

As always he was solicitous about Gwen John's health. He had heard that the winter of 1923–4 had been as bad as the previous one had been good, bedevilled by 'grips' (as he called them) and toothache. Gwen John who had not visited a dentist for years, had been brought to the dental chair with an agonising ulcer and had been obliged to return to it many times. Quinn sympathised and concluded his letter by announcing his last and greatest discovery, Rousseau's 'Sleeping gypsy'. It was fifteen years since Gwen John had brought to his attention the work of a *douanier* who 'felt he must paint'. Rousseau's work was now much sought after. 'It is a night scene, full moonlight,' Quinn wrote after he had seen Roché's photograph. 'A grave beautiful scene in the desert . . . a great lion in the middle, sort of sniffing at the arm of the woman, who is facing away from the lion. One does not know whether the lion is going to devour her or go away and leave her alone. But he has a wicked eye.' The letter ended with the words, 'It will soon be spring now in Paris and very lovely.' Gwen John wrote back an almost equally long one, concluding with the words, 'I have more to tell you.' Neither she nor Quinn guessed that he had only months to live.

Quinn had known he was ill for some time but would not admit how ill. When Mrs Foster returned from France she was shocked to see how much weight he had lost. At first the only change in his behaviour was an increased determination to take exercise. Every Sunday he tramped over the grounds of the Sleepy Hollow Club or the hills around White Plains with his friend F. J. Gregg, although these expeditions increasingly exhausted him. Then he became cautious about buying pictures. He turned down the opportunity to buy a Daumier, a Van Gogh, two Toulouse-Lautrecs and four Rouaults. And his attitude even to Gwen John changed. A month *before* writing his last letter to her he had already confided to Roché, 'I don't think I shall bother Gwen John very much now. She intimated to Mrs Foster that she would have no paintings to sell for some little time. She wants to give her next three or four paintings to me, and then we shall be even.'

Quinn cannot be blamed for treachery. By now he could neither eat nor drink normally, he could not sit comfortably in any position and he could not sleep. But still he went to the office in Nassau Street, made scenes with the telephone company and insisted there was nothing seriously wrong with him. 'It is not malignant,' he told Lady Gregory, 'but it's very uncomfortable.' In fact it was cancer of the liver.

By 21 July John Quinn was barely alive. Mrs Foster nursed him night and day in the flat on Central Park West among the shrouded Brancusis and Modiglianis. In her diary she wrote an entry that, in better times,

Quinn would have enjoyed. 'His head is a skull with yellow skin drawn over it – his face a mask of pain, his eyes faded to a light blue. His arms are flails of bone, his poor body a skin swelled with water.' Seven days later Quinn was dead. He was fifty-four.

Because he had been so secretive about his illness Gwen John knew nothing of his death until a letter arrived from Ursula Tyrwhitt who assumed she already knew. Gwen John had opened the letter with eager hope, thinking it would contain an explanation of Ursula's abrupt departure from Paris. The shock was considerable. The relationship with Quinn had become closer since he had visited her in Paris three years ago. Now it was severed without warning. She wrote to Ursula, her hand shaking with emotion, 'Is it really true John Quinn is dead? Is it a mistake? I had not heard. I feel very unhappy and must write a note to Mrs Foster who must be very unhappy and then go to sleep. It is strange how being very unhappy makes one sleepy.'

The passing of Quinn was a passing into instant oblivion. He left one of the finest private collections of modern art in the United States (possibly three thousand items), a collection that could have been the nucleus of a museum of modern art.[14] It was dispersed by his sister, Mrs Anderson, who cared only to turn 'wild art' into cold cash as quickly as possible, in spite of the horrified protests of Roché and Mrs Foster. It must, however, be admitted in Mrs Anderson's defence that it was Quinn's wish to see his collection dispersed. Like de Goncourt he wished that 'these things of art which have been the joy of my life shall not be consigned to a cold tomb of a museum and subjected to the stupid glance of the careless passer-by. I require that they shall be disposed under the hammer of the auctioneer so that the pleasure acquiring each of them has given me shall be given again.' It should also be said for Mrs Anderson that she did not sell her Gwen Johns, perhaps because they were not 'wild' like Picasso's or 'large' like Augustus's. It is possible that she kept them because she knew Mrs Foster wanted them.

Mrs Foster's tears for Quinn can hardly have been dry before she approached Gwen John with the suggestion that she should not only inherit Quinn's right to Gwen John's entire production, but that, if she did not choose to buy the pictures herself, she should decide what pictures Gwen John might sell and to whom. Gwen John appeared satisfied with this extraordinary arrangement, merely remarking, 'I don't think I'll be in want unless Mrs Foster takes all my work and

[14] A few years later the Museum of Modern Art in New York was established and many of Quinn's best pictures found their way into it. It would be a fitting memorial to Quinn if the authorities there would place a plaque at least under Rousseau's 'Sleeping gypsy' to commemorate Quinn's purchase of it.

doesn't send much money.' In fact the contract appears to have fallen through, for the 'American woman' did not write often and Gwen John had nothing she was ready to part with.

The exhibition

1925–7

After 1925 Gwen John's desire to paint in oils declined sharply. Free from
Quinn, she turned gratefully to watercolours and gouaches. Her portrait
of Louise Salaman's daughter, Miss Bishop, may well have been her last
oil painting. Miss Bishop's account of that sitting is therefore doubly
precious. She recalls the attic in the rue Terre Neuve as light, pleasant and
sparsely furnished. She recalls the cats asleep on all the window sills, or
demanding to be let out or let in. She recalls the curé knocking on the
door and not being let in. Gwen John herself was shy and kindly in a long
purple cloak and a large felt hat. There were protracted silences while she
worked.

The ten year period of activity (1915–25) which had coincided with the
period of Quinn's patronage was now at an end. In the spring of 1925
Gwen John found she could not even produce a watercolour. She had
waited anxiously for the spring to come and bring with it the flowers and
landscapes she longed for, but when it came she was busy. She had to
paint her studio 'flesh colour and apple green'. Then she had to prepare
the room for work. But she still did not work. She complained that the
people in the house talked too much and that the curé had asked for
another portrait from a photograph,[1] and, 'I can't refuse *anything*.' To
cap it all, she sat on a needle and had to go to hospital for two days to have
it removed.

She was also have difficulty in obtaining good Japanese watercolour
paper. She told Ursula Tyrwhitt she needed this paper because on it the
'coulours don't run into each other. The paper absorbs the coulour with
each touch of the brush so that it is final, there is no retouching.' Ursula
Tyrwhitt suggested washed Ingres paper as a substitute and it seems to
have been successful, though Gwen John found the preparation of the

---

[1] Possibly the 'Woman in a turban' series, now at Cardiff.

large sheets tiring. Finally there were cat problems. 'Tragedies have happened in my home and the cat I loved best has died and another. It has stopped me in my work and all the exquisite flowers I was going to do pictures of have passed now. There remains the acacia trees that I can see from my windows but I cannot do them yet.'

There was one subject, apart from cats and still-lifes, that was always available, in all weathers and in all seasons. It was people in church. Louise Roche, a neighbour in Meudon, remembered a vespers service around 1923 when a woman in a broad-brimmed felt hat and a long dark cloak slid discreetly to the back of the church and there, instead of kneeling, commenced to draw in a sketch-book throughout the service. When Madame Roche heard that the strange creature was a convert, and an English one at that, she thought no more of the matter. Gwen John was in fact making what she called 'the little drawings in colour I do'. Her subjects were the back views of the Sisters of Charity with the uniformed rows of orphans in their charge. Also the well-dressed mothers of the parish with their daughters.

These gouaches, often executed on small squares of paper cut from discarded drawings, are the most personal things Gwen John ever made. The figures are sometimes single and sometimes in groups of two, three or four, without background or properties save the wooden chairs they sit on or kneel behind. All is pared down to the simplicity of the primitive Japanese prints she admired. Usually the figures convey devotion but sometimes they are frankly comic. A child with a dot for an eye and a pom-pom on her hat turns to show her tilted snout in profile.[2] An old nun, her head-dress disappearing below her hump, dozes quietly.[3] Gwen John had a sense of the ridiculous and occasionally allowed herself an unofficial caricature in a margin which showed a wicked power of observation. At Cardiff there are two examples. In one an ugly woman in a cloche advances her lower lip towards a cup of tea.[4] In the other two old ladies wag their beaks and their lorgnettes at each other under large hats.[5]

The colouring of the church studies is extraordinarily subtle. The isolated figures are bathed in an unworldly light, an effect achieved by a very limited range of tone. The 'Girl with long hair kneeling in church seen from behind,[6] confines itself to two colours, prussian blue and ochre. The dress is a thinner wash of the blue of the hat, and the glowing auburn of the hair is a mixture of the ochre of the background with blue.

[2] 'A girl wearing a hat and coat with a fur collar seated in church', no. 37, 1976 Exhibition, Cardiff.

[3] 'Seated nun in church', no. 81, 1976 Exhibition, Cardiff.

[4] Sheet of drawings of Saint Teresa and her sister, no. 47, 1976 Exhibition, Cardiff.

[5] 'Two women talking', no. 20, 1976 Exhibition, Cardiff.

[6] No. 32, 1976 Exhibition, Cardiff.

The same colour range is used in 'Two women seated in church, one wearing a check coat',[7] described by Fraser-Jenkins in the catalogue to the 1976 exhibition as, 'a brilliantly witty design, much of which is painted directly without outline. The texture of the thin wash paint is so even throughout the painting that the browns of the chairbacks and the square pattern on the coat almost look like surface designs.'

Gwen John was now beginning to feel a serious need for money. Mrs Foster appears to have sent nothing and the dreadful necessity for a show began to loom. Gwen John suggested a joint exhibition to Ursula Tyrwhitt, a *small* one. 'Big ones are so tiring and stupid, like Madge Oliver's[8] was,' she added. Ursula Tyrwhitt meanwhile was painting in Venice. 'You're in a lovely place arnt you?' Gwen John wrote. 'It must be a pleasure to see strange places and people.' By June Gwen John had thought of some reasons why she couldn't exhibit. Her little drawings in colour would be too small. She only had five canvases ready and they all needed retouching. Mrs Foster wanted a painting. How many pictures went to the smallest exhibition? And there was another problem. Gus had offered to arrange a show for her and he might be offended if she exhibited without his patronage. 'He is offended at everything I do or don't do.' But Gus was in New York, following his reconnaissance of the previous year with a more serious campaign. He had hired a studio in New York and millionaires were flocking there for their portraits. Unfortunately he was drinking heavily. 'Life,' he wrote, 'is full of pitfalls (and gin).' At the end of one dinner he broke his silence to boom an apology for having monopolised the conversation. At a lunch, when a lady asked him which young artist of promise he was watching he replied, 'I am watching myself, madam, with considerable anxiety.' His behaviour was beginning to resemble that of his young friend and fellow-countryman, Dylan Thomas.

In November the New Chenil Galleries wrote to Gwen John to say that Augustus definitely wanted to exhibit with her and that they could promise a warm welcome and a highly satisfactory result, 'as if they could tell,' Gwen John commented. The New Chenil Galleries had been opened in 1907 near the Chelsea Town Hall in the King's Road. The two exhibition rooms were upstairs. One held a permanent show of works by Augustus, Ambrose and Mary McEvoy, William Orpen and William Rothenstein. This was hardly surprising since Jack Knewstub, the managing director, was the brother-in-law of both Orpen and William Rothenstein and a close friend of Augustus. 'Curly' Knewstub had fair wavy hair and a north country manner. His father had been Rossetti's

---

[7] No. 33, 1976 Exhibition, Cardiff.
[8] A fellow pupil at the Slade who lived in Cassis and painted landscapes. There are two interiors of her house at Cassis at the Tate. Gwen John did not know she had just died.

assistant but he had no artistic gifts, only an artistic temperament. He worshipped Augustus and modelled himself on him. He envisaged the Chenil Galleries as a flourishing centre for all the arts, with a restaurant included. But the restaurant never materialised. A notice at the back of every catalogue even promised 'Perfect acoustics and spring-supported oak dance floor.' But there was little dancing, and Gwen's was to be virtually the last show held at the gallery.

As the date of the opening approached, the old panic began to appear in Gwen John's letters to Ursula Tyrwhitt. Since Rodin's death she had written fewer letters, claiming that they tired her, but now Ursula received them by almost every post, first in Venice and then at the villa in Taormina where she and Walter were staying amid orange groves. Would Ursula send a picture she possessed? Would she write a short introduction for the catalogue? Could she deal with a magazine editor: '*I* won't spend a franc on him.' Finally, in despair, she declared, 'The exhibition is a nightmare.'

Gwen John's first and last one-man show[9] took place in May and June 1926. It consisted of about a dozen oils and fifty drawings. Four albums of further drawings were included to bulk out the material. One was entitled 'Studies of a child' and another 'Meudon at night'. These were left about on tables for the public to inspect. The oils were not all recent apart from 'The blue dress',[10] 'The precious book'[11] and two interiors. There were some earlier paintings like 'The little model', a version of 'Mère Poussepin', 'The letter' and, oldest of all, Ursula Tyrwhitt's 'Dorelia in a black dress', painted at Toulouse. Among the drawings were several of cats and children. But the newest and certainly the most significant section was sixteen gouaches entitled 'Group of studies in church'.

The Chenil Exhibition of 1926 marked a turning point in Gwen John's life as an artist. The productive decade of 1915–25 was over. After 1926 there were to be only four more oil paintings. But the period of the gouaches had five years to run. The exhibition was a success, for Gwen John had begun to acquire a standing in the London art world. Three pictures from the early Paris period already hung at the Tate: the naked Fenella, 'The lady reading'[12] and the first portrait of Chloë Boughton Leigh[13]. As a result prices were high. The portrait of Dorelia was bought

---

[9] The show has been described as a joint one with Augustus, but Gwen John's exhibits were listed in a separate catalogue.

[10] 'Girl in a blue dress' appears as 'The blue dress' in the Chenil catalogue. It must not be confused with Quinn's child portrait, 'Girl in blue'.

[11] A small canvas painted for Ursula Tyrwhitt.

[12] Presented by the Contemporary Arts Society, 1917.

[13] Bought from the sitter, and presented by the N.E.A.C., 1925.

by the Duveen Paintings Fund and exhibited the following year at Vienna in the *English Masterpieces of the Last Two Hundred Years* show. Eventually it also was bought by the Tate.

Gwen John's friends were warm in their congratulations. The paintings of nuns made an especially strong impression at a time when, it should be remembered, London was solely obsessed with the Blackbirds and Diaghilev.

Those cool nuns, [wrote William Rothenstein,] with their quiet and beautiful hands, the remembrance of them will be with me all day. If they have found the wisdom of quietness and peace you have given them, they are happy women. Dear Gwen, you can't think how the likeness of your paintings to your own self touches me, and how powerfully your pictures evoke the shy loving being whose heart I could sometimes almost hear throbbing at times of pain and disturbance. It is as though you fought against Augustus's flowing, undisciplined genius and now an exquisite peace and perfume, which mystics say fills the air for them, has entered your spirits.

William Rothenstein was now the principal of the Royal College of Art and was about to become a trustee of the Tate. But there was a more mystical side to his nature that was shown in his friendship with the Indian poet, Rabindranath Tagore, whose fine head he drew.[14] Augustus now called him 'the parson' and went out of his way to shock him. It was to the parson in Rothenstein that Gwen John's nuns appealed. The pictures struck a similar chord in Louise Salaman. She wrote, 'It was a christening joy to stand among those pale quiet songs of yours . . . My thoughts went back to our youth with its aims and its hopes and you seemed to be the only one of that eager band who had been utterly faithful to those aspirations but who had achieved more than we dreamed of.'

One person failed to make money out of the Chenil Show and that was Curly Knewstub, who went bankrupt. The artists whose work he had regularly exhibited now turned their backs on him, and Augustus in particular refused to help him in his hour of need because he was said to have cheated Gwen of fifty pounds, presumably in connection with the show.

As soon as Gwen John's money from the Chenil came through, presumably in the late autumn of 1926, she spent it on a big present for her five cats: a piece of land with a wooden garage at the end of it.[15] The

14 Now in the Tate.

property was situated at No. 8 rue Babie, a quiet leafy street not far from the rue Terre Neuve. Augustus was horrified. He wrote, 'It consisted of a mere shed, hardly weatherproof, erected in half an acre of waste ground. My objections to this policy of self-neglect, entirely motivated by my regard for her well-being, were met with ridicule. I was only betraying an absence of sensibility and a fundamentally "bourgeois" state of mind.' Gwen's great-niece, Sara, however, who knew it better, describes it as, 'an adorable little place . . . a wooden house on stilts'.[16]

Gwen John's half-acre had been part of the fine estate of General Jacqueminat (who had served under the empire). Her first act on moving into it was to build a high wall between it and the road and lay some paths made from paving stones. She made no further improvements. The acacias by the gate were allowed to grow unchecked, the row of limes that led to the garage went likewise unchecked and indeed were greatly loved for the green vault they raised over the head of their owner. Otherwise the *mauvaises herbes* (weeds) flourished in the sunshine.

One thing only troubled Gwen John in this paradise and that was what the cats, whom she loved, did to the birds, whom she loved. She loved birds so much that she once bought Madame C.'s caged blackbird, which she passed every day on her way to church. Louise Roche, who now lived across the street from her, entered Gwen John's garden half an hour after the door of its cage had been opened. The bird was still inside, refusing to accept its liberty, and Gwen John was hovering in the background, anxiously praying the cats wouldn't come. Too often, alas, they did come and their owner would be discovered peering up with horror into the branches of a tree where some poor little victim was meeting its end beyond her reach. The only serious quarrel between Louise Roche and Gwen John occurred over birds. Gwen's cat killed the parents of a nest of young tits located in a hollow pillar in Madame Roche's garden. Gwen, anxious to defend her cat, said the Roches had better stop up the hole next time. Louise said she would kill the cat if it happened again.

Augustus was so distressed about his sister's new residence that he hit upon a way of persuading her not to move in. He bought her a better one, a cottage near the New Forest. He had another motive for this purchase. He hoped the presence of Gwen John in England would encourage Edwin, now eighty, to die. Old Edwin John kept in touch by means of a series of epistolary weather reports. 'What is the weather like in Paris?' he would ask Gwen John, and would inform her in return of its behaviour in America and Canada where Winifred and Thornton lived, and in Jamaica

---

[15] Edwin John lived there after Gwen John's death. The shack has now been replaced by a modern villa.

[16] Edwin probably carried out improvements.

where Augustus happened to be on a visit. ('Very hot but usually tempered by a breeze from the sea.') At home he was always finding himself overtaken by some 'nice breeze', afflicted with 'unbearable heat waves' or 'in the grip of a fierce blizzard' . . . As he advanced into his nineties the climate hardened, 'the present weather being I think the worst I have experienced. How is it going to end?'

How indeed? And when? Augustus often thought the end was near. The old man would summon him to Tenby in urgent tones, and Augustus would set out in his saloon car. On these 'death-trips' he stayed at Richard Hughes's castle in Laugharne. On returning from Tenby he once said gloomily, 'My father is on his death bed but refuses to get into it,' for he always found the old gentleman miraculously recovered.

In 1926 there were more hopeful tidings. 'My father speaks of the uncertainty of life and his Will – so I suppose he is thinking of moving onwards,' Augustus told Dorelia, probably from America. 'He would prefer to wait till Gwen and I have returned.' No obstacle, Augustus considered, should be put in the old man's way. Yew Tree Cottage was made available to Gwen. She rose to the bait, went over to see the cottage in June 1927 and was immediately enthralled by it, in spite of the fact that it was less than a mile from Fryern Court to which Augustus had just moved.

It stood, and still stands, in the village of Burgate Cross, just by the turning which leads to Fryern. It was the kind of cottage one might embroider on a tea-cosy, with rough timber-framed walls, a window on each side of the front door and a thatched roof in need of repair. Decayed country houses were irresistible to Gwen John, and this, owing to Augustus's forethought, had the added charm of lacking furniture (he had supplied only a small painting by himself, a dresser and a 'thing for sharpening pencils'). 'I looked through the window and saw a lovely dresser,' Gwen John told Ursula Tyrwhitt. 'It is a very dear cottage and the countryside is exquisite. The ground is bordered on one side by lovely little fir trees.'

Gwen John set to work to furnish the place on five pounds, but found that that sum would only cover the cost of the sofa on which she planned to sleep in the sitting-room. An S.O.S. went out to Ursula Tyrwhitt, the provider, for an old chair, a table and a bed (for visitors). Ursula sent a carpet, an overcoat and a collection of shells which were received raptuously.

But work was in progress. Workmen were pulling down partitions to enlarge rooms, whitewash was being applied and Ursula's carpet was now laid on the sitting-room floor and her shells arranged on the mantelpiece. 'It takes much longer getting settled here than I thought,' Gwen John wrote to Ursula. In July she had had to return to Meudon, perhaps to see the cats, one of which immediately took up residence in the Meudon-Versailles railway tunnel for four days. (The tunnel, according to Gwen John, was three miles long.)

The cats had been constantly on Gwen John's mind while she had been away. There was one in particular, Valentine, old and hideous beyond belief in the opinion of Louise Roche. Valentine had no teeth and Madame Roche had been requested to feed her 250 grammes of minced meat daily. 'I thought of writing to tell you to give her calf's liver but I didn't because I knew you wouldn't,' Gwen John told Madame Roche. '*Oh! Certainement non!*' Madame Roche commented in housewifely horror. Gwen John, who would not cook for herself, thought nothing of walking to the market to buy a cod's head for the cats which she would make into a delicate pâté.

In August Gwen John returned to England for five weeks, bringing blue cups with white spots for the dresser. Because of the state of the cottage she was obliged to stay with Augustus and Dorelia, as, no doubt, Augustus had intended. Gwen liked Fryern, a mediaeval friary masquerading behind a Georgian front. The facade was bisected by a porch with columns and there were five windows which reached to the ground. Behind the three on the right was the dining-room with a long refectory table. The sitting-room on the left gave on to the garden and contained signed copies of books by Hardy, Strachey, T. E. Lawrence, Yeats and Shaw. Several of Gwen John's paintings hung between the windows along with a watercolour by her nephew, Edwin. Up the side wall of the house clematis and roses grew in a tangled mat and the cats made hammocks for themselves among them. These cats were a feature of Fryern. They were of all colours, and usually sat on the kitchen table when indoors.

Dorelia was the queen of Fryern, for Augustus was often in London for months at a time. She had of course changed since Gwen John had last seen her in Paris twenty years before, but her style had not. She still wore flowing dresses with high waists and long sleeves. She had set a fashion of dress for three decades now among art students, and never defected to the shift or the cloche. She still maintained her air of mystery, and people of both sexes continued to fall in love with her. Carrington, while fighting Augustus off at one of his wild parties, saw Dorelia 'like some sybil sitting in a corner with a basque cap on her head and her cloak swept round her in great folds, smiling mysteriously. She was so amazingly beautiful.' Kathleen Hale also describes her as the most beautiful woman she had ever seen. Lady Pansy Lamb, with the historical accuracy of the Pakenhams, adds that by the time she was forty-five her waistline had thickened and her chin was tending to disappear into her neck. (Lady Pansy was to marry Henry Lamb shortly after Gwen John left.) During

Gwen John's visit Lamb was still Dorelia's admirer and a constant visitor to the house, having bought a place in Poole to be near her. At Fryern he filled the role that Augustus so abysmally failed to fill. He played piano duets with Dorelia and taught Poppet and Vivien to ride.

Fryern Court was a cheerful if not excessively tidy place. Dorelia's brightly coloured bits of sewing littered every room, an atmosphere of wood smoke left a film on everything, and no unnecessary housework was done. Lord David Cecil claims to have been able to retrieve his hat from the same spot on the sitting-room floor six weeks after he left it there. The entertainment was prodigious. Sometimes twenty-two people sat round the candlelit refectory table and were plied with Mediterranean food and red wine. A great deal of drinking was done and there was a special ceremony for the making of the salad dressing. This could only be done by the senior virgin present, and she must toss the salad by hand. Afterwards Augustus would sing folk songs, puffing at his pipe and rolling his eyes. Surplus guests slept the night in the yellow and blue caravans in the garden.

Dorelia did not manage this circus alone. She had her 'squaws', just as did Augustus. His were models, dancers and actresses. Hers were her sister Edie, Fanny Fletcher and Mrs Cake. Dorelia's sister Edie was a permanent presence in the busy kitchen at Fryern. In her portrait by Augustus she appears small with vast brooding eyes under a black fringe. She dressed in the same gypsy style as Dorelia and eventually became the wife of Francis Macnamara, father of Caitlin Thomas and Nicolette Devas. Fanny Fletcher was an art student who helped Dorelia with dressmaking, and who was to become better known for her potato-print wallpapers. She was said to be a witch. During her spell as senior virgin she was suspected of mixing spells with the salad dressing. Mrs Cake, a native of Dorset, was the cook. She and her husband had been at Alderney Manor and, although always promising to leave, remained with the family for over thirty years. She was cheerfully convinced she was a great beauty. 'Old Cake was very lucky to get me,' she would say. 'All the boys were after me. It was my hair.' Old Cake now preferred to walk the mile to the pub in the evenings. A small silent hunchback with a limp, he helped in the garden. In a cottage in the grounds lived Dorelia's mother, a hard-headed Scottish housewife with white hair and a round pink face. She made the quilts that covered every bed at Fryern.

Gwen John's relations with Augustus appear to have improved. She told Ursula Tyrwhitt, after her stay, 'I don't mind seeing Augustus now, or that family.' Augustus wrote to her, at this time, 'Few on meeting this retiring person in black, with her tiny hands and feet, a soft, almost inaudible voice, and delicate Pembrokeshire accent, would have guessed that here was the greatest woman artist of her age, or, as I think, of any other.' (It is a strange fact that Gwen John's Welsh accent became more pronounced after her stay in France.)

Gwen John spent some hours each day on the beach at Bournemouth (fourteen miles away by bus). She insisted that Fanny Fletcher should accompany her there. But she found the English summer cold and wore Ursula Tyrwhitt's overcoat everywhere. Henry Lamb had a memory of Gwen John at Fryern. They were passengers in a car together. She was sitting beside him, 'a little old lady in a shawl'. Suddenly for no apparent reason she clutched his arm feverishly. He interpreted the gesture as an amorous advance. It seems more probable that Augustus was driving.

Augustus was an appalling driver, but, like Mr Toad, he found motors irresistible. In 1920 he had acquired a blue two-seater Buick with yellow wheels in exchange for a picture. After half an hour of instruction he drove it home to Hampshire in first gear. He soon learnt both how to change into top and to put his foot on the accelerator, but little else. When at the wheel he would often forget he was driving at all, allowing the car to continue on its course while he stared back over his shoulder to admire some receding view. Once, when hurtling towards a fork in the road, he demanded of his passenger which direction to take. On receiving no reply he bisected the angle and ploughed into a field. By the time Gwen John stepped into the passenger seat the Buick had been abandoned (upside-down) somewhere near London, and a more respectable saloon model had been acquired.

Gwen John's six grown-up nephews all drove the car with the same passion as their father when they were at home. As they were now aged between twenty and twenty-five, this was not very often. Apart from young Edwin, they were almost strangers to her. Edwin had visited her in Paris while he was a senior student at the Collège de Normandie. Perhaps Gwen John was lucky to have missed the boisterous untamed boyhood of David, Caspar, Robin and Romilly at Alderney Manor. There they had run amok, partially uneducated and wholly naked, climbing trees, lighting fires and screaming in terror as their father pursued them with a stick. Now the only children at home were the two daughters, the darkly sensuous Poppet, aged twelve, and Vivien aged ten. And they were *permanently* at home. Their father did not hold with sending girls to school. Women, in Augustus's opinion, were created to be the mistresses and models of men.

Vivien still remembers Gwen John at this time. She writes,

She could hardly bear to leave her cats in Paris, but eventually she did make the necessary arrangements and she did arrive. Unfortunately there were rather a lot of other guests in the house at the time. As she was extremely shy, this made it necessary for her to have her meals in her bedroom. I remember her very well, because I was terribly struck by her appearance – so very like my father, but very very tiny, like a miniature Augustus, with eyes that filled with tears almost continuously as she talked; very pale, bluey eyes and she wore dark, dark clothes.

A physical change came over Augustus in the early years at Fryern. Although he wasn't quite fifty his hair was already grey and his eyes bloodshot. The cause of this change was alcohol. He drank more in the 'twenties than in any other period of his life, both at parties in his studio in Mallord Street, and in the pubs of Fitzrovia. Drink banished his shyness and his sense of emptiness, made him forget that he had ceased to paint well and unlocked his amazing gift of the gab. It also made him violent. A period of drying out at a sanatorium only had a temporary effect. Fortunately for Gwen John he drank less when at Fryern, where Dorelia had the key of the cellar.

Augustus was feared rather than liked by his sons, and his relationship with them deteriorated as he saw them decline from visual objects into thinking beings. Romilly recalls the awful silent mealtimes when Augustus was in one of his 'glooms'. These silences were not necessarily broken when there were visitors present, for the Johns despised small talk. Old Edwin's soundless board at Tenby was coming perilously close to being duplicated. Augustus wanted his sons to succeed, but only because their success would reflect glory on him. He invariably gave them the wrong advice and this, combined with an abnormal upbringing and education, ensured that some of them failed spectacularly, although Caspar was to become First Sea Lord and Chief of the Naval Staff. The case of Henry, Ida's last child, was the most tragic. Henry is the only one of her nephews Gwen John is known to have met at Fryern. During the panic after Ida's death Henry had been left with the Nettleships. He had been brought up by a Catholic cousin, Edith Nettleship, in a village in Hampshire and sent to Stonyhurst. During the holidays he had come to Alderney Manor for the odd week, looking strangely out of place in his grey flannel suit and tie. He was an attractive figure to his brothers for he had striking good looks and a vehement personality but he was always an alien. The constant talk of love and physical beauty at Alderney both alarmed and attracted him.

Just before Gwen John came to Fryern, Henry had decided to become a priest. At the age of nineteen Father d'Arcy had taken him to Rome. It was this experience that had convinced him he had a vocation. By the time Gwen John reached Fryern he had completed his first year of training as a Jesuit at Manresa and was spending his summer vacation at home. Strangely enough Gwen John does not appear to have taken to this apparently desirable nephew. Her relations insist that she disliked priests, and Henry behaved as if he were one already. (He had already persuaded his father to paint him in Jesuit robes.) Augustus recorded an occasion when Henry had been attempting to convert him. He had pointed out how much Augustus had to gain, how little to lose by taking the step. Hearing Henry's argument Gwen John at once contradicted him with the statement that one accepted the truth, not as a business transaction, but for the love of God, even if it meant disaster or death itself – 'as if *that* mattered,' she added contemptuously.

The rest of Henry's story is quickly told. At Campion Hall, Oxford the conflict between the paganism of the Johns and the asceticism of Jesuits became intolerable and he submitted a dispensation of his vows. (The deterioration of his handwriting at this time of extreme perturbation is extraordinarily reminiscent of that of his aunt at similar periods.) At the end of his last term at Oxford Ethel Nettleship (Ida's sister) lent him a bungalow on the Cornish cliffs. Here, during June, Henry waited for the beautiful but complicated Olivia Plunket-Greene to come and relieve him of his virginity. Olivia did not come. On 5 July his body was found washed up on the beach at Perranporth, after what may have been a cliff climbing accident. His dog was waiting inconsolable on the shore. He was twenty-seven years old.

Gwen John would see nobody apart from her family while she was at Fryern. She begged Ursula Tyrwhitt not to tell even old friends from the Slade she was there. 'I count on you not to tell anyone. *I will not be troubled by people*. If I saw Gwen Salmond and others it wouldn't do because my mind is not strong enough to keep its harmony when any difficulties or obstacles come. But if you came it would not be the same as we come into each other's solitude or harmony. We're part of each other's atmosphere.' Ursula Tyrwhitt was invited to stay at Fryern in September. 'It is nice here,' Gwen John added.

Gwen returned to France on 19 September, after spending only three nights in all at Yew Tree Cottage. Augustus had hoped she would stay the winter. She promised to return when she had sold 'a few paintings' (with which she hoped to repay him for the cost of the house). 'I can't say how long they will take,' she added. They took her the rest of her life. It was Fanny Fletcher, the witch, who took up residence at Yew Tree Cottage, with the blue spotted teacups on the dresser.

Véra

1928–32

There was another reason why Gwen John never returned to Yew Tree Cottage, although, as she confided to Ursula Tyrwhitt, she sometimes wanted to 'very much'. She was emotionally engaged once more. Since the death of Rodin ten years earlier she had formed no sentimental attachment to a man. She had, however, had a passing feeling for an Englishwoman called Nona.[1] One of the letters to Nona runs, 'Suddenly I hear your words, "My dear Gwen". Nona, what angel made you say it? Nona, when you look at me so thoughtfully and write to me you don't know what you do. In Brittany at night I used to pluck the leaves and grasses from the hedges all dark and misty and when I took them home I sometimes found my hands full of flowers. Nona, you are like a sculptor who models the clay in his hands without thinking and suddenly he finds a lovely form.'

Now Gwen John was to meet someone who came to mean much more to her than Nona. She met Véra Oumançoff as a result of Rilke's death. The poet had developed leukaemia while living at Muzot, his remote tower in Switzerland. He died alone in the clinic by the lake at Valmont at the end of 1926. Gwen John reacted strangely. Although she had been a

---

[1] The identity of 'Nona' is unknown. Augustus, who found a copy of the letter among Gwen John's papers, may have misread the name. Nora Summers and her husband Gerald were close neighbours of Augustus's at Fryern. They had been at the Slade with Gwen, but, having a private income, had allowed goats to supersede art in their lives. Nicolette Devas gives a vivid picture of Nora in her autobiography, *Two Flamboyant Fathers*: 'In the Summers' marriage Nora was the dominant personality with an over-sensitive intellectual type of beauty, refined and perfect in its way, though it verged on the sickly. Her appearance described exactly what she was like in character; physically delicate, she was temperamentally delicate too . . . Augustus painted her at this period, leaning against an upright piano, wearing baggy black velvet trousers, a shantung shirt, her very long pale hair parted in the middle and gathered in a thick coiled bun in the classic style.'

Catholic for fourteen years, she was uncertain whether she could pray for the soul of the dead man anywhere but where he had died. She had in fact already begun to pray not only *for*, but *to* the poet. A note found in her studio after her death begged him to hold her hand and guide her when her 'brain slept'. He had begun to help her, he must continue. Now she did not go to the curé for advice but to Jacques Maritain, the Catholic philosopher, who lived a few doors away from her hut.

Jacques Maritain, with his wife Raïssa and her sister Véra Oumançoff, were people she saw regularly in church. They had moved to a gabled black and white villa at 10 rue du Parc three years earlier[2] and it was from this house that they were carrying out their 'apostolate of the arts', an attempt to bring Christianity to the world of painting, literature and philosophy.

Maritain had married Raïssa, the daughter of Russian Jewish *emigrés*, while they were both students at the Sorbonne and together they had been converted to Catholicism by the poverty-stricken Léon Bloy, a man who came as close to being a prophet as anyone is likely to in this century. From that time on Maritain had made it his mission to reconcile the philosophy of the Greeks to the Christian ethic. In this endeavour he had found a staunch ally in St Thomas Aquinas, 'the divine doctor'. By the time Gwen John met him Maritain had already published his *Art and Scholasticism* and several other books on neo-Thomism.

Jacques Maritain was a charismatic figure, often confused with Christ by his more emotional converts. Cocteau and his lovers, Maurice Sachs and Jean Bourgoint, were captivated by the beauty of his pale eyes, 'damp with tenderness', the childlike lock of fair hair that hung over his forehead and the thin golden beard. Raïssa was the dark flame to Jacques's pale one. She was physically frail and spiritually heroic, given to long hours of meditation. She also had written several books, including *The Prince of this World* about Christianity and the arts. Like her husband, she had charm and Cocteau, when he heard she was dead in 1960, considered becoming a monk.

Then there was Véra, Raïssa's younger sister, who had lived with the couple since Raïssa's first serious illness in 1908. She was plump and fair like a Russian peasant and she wore her hair in plaits round her head. She mostly ran the household and looked after Raïssa who was often gravely ill. It was with Véra that Gwen John fell in love. On 30 December 1926, the day she heard of Rilke's death, Gwen had followed Véra and her 'little brother' (Jacques Maritain) home from Mass. She had been encouraged

---

[2] The street is now named after General Gouraud, whom Gwen John had drawn from a photo. Gouraud came from Meudon. The house still stands, with a plaque commemorating the hospitality to be found there between 1923 and 1939.

many times by Mother Superior to call at the house where all those in trouble were welcome. Now at last she found the courage. Ten rue du Parc was a house dear to many. Maurice Sachs remembered it with nostalgia: the crunch of the gravel on the path, the barking of the dog and the welcoming smell of the sitting-room where everything was scrupulously clean and bright. The copper shone, the books were in line and the flowers stood to attention in their vase. On the wall were portraits of Léon Bloy and St Thomas. There were also paintings by Rouault and Severini (who lived at Meudon).

On her first visit Gwen John was received by all three members of the household. On future visits she saw only Véra. Certainly Véra lacked Jacques and Raïssa's intellectual brilliance, but she had shared all their religious experiences. She had been received into the church with them. In the early days of their religious fervour she had even formed a lay community with them. They had called themselves Brother Placide, Sister Gertrude and Sister Agnes.[3] Placide and Agnes had mortified the flesh by sprinkling bitter powder over their food and wearing hair shirts. Gertrude (Raïssa) had considered daily Mass a sufficient mortification. They had now dropped these practices but in the privacy of their rooms both Raïssa and Véra spent many hours in prayer. Raïssa's profound and agonising meditations were committed to her diary. But it was to Véra that God spoke directly and simply, 'in a sort of loud whisper'.

There was something innately motherly about Véra. She looked like her own round-faced cheerful mother who also lived at No. 10 and ruled the kitchen. Raïssa always called, Véra 'little mother' although Raïssa was the older sister. When the two girls were children at Rostov-on-Don they had a favourite game in which Véra was Mimi and Raïssa was Pifo, her little boy. They inhabited a world where there was no crying, the flowers bloomed all the year round and grown-ups were never cross. It was as a spiritual mother that Gwen John valued Véra, just as she valued the Mother Superior at the convent. She had a breadth of understanding that Gwen John had never found in the curé. When consulted about the morality of sketching during Mass, Véra declared stoutly that it was *not* a sin. Gwen John replied that the curé said it *was*. But Véra gave her the courage to continue drawing at other services than Mass, such as Vespers and Benediction. She also drew during retreats. She explained to Véra that the orphans with their black hats and white ribbons and their black dresses with white collars charmed her so much, as did other *créatures*. 'If I gave up all that there would not be enough happiness left in my life,' she said.

There were other problems with the curé. In the church he had

---

[3] *Carnet de Notes* by Jacques Maritain, is a series of biographical fragments. There is a chapter on Gwen John which is chiefly concerned to prove that she was never his friend.

replaced the old Stations of the Cross, which were 'simple and good' with modern 'horrors'. And on the parish picnic he had made jokes suited to the intellect of the lowest. 'You could hardly be as gross and stupid as Suzanne, now could you?' Gwen John added.

Véra, who longed to devote her life to nursing the poor, felt compassion for Gwen John, seeing her as a lonely and destitute artist. She recognised her as a contemplative so lost in solitude that she did not always know reality from fantasy. When Gwen John claimed never in her life to have visited the Louvre, Véra privately discounted this piece of invention. Gwen John told Véra about Rodin. She even asked Véra to call her Marie, the name by which *he* had called her. And she started to write long letters to the *Chère Mademoiselle*, as she had to the *Cher Maître*. Into these letters she poured the torrent of devotion Rodin had once inspired. She loved Véra, she told her, as she loved flowers. She loved her so much that she dared not look into her eyes; but like a small hurt animal she needed to be loved in return.

Véra, who was merely attempting to do her share for the apostolate of the arts, found these outpourings trying. She endured being followed home after Mass every morning for some months. Finally Jacques and Raïssa intervened and insisted that once a week, on Mondays, was sufficient. Even these Monday visits were not always satisfactory. Véra complained that Gwen John sat and stared at her as if she were not listening. Gwen John insisted that she only gave an *impression* of inattention, that she was attending to Véra's *presence*. Véra's words, she said, she inscribed on a tablet in her brain and read through later. Although Véra could limit the number of Gwen John's visits she could not limit either the length or the number of the letters. 'Do you really have to write to me every day?' she enquired. 'I think not, and I even think it is injurious to your soul, for you are becoming too attached to a fellow creature whom you hardly know. You have strong feelings but they should be turned towards Our Lord and Our Lady.'

'You told me my letter was too long,' Gwen John replied. 'Too long for what? I think the souls in Purgatory must feel like me. I don't live calmly like you and the rest of the world. When you leave me you will have a tomorrow and a day after and all the days of the week. For me it's the last day.' In another letter Véra was told what God the Father would have to say to her when she got to Heaven:

God the Father: 'Well, little one! Come here! There is something I want you to explain to me. Marie, who has been here with me for some time, tells me you have not been kind to her.'

  You: 'Holy and Eternal Father! There were several reasons for that! One is that I didn't understand her very well – it's true that Mother

Superior said that she could speak to me and that I would understand, but, but, oh, most Powerful Father, it wasn't as easy as all that.'

God the Father: 'Well, for Heaven's sake forget about Mother Superior. It was as clear as daylight. That morning when she ran after you and your little brother, at that moment all was said about her, ALL, ALL, ALL. Come now! No regrets! I can't be angry with you my little Véra! Go and find Marie, she's in the Joan of Arc room drawing the children in the catechism class. St Peter will show you the way.'

More despairing, and more reminiscent of the Rodin correspondence, was the tone of another letter. Evening had come, she was unhappy, she could do nothing. She could not even get dressed or do her room. She had decided to go and look for a lost cat but then remembered that Véra had told her not to follow chimeras but to associate with serious people like Miss O'Donnell. 'But the trouble is you and she are *too* serious for me. I do not want to live any more.'

This last letter suggests a state of clinical depression. The inability to do anything or even to get dressed, the indecision, the fear of going out, the conviction that she was unlovable, the thoughts of suicide, all are typical of a pathological state. In her notes of this time Gwen John spoke of 'the cloud descending'. This image of the cloud (so similar to Sylvia Plath's bell jar), exactly describes the sensations of the depressive when he foresees a new attack. In her efforts to ward off 'the cloud' Gwen John sought another spiritual adviser, a Frenchman who signed his letters 'Y.M.', standing for 'Your Master'. When Augustus found Y.M.'s numerous letters in Gwen John's studio after her death he assumed that they were from J.M., Jacques Maritain. But Maritain has hotly denied that he would express such sadistic sentiments in any language, let alone Y.M.'s 'English of the kitchen'. One of the letters runs: 'Your answer . . . is too much conceit, I don't know what you wrote at more length at first, and I am regretting you don't to have sent me your first writing, since I ordered you to tell me long and entirely what your mind finds about that subject. I'm *sole* judge of my orders and your *sole* duty is to obey me.'

As humanity turned its back on her, like the people in the church studies, Gwen John turned increasingly to flowers. 'Which region can you wander in?' she asked herself in a note, and answered, 'The land of flowers.' The titles of her flower gouaches give an idea of their subjects: 'Faded dahlias in a grey jug', 'Green leaves in a white jug', 'Fern leaves in a painted vase', 'Jar of white flowers'. Sometimes her subjects were pulled out of the hedge, sometimes, rather surprisingly, she used artificial flowers.

In the spring of 1928 Gwen John felt she was on the point of a breakthrough in painting. 'But it will be months or years perhaps.' In fact she painted two pictures that suggest a change of style *had* taken place. Both measured eight and a half inches by six and a half inches, both were gouache portraits of children. One was entitled 'Little girl with a large hat and straw-coloured hair',[4] the other, 'Boy with a blank expression'.[5] The boy is shown three-quarter length, a clearly defined dark shape against a light ground, his face bearing an expression of what Gwen John described as 'stupid fear'. The girl is shown only to the waist and she has a pale elongated face, also with a sad expression. Both pictures have something of the Japanese print in their simplicity, and something of Modigliani and Maurice Denis in their distortion.

And then the person from Porlock arrived and brought the new beginning swiftly to an end. He took the form of a developer eager to build in the rue Terre Neuve. Gwen John set up her easel at the windows of the attic studio and commenced to record the beloved curve in the street for the last time in a series of small swift gouaches. These also show a change in approach. A typical one, 'Rue Terre Neuve, Meudon', is to be seen at Cardiff.[6] David Fraser-Jenkins has pointed out that the style of this gouache, like that of the flower paintings, is more impressionistic than the church studies which were worked over later in the studio. An even wilder one is the fine study of the wind-tossed branches of an acacia.[7] The leaves are represented by a few brush strokes against a sky mauve with storm clouds.

This occupation in turn was rudely interrupted by another 'terrible event' in the form of a letter telling Gwen John she must get ready for an exhibition in the autumn. The 'picture man from New York' was in Paris, she told Ursula Tyrwhitt. He wanted to 'finalise' arrangements for a one-man show in America in November. The picture man was Maynard Walker, an employee of the Ferargil Galleries. This gallery, owned by Frederic Price, had the authority of Quinn's sister, Mrs Anderson, behind it. Mrs Foster appears to have faded from the scene.

Maynard Walker had in fact approached Gwen John at Meudon a year earlier and had selected paintings, still unfinished, for a show. Now, when they did not arrive, he returned to Paris. For the first ten days of July 1930 Gwen John worked all the daylight hours, and as a result did have something to show him when he visited her studio. He was pleased, she wrote, 'as far as one can tell', and had taken what she had while insisting that he required ten more paintings. Maynard Walker, in a letter

[4] No. 85, 1968 Arts Council Exhibition, now in Bristol City Art Gallery.
[5] No. 95, 1968 Arts Council Exhibition. Private collection.
[6] No. 39, 1976 Exhibition, Cardiff.
[7] No. 43, 1976 Exhibition, Cardiff.

to Cecily Langdale written in September 1975, firmly denies that he received a single painting from Gwen John. 'She promised however to get busy that summer and to go ahead with the show and to get everything ready for it. But the pictures were never worked on, and the show never came to pass.' He did in fact receive one drawing, sent in 1929. It was a head of Gwen John, drawn by herself in the year she met Rodin. Augustus remained convinced to the end of his days that a cache of Gwen John's paintings and drawings, accumulated for despatch to the Ferargil Galleries at Pottier's in Paris, had disappeared.

In the summer of 1930 Gwen John was again distracted by visitors to Paris, young Edwin and Ursula Tyrwhitt. Edwin was now twenty-two, large, pale and awkward. But he had a real gift for watercolour, which appeared when he drew Poole Harbour at the age of fifteen, and he also played the flute. He was now studying art in Paris which pleased his aunt. He had also taken up boxing, which did not. When he returned to England he became 'Teddy John of Chelsea', winning seven of his nine professional fights. Augustus crowed. He brought parties of festive spectators and once entered the ring himself and squared up opposite his son for a photo. 'I like him immensely,' he wrote. 'He has become a tall hefty fellow full of confidence, humour and character.' (Augustus was also convinced Edwin would make a good career as a clown.) Eventually, largely as the result of Gwen John's influence, young Edwin gave up the ring in favour of the brush, coming to live in Paris between 1935 and 1938 with his wife and baby son. He was to visit Gwen frequently and she eventually made him her heir.

Gwen John introduced Edwin and Ursula Tyrwhitt to the paintings of Rouault and Chagall. Rouault and Chagall were both close friends of the Maritains and Rouault was later to rate a chapter in Raïssa's autobiography, *Les Grandes Amitiés*. He was a mystic, some said a madman, who shared his hatred of hypocrisy and cruelty with his friend and master, Bloy. Like Léon Bloy he lived in poverty because he would not lower himself to produce work that would merely sell. According to Raïssa he could have painted pseudo-Rembrandts for the bourgeoisie for the rest of his days. Instead he preferred to paint stark black and white crucifixions, and clowns with elongated ivory faces and blue eyes. He supplemented his meagre earnings by being curator of the Gustave Moreau museum. When Gwen John told Edwin that she considered Rouault the greatest painter of the day he gave 'a snigger of contempt'. Then 'having heard at his academy that Rouault was great', he came to Gwen John and told her about him as if he had discovered him. 'But boxing interests him much more', she added in a letter to Ursula Tyrwhitt. If Rouault fascinated Edwin, it was Chagall who enchanted Ursula Tyrwhitt. Gwen John was not surprised, for some of Ursula's sketches of people had a feeling of Chagall. Gwen John, too, found Chagall's work 'calm and natural at heart', in spite of the bizarre subjects.

Ursula Tyrwhitt's visit as usual ended in misunderstanding. She had dashed back to England to be with Walter and Gwen John was only told at the last minute. Gwen had made great efforts with her toilette for their last afternoon outing. She was planning tea in the Avenue de l'Obser-vatoire and a visit to Constance Lloyd and her tapestry, then dinner at one of the little restaurants by the river at Bas Meudon that were so expensive she'd never dared to eat in them. Her afternoon now lay in ruins, she wrote.

A man of the same age as Edwin, who Gwen John was also seeing at this time was Tom Burns, later editor of *The Tablet*. He had been at Stonyhurst with her nephew, Henry and attended the Maritains' Sunday afternoon receptions regularly. The young man and the middle-aged woman became friends and spent many hours talking about God at café tables in Montparnasse. Mr Burns observes that Gwen John was small and thin, wore 'rather mauve' clothes and never took anything to eat or drink. Henry John also paid a call on Jacques Maritain this year, but made a far less favourable impression, since he dared to argue the validity of neo-Thomism with the Master. Gwen John was deeply shocked.

Gwen John's friendship with Véra came to a close at the end of 1930 when the Monday visits ceased, although the final parting was not until 1932. It had lasted for four years and was one of the casualties of a ukase that Jacques proclaimed in the spring of 1930. 'To defend us all from invasions from our neighbours, we are going to try and see if it is possible to live at Meudon without losing all leisure for prayer, and without endangering our very lives,' he declared. Gwen John's life was the one that was sacrificed. Véra had made the mistake religious people some-times make in their enthusiasm for converts. She had used her personal charm as a tool and it had become a master. Gwen John was more fascinated by Véra than by her teachings. Now she must pay the price. Véra promised she would always pray for her. Gwen confided to Louise Roche that Véra was too authoritarian to make a good friend.

A memorial to the friendship of the two women was the collection of drawings that Gwen John gave Véra, drawings which she always refer-red to as *Les Dessins de Lundi*. Every Monday morning, when she paid her call on Véra after Mass, she took with her a gift of a drawing, a gouache or a watercolour. On the back of the drawing was written the date of the visit (dates which ranged between 1928 and 1930) and occasionally an explanatory message. By the end of 1932 Véra had accumulated about a hundred works. The drawings covered the full range of Gwen John's working life. There were early ones of Tiger (now twenty years dead), some of the children at Pléneuf (now all grown up) and more recent church and flower studies. Of the contemporary portraits most seem to have been done in the train on the way to Paris for Gwen John could no longer afford to pay models. On the back of 'Little girl with a large hat and straw-coloured hair' she wrote, 'Little girl in the train (you)'. On 'Boy with a blank expression' she wrote, 'At the station (me)', and on the absurdly becloched 'Woman in a railway carriage' she inscribed, 'A *créature* writing a love letter in the train'.[8]

Oddly enough *Les Dessins de Lundi* were not appreciated in the cultivated household at Number Ten. 'I can't tell you how strange it is to hear you talk of my drawings,' Gwen John once wrote to Véra. 'If you don't like them *tell* me and I'll change them as I would my clothes if you disliked them.' Perhaps Véra had hoped that Gwen John would develop into a religious painter like the admired Maurice Denis. Certainly she was quite unaware of Gwen John's standing as an artist. She thrust *Les Dessins de Lundi* to the back of a cupboard where they were found after her death and assumed to be the efforts of Véra's friend Christine van der Meer, a nun who did 'little pictures' to raise money for her convent. Most of *Les Dessins de Lundi* have now been sold at very high prices through Sotheby to raise funds for the Jacques Maritain Study Centre in Alsace. Among the thirty that remain unsold are drawings of the Bishop of Versailles (with 'Your Bishop' written on the back), of St Teresa (copied from a photograph), and of the rue des Clos Moreaux (down which Gwen had run during the 1917 bombing). An experimental oil on paper, 'La boutique de Mme Caiffa', dated 31 September 1932, must surely have marked the final parting of the ways.

[8] It can be assumed that those drawings bearing messages were of recent production.

The hut in the garden

1932–9

When Véra closed the ever open door of 10 rue du Parc, the cloud descended for the last time. The final seven years of Gwen John's life were spent in almost total isolation. She had written in her diary earlier, 'Leave everybody and let them leave you. Then only will you be without fear.' Now she wrote, 'Don't think (as before) to work for years ahead. You work for one moment.'

But what seemed like a death to others was to her a new life. 'God has taken me to enter into art as one enters into religion,' she wrote. She now spent many hours copying out passages from the lives of the saints and other books of a spiritual character. She also copied out her own prayers and meditations, as well as the letters she sent and the letters she received. She made not one but many copies, as she was to do with her late gouaches. Her studio was littered with these copies after her death.

Among the spiritual books she read there was one secular one, *The Idiot,* to which she was faithful. The story of Prince Mishkin could always move her to tears. Perhaps in his innocence she saw a reflection of her own. But for spiritual direction she still read Father Faber daily. He alone could convince her that she was God's child, enclosed in His hands, that *He* was the father and mother she had sought all her life. The creature had come back, like a bird, to roost with the Creator. And the vocation of the creature was to paint. From now on she was 'God's little Artist'.

But she did not paint. 'Forgive my sins and my time wasted,' she had written back in 1929, 'and tell me how to love Véra.' The difficulties of her relationship with Véra had driven her to seek escape in a large department store. At the Grands Magasins du Louvre there was a reading room of amazing splendour.[1] Potted palms and marble tables stood beneath an elaborate plaster ceiling and ladies sipped tea in the English fashion. Nobody appears to have done much reading,

[1] Recently destroyed to make room for an antique hypermarket.

but Gwen John, using the headed notepaper supplied by the management, did seven hundred and thirty-four drawings of two small girls in Victorian dress, covering sixty-eight sheets of paper.[2] The fact that she dated these sheets suggests that she had originally intended to write letters on them (probably to Véra) and had then commenced to doodle. In her studio Gwen John was also making minute gouaches of the same subject, some of them very small indeed.[3] In these she introduced decorative features, like swagged velvet curtains, and varied the colour of the girls' dresses.

The two Victorian girls were not observed from life but from a popular photograph of St Teresa, at the age of eight, with her sister Celine, aged eleven. St Teresa of Lisieux was a saint to whom Véra and the Maritains had a deep devotion. She had been born only three years before Gwen John, to a shopkeeper's wife at Lisieux in Normandy, and had entered the local Carmelite convent at the age of fifteen. There, after leading a life of quiet virtue and suffering many privations, she died of tuberculosis at the age of twenty-four. She had vowed she would spend her heaven doing good on earth and she performed so many miracles that in 1925 Pope Pius XII was obliged to canonise her before the people did.

Teresa left behind her an autobiography which became a bestseller. *L'Histoire d'une Ame* gives a picture of a saint who was totally unassuming. Hers was the 'little way', of trust and self-surrender. Her sacrifices were the little ones: to smile when the sister next to her at the wash tub repeatedly splashed her with soap suds, or when a sister in chapel rattled her beads to distraction. 'I do not aim,' she wrote, 'to do extraordinary things, but to do ordinary things extraordinarily well.' Like Gwen John, Teresa was not an intellectual. 'Whenever I open a book my heart dries up,' she wrote. Like Gwen John she was 'an exile on this earth'. Human affections, she said, brought nothing but bitterness. 'How can a heart that is taken up with human love be fully united to God?' Yet there was one heart that was very close to that of Teresa, and it was the heart of Celine, the sister who was three years older than her, but as close to her as a twin. When they were children the sisters were never separated. They slept under the same coverlet like 'two little white chickens'. Sister Teresa's greatest sacrifice in Carmel was to pass her sister in the corridor without a word (for Celine also took vows). The relationship between them must have reminded Gwen John of her own with Winifred.

The St Teresa sketches were not Gwen John's only religious drawings at this time. She also did a set of nine entitled *Madonna and Child in a*

[2] No. 47, 1976 Exhibition, dated 1929, now at Cardiff. Others were dated 1927 and 1932. The sheets measure 5" by 7".
[3] 'The Victorian sisters', no. 93, 1975 Exhibition, New York, was 4" by 3". Private collection, New York.

landscape.[4] These were in harsh black wash on paper six inches square and portrayed a veiled woman with a halo standing on a mountaintop with a chasm behind her. The style is strangely crude and angular and they were once considered to be late works until their resemblance to other drawings found in Gwen John's studio was noticed. These were in a naturalistic style that could not have been later than 1930.

The Virgin standing on the edge of a precipice is most probably Our Lady of La Salette who appeared to the shepherdess Mélanie in the department of Isère in 1846 and wept because she could no longer shield the human race from impending disaster. A statue of this apparition stood above the altar in the Maritains' chapel at 10 rue du Parc. Our Lady of La Salette had had a profound effect on Léon Bloy who wrote *Celle qui Pleure* under her influence. The Maritains were in the habit of making regular pilgrimages to her shrine with Véra.

After 1930 there were no more religious drawings apart from the studies in church, and these were constantly repeated and grew smaller, as if their author was attempting to reduce them to a mere point in infinity. A series of watercolour profiles[5] of a girl in a cloche hat ended with one that was two-inches square. As it grew smaller it grew so simplified as to be practically an abstract.

Flower studies now received the same treatment, being repeated time and again and growing smaller. It was as if painting had become for Gwen John what saying the rosary is to others. A subject repeated many times was 'Flowers in a jug'.[6] Bright poppy-like blooms crowd at the mouth of a tall jug that leans towards the centre of the picture. Countless ink sketches for this were found in the late sketch-books. The smallest versions could grace a millionaire's dolls' house.

By 1936 even the mini gouaches seem to have ceased, for Gwen John had something else on her mind. 'You *must* be a saint,' she wrote in her journal. St Teresa had said very similar things in her journal. But to be a saint Gwen John had to be absolutely alone. People broke into her thoughts with their opinions and left her angry and hurt. She hated them too because they told her horrors about animals. There were too many people at the rue Terre Neuve. She now decided to move completely into the hut in the rue Babie[7] where she already lived in summer, retaining

[4] No. 46, 1976 Exhibition, Cardiff.
[5] *A girl seated in church in profile.* Four watercolours, no. 42, 1976 Exhibition, Cardiff.
[6] No. 96, 1975 Exhibition, New York. Private collection, New York.
[7] There is some disagreement about the date of this move. Gwen John acquired the shed in 1926, but in a letter to Ursula Tyrwhitt dated ten years later she spoke of being about to move into it and still used the rue Terre Neuve address on her notepaper. On the other hand, some traditions have it that she moved into the hut soon after she bought it. Probably she inhabited both places until she moved into the hut definitely in 1936. This is what Maynard Walker says in his letter to Edwin John, 6 May 1946.

only the storage *grenier* at the rue Terre Neuve. The hut needed repairs before she could pass a winter there. Workmen with planks were called and Gwen John slept out of doors while the work was being done and often thereafter. When the workmen left she was truly alone at last. All her thirty years in France she had lived in lodging houses where the *locataires* were in and out of each other's rooms. Now she had her island and could commence being quite alone. She survived three years in this way.

Imitating Véra, she mortified the flesh, keeping before her St Teresa's 'little way of trust and self-surrender'; Teresa who, after she entered the convent, never again ate meat or sat on a chair, slept on a bed or entered a heated room; Teresa who drenched her handkerchief in blood each night and told nobody. Gwen John's diet at this time was rather less nourishing than the diet at Carmel. She had taken to living on liquids because it was 'less trouble'. Time spent in cooking she regarded as so much time lost. She described to Ursula Tyrwhitt how she made an infusion of malted barley, grinding up the grain like coffee beans. She used to prepare a three-day supply and drink it with milk. 'You will find it sustains you very much,' she assured Ursula.

But these privations began to take their toll. Her letters to Ursula became strangely disjointed and often contained references to illnesses. First it was her hand which hurt too much to hold a brush. Then her head ached continuously. She invented an elaborate method of scalp massage which she passed on to Ursula. 'Press very firmly, not on temple but down sides of eyes *plutôt*, elbows supporting body.'

But she still attempted to paint. Just as an old author will sit at his desk with his pen in his hand because he does not know where else to sit, so she still turned over the *grenier* canvases that Quinn had lusted for. In 1936 the Ferargil Galleries of New York once more planned an exhibition of her pictures and sent over a woman director ('so it is not so terrifying') to take them back with her. In a letter to Ursula Tyrwhitt Gwen John claimed she had five paintings ready (presumably from the *grenier*). These never reached New York, nor did the six new ones that she promised, although, according to Louise Roche, one day a van waited all day outside the house to take them away, while she remained inside putting finishing touches. With this fiasco the efforts of the Ferargil Galleries ceased, but another American gallery owner, Mrs Cornelius, now went into battle. She had been a friend of Quinn and perhaps hoped this would give her an entry at 8 rue Babie. It did not. She hammered in vain on the door. Gwen John, locked inside, would not unlock.

In another letter the same year she did, however, show a new interest in the *theory* of art. This had been aroused by a visit from Ursula Tyrwhitt in July. 'I needed the stimulus you gave me,' she wrote afterwards. Ursula was at this time under the influence of L'Hoté, art critic and artist. She warmly recommended his book to Gwen John who filled her reply with the technical art terms he uses. Gwen John also quoted Cézanne at Ursula and offered to send a 'very precious little book' on him. She said she would also send Fieren's book on Ensor (a Belgian artist who painted macabre pictures in the style of Manet). She admired the pure vermilions and emeralds of his carnival masks.

Gwen John's interest in colour was as strong as ever. The letters to Ursula were full of references to the exact shades of watercolours available from the colourist Le Franc.[8] She memorised tones by associating them with parts of plants. Thus *Cinabre clair* was 'the colour of the little ball holding the snowdrop petals', *Rouge Phénicien* was 'the colour of the stem of the wild geranium', and *Laque de Smyrne foncé* was the colour of the 'roses in tufts now in flower'. *Anglais*, she added, was the green of the tubs in front of Ursula's hotel.

This keen interest in the theory of painting suggests some practical activity. But in fact it was a substitute for it. Gwen John referred to her own 'little paintings' at times, but only to say that she could not *réaliser* them. She added, '*Réaliser* is Cézanne. I think *finish* would be a better word in my case.' In another letter she spoke of her inability even to start a painting. Elsewhere she told Ursula that she had nothing done or even commenced.

Maynard Walker made a final bid to wrest some *grenier* paintings from her in 1937. He now owned the Walker Galleries at 108 East 57th Street. His is the last known account of her. On 3 July he wrote his farewell to her. 'I am leaving Paris with the greatest feeling of peace and joy after my visit to you this afternoon. I think the same spirit that emanates from your paintings is in that garden and surrounds you. I don't know whether you are religious or not, but in any case you have got a halo.' Writing to Edwin John ten years later Maynard Walker recalled that last visit to Gwen John, when 'she gave me tea underneath those great brooding trees at the back of that wild garden. We talked of Proust and saints and angels and sinners and painters.' Less heartening was the sight of thirty-odd *grenier* paintings, now transferred to the garage studio. 'The little place she now lived in,' he wrote, 'was far from weather-proof and there were sad signs that moisture had got into some of the canvases and damaged them'.

Walker once more begged to have a selection sent to New York. Gwen John would only consent to let him have one and that he must accept as a gift. When he refused to accept it she said she would send it anyway. No picture was ever sent and when the garage studio was cleared by Edwin after her death it was found to contain no paintings.

[8] Ursula Tyrwhitt was chiefly a watercolourist by now.

Two months after Maynard Walker's visit Gwen John became gravely ill. She described her complaint as a 'chill inside' caused by sitting on her doorstep to draw a flower. It was certainly something more serious but she refused to see a doctor. When she wrote to Ursula on 21 September she could neither stand nor walk without pain. She begged her not to visit Paris as she would not be able to accompany her to exhibitions. This letter of 21 September 1937 is probably her last to survive. Two more, written earlier that year to a young man who had suggested calling on her were equally discouraging. The young man was Michael Salaman, son of her old friend Michel. In the first she told him, 'I've got *la grippe*. (You won't catch it by this letter. I shall put the letter out in the wind.)' In the second she told him she would be away the whole summer (almost certainly untrue).

For the last two years of her life Gwen John was not much troubled by people. Louise Roche was almost the only person who saw her. She was appalled at Gwen John's self-neglect. She described how, 'To go to a doctor inconvenienced her, to take solid nourishment inconvenienced her. She treated her body as though she were its executioner.' Those last years, alone with her God, are distressingly reminiscent of the last years of Camille Claudel, Rodin's earlier mistress, before she was removed to the asylum. Like Camille, Gwen John was now living in a twilight world. Raïssa had a vision at this time that might well have applied to her. 'I was seized with a new sensation. It was as if the bitter taste of *poverty* had filled my mouth and all my being. A total and all enveloping poverty, without issue to the fresh air or the slightest consolation.' That was the poverty of Gwen John.

One friend Gwen John could ill afford to lose was struck down very suddenly about this time. It was the curé, who despite his poor taste in art and jokes, had developed an understanding and broad-minded attitude towards her. He had refused to join forces with her critics when she failed to turn up at Mass for a month because she was engaged on a picture, knowing that artists sometimes require a bending of the rules. Now he was on his deathbed and she sat with him all day for several days drawing his face in profile. When he died she remained deeply shocked for some months.

She was now left without a spiritual adviser, for the only other curé she knew at Meudon was not a parish priest but a historian, the author of a life of Queen Elizabeth. She had been commissioned to draw his portrait and chose to do it when he was saying Mass, for the church continued to be a favourite studio. Louise Roche recounts that when her illness was already far advanced she spent a whole day in the church without food or rest, drawing children who were making a retreat before their First Communion. She would not go home until she had conveyed satisfactorily the modelling of one small girl's cheek.

The spring of 1939 was cold and wet. The pain of Gwen John's illness (surely a cancer of some abdominal organ) was making it hard for her to sleep at night, and as a result she was afraid of not waking in the morning and so missing Mass. To remedy this she moved her bed to the small garden shed which she sometimes used as a studio or summer house in hot weather. The shed had no door and the icy rain on her coverlet woke her in good time, to her satisfaction, but the horror of Louise Roche.

On 1 September 1939 Hitler invaded Poland and two days later France and England declared war on Germany. In Paris panic was instant. Véra and the Maritains escaped to the country and foreigners hastened home to avoid internment. Augustus was among those who hurried home. At sixty, now the Grand Old Man of Bohemia, he had come with Dorelia to a farmhouse at St Remy in Provence for three years running, bringing a selection of young people of both sexes whom he had fathered on different mothers. This year he had with him Vivien, Zoë and Tristan. He seems to have been strangely out of touch with Gwen in the previous two years. In 1937 she had sent an urgent note to Maynard Walker asking him to visit Augustus at Fryern to find out how her brother was. Such enquiries on her part had been rare in the past. It was more often the other way round. There is no record that Augustus even informed her of her father's death in 1938.

For some time Augustus remained at St Remy, refusing to believe in the war. Finally a phone call from Poppet convinced him of its existence and he packed the two cars and set off. There was no thought of Gwen in his mind. He made straight for Le Havre before the petrol ran out. The port was in confusion. The last boat was preparing to leave and passengers were told they must abandon their cars and take only what luggage they could carry. By distributing bribes Augustus got himself and his cars on board but left all his wine behind.

Eleven days later Gwen tried to follow his example. No doubt she felt unable to face another war in France, a war which promised to be far worse than the first. She was ill, Yew Tree Cottage awaited her and Louise Roche was willing to feed the cats for the duration. She made for Dieppe and freedom, perhaps with the poem 'Dieppe' by Arthur Symons (now blind, widowed and a recluse) ringing in her ears.

> O I am lost, you will not set me free
> Unless I turn again and seek the sea
> Some vague new world of waters, bounded by
> The soft and sudden barrier of the sky.

On alighting from the train on 1 September she collapsed in the street. She was found to be without luggage, assumed to be a derelict and removed to the Hospice de Dieppe, Avenue Pasteur, where she died shortly afterwards. Her death certificate gives no cause of death, and the whereabouts of her grave is unknown.

Augustus was to design a gravestone, 'but never got round to it', perhaps because her grave has been untraceable. 'As if it mattered,' one seems to hear her say.

APPENDICES

EXHIBITIONS OF GWEN JOHN'S WORK

1900–11 New English Art Club (N.E.A.C.). Exhibited irregularly.

1903 Carfax Gallery. Works by Augustus and Gwen John. 3 paintings.

1913 New York, Chicago, Boston. *The Armoury Show*. 1 painting.

1919–25 Paris, Grand Salon, Salon National, Salon d'Automne and Salon des Tuileries. Exhibited altogether 15 paintings, 29 drawings and watercolours.

1922 New York, The Sculptors' Gallery. *Modern English Artists* (from John Quinn collection). 5 paintings and 10 drawings.

1925 N.E.A.C. *Retrospective Exhibition*. 4 paintings.

1926 New Chenil Galleries. 44 paintings and drawings and 4 albums of drawings.

1940 National Gallery. *British Painting since Whistler*.

1946 Matthiesens Ltd. *Gwen John: Memorial Exhibition*. 217 paintings and drawings.

1952 Tate Gallery and Arts Council. *Ethel Walker, Frances Hodgkinson, Gwen John: A Memorial Exhibition*. 55 paintings and drawings.

1952 Edinburgh College of Art. 63 drawings and watercolours.

1957 Brighton Art Gallery. *The Influence of Wales in Painting*. 13 paintings and drawings.

1958 Matthiesen Gallery. *Gwen John*. 67 paintings and drawings.

1961 Matthiesen Gallery. *Gwen John*. 82 paintings and drawings.

1964 Faerber & Maison Ltd. *Gwen John*. 60 paintings and drawings.

1965 New York, Davis Gallery. *Gwen John*. 35 paintings and drawings.

1968 Arts Council. *Gwen John: A Retrospective Exhibition*. 141 paintings and drawings.

1970 Faerber & Maison Ltd. *Gwen John*. 48 paintings and drawings.

1975 New York, Davis & Long. *Gwen John*. 102 paintings and drawings.

1976 Anthony d'Offay. *Gwen John*. 62 paintings and drawings.

1976 National Museum of Wales. *Gwen John*. 48 paintings and drawings.

we are getting homesick
I think, we are always
talking of beautiful
places we know of
beyond the suberbs of
London o Fitzroy St. o
Howland St. seem to
me more than ever
charming o interesting
We shall be going home
in the Autumn I think
or before.
I am getting on with
my painting, that makes
me happy. We expect
Gus to come over here
next week. The room
is full of pieces of

Two examples of Gwen John's handwriting in letters to Alice Rothenstein. The earlier, above, was written in 1903, the second, opposite, in 1926. The childish character of Gwen John's later hand seems to have resulted from her sense of abandonment after her affair with Rodin in 1904. (From the Houghton Library, Harvard University, Cambridge, Mass.)

Ingen court
Nr Fordingbridge
Hants
May 31st

Dear Alice,

Thank you for your charming little letter.

I have an appointment in Paris so cannot stay longer now.

Don't talk sentimentaly about not being here if I "put off coming to you for long" You will be here much longer than me of course, but I shall see you and Will soon. I'm not going to be so "sauvage" in the future.

Your loving
Gwen

SELECT BIBLIOGRAPHY

Baron, Wendy: *The Camden Town Group* (Scolar Press, 1979)

Batterby, K. A. J.: *Rilke and France* (Oxford University Press, 1966)

Bertram, Anthony: *A Century of British Painting 1851–1951* (Studio Publications, London/New York, 1951)

Brenan, Gerald: *St John of the Cross*, Life and Poetry (Cambridge University Press, 1973)

Browse, Lillian, ed: *Augustus John: Drawings* (Faber and Faber, 1941)

Bruno, Father, O.D.C.: *St John of the Cross*, Introduction by Jacques Maritain (Sheed and Ward, 1932)

Butler. E. M.: *Rainer Maria Rilke* (Cambridge University Press, 1941)

Cecil, Lord David, ed: *Augustus John: 52 Drawings* (George Rainbird, 1957)

Chapman, Ronald: *Father Faber* (Burns and Oates, 1961)

Chassé, Charles: *The Nabis and Their Period* (Lund Humphries, 1969)

Cladel, Judith, *Rodin* (Kegan Paul, 1938)

Cocteau, Jean: *My Contemporaries* (Chilton, United States, 1968)

Coquiot, Gustave: *Le Vrai Rodin* (Jules Tallendrier, Paris, 1913)

Descharnes, R. and J. F. Chabrun: *Auguste Rodin* (Macmillan, 1967)

Devas, Nicolette: *Two Flamboyant Fathers* (Collins, 1966)

Easton, Malcolm and Michael Holroyd: *The Art of Augustus John* (Secker and Warburg, 1974)

Elsen, Albert: *Rodin* (Secker and Warburg, 1972)

Faber, Frederick William: *Creator and Created* (Burns and Oates, 1961)

Forge, Andrew: *The Slade 1871–1960* (privately printed, 1961)

Fosca, François: *Maurice Denis* (Gallimard, 1924)

Fothergill, John: *The Slade 1893–1907* (privately printed, 1907)

Greer, Germaine: *The Obstacle Race* (Secker and Warburg, 1979)

Holroyd, Michael: *Augustus John* (Penguin 1976)

Hone, Joseph: *The Life of Henry Tonks* (Heinemann, 1939)

Hopkinson, Tom: *Love's Apprentice* (Jonathan Cape, 1953)

John, Augustus. Autobiography: Part 1 *Chiaroscuro*; Part 2 *Finishing Touches* (Jonathan Cape [1952 and 1964] 1975)

John, Romilly: *The Seventh Child: A Retrospect* (Heinemann, 1932)

Levenson, Samuel: *Maude Gonne* (Cassell, 1976)

Lewis, Percy Wyndham: *Rude Assignment: A Narrative of My Career Up to Date* (Hutchinson, 1950)

Lewis, Percy Wyndham: *The Wild Body* (Chatto, 1927)

Llhombreaud, Roger: *Arthur Symons: A Critical Biography* (Unicorn Press, 1963)

Maritain, Jacques: *Carnet de Notes* (Desclée de Brouwer, Paris, 1965)

Marriott, Charles: *Augustus John* (Masters of Modern Art Colour Ltd., 1918)

Mellow, James R.: *Charmed Circle. Gertrude Stein and Co.* (Phaidon, 1974)

Morphet, Richard: *British Paintings 1910–1945* (Tate, 1967)

Owen, Roderic, with Tristan de Vere Cole: Beautiful and Beloved: *The Life of Mavis de Vere Cole* (Hutchinson, 1974)

Perry, Gillian: *Paula Modersohn-Becker* (Women's Press, 1979)

Read, Herbert: *A Concise History of Modern Painting* (Thames and Hudson, 1959)

Reid, B. L.: *The Man from New York: John Quinn and his Friends* (Oxford University Press, New York, 1968)

Richardson, Samuel: *Clarissa Harlowe; or the History of a Young Lady* (Chapman and Hall, 1902)

Rose, W. K., ed: *The Letters of Wyndham Lewis* (Methuen, 1963)

Rothenstein, John: *Modern English Painters* Volumes 1 and 2 (Eyre and Spottiswoode, 1952, 1956); Volume 3 (Macdonald and Jane's, 1974)

Rothenstein, John: *Time's Thievish Progress: Autobiography III* (Cassell, 1970)

Rutherston, A. D., ed: *Augustus John* (Ernest Benn, 1923)

Saint Teresa of Lisieux: *The Story of a Soul* (Burns and Oates, 1951, Translated by Michael Davy)

Sandel, Cora: *Alberta and Freedom* (Peter Owen, [1931] 1963)

Speaight, Robert: *William Rothenstein. The Portrait of an Artist in his Time* (Eyre and Spottiswoode, 1962)

Steegmuller, Francis: *Cocteau. Biography* (Little, Brown, United States, 1970)

Stein, Gertrude: *Picasso* (Beacon, Boston, United States)

Sutton, Denys: *Rodin: Triumphant Satyr* (Country Life, 1966) .

Symons, Arthur: *From Toulouse-Lautrec to Rodin* (Bodley Head, 1929)

Symons, Arthur: *Wanderings* (Dent, 1951)

Thornton, Alfred: *Fifty Years of the New English Art Club* (Curwen, 1935)

Thornton, Alfred: *The Diary of an Art Student* (Pitman, 1938)

Twitchin, Annella: *Gwen John: Her Art and Her Religion* (Courtauld Institute M.A. Report [unpublished] 1972)

Wydenbruck, Nora: *Rilke; Man and Poet* (Lehmann, 1949)

NOTES ON SOURCES

Abbreviations:
- G.J.   Gwen John
- A.J.   Augustus John
- U.T.   Ursula Tyrwhitt
- J.Q.   John Quinn

Chapter 1 **Haverfordwest** 1876–84
20 John grandparents: *Chiaroscuro*, A.J.
21 Mimi's home: *ibid.*
23 Broad Haven: *ibid.*
23 Broad Haven: *ibid.*

Chapter 2 **Tenby** 1884–95
25 Motherless Winifred: *Augustus John*, Michael Holroyd.
26 Winifred's memories of Victoria House: author's interview with Mrs Robins, proprietor of the Victoria Hotel.
26 Silent meals: *Augustus John*, Michael Holroyd.
29 Edwin John on A.J. and G.J.: 'The education of Augustus John', *Evening Standard*, 19 January 1929, in an occasional series called 'Makers of Men'.
30 Surrounding countryside: *Chiaroscuro*, A.J.
30 Younger brother homecomings: G.J. to Rodin, 1908.
31 Jimmy: *Chiaroscuro*, A.J.
32 Edwin John: *ibid.*
33 Edwin John: *ibid.*
33 Tenby's relaxing air: G.J. to U.T. undated.

Chapter 3 **Slade** 1895–8
36 A.J.'s first Life Class: *Horizon*, Vol. III, no. 18, June 1941, p. 394. *Chiaroscuro* originally appeared as eighteen instalments in *Horizon*.
38 Whistler at the Slade: *Chiaroscuro*, A.J.
38 Wilson Steer: *Finishing Touches*, A.J.
39 G.J. to Michel Salaman: written from Peveril Tower, Swanage, 1899.
40 U.T.'s background: Catalogue to Tyrwhitt Exhibition, Ashmolean, 1946, by Richard Buckle.
40 The Grand Epoch at the Slade: Obituary of Lady Smith (Gwen Salmond) by A.J., *The Times*, 1 February 1958.

40 The Three Musketeers: *Men and Memories*, William Rothenstein.
41 A.J. on art students: *Chiaroscuro*, A.J.
43 A bang on the head: *Finishing Touches*, A.J.

Chapter 4   **Ambrose McEvoy** 1898–1903
46 Tenby summer vacation: A.J. to Michel Salaman, June 1898, quoted in *Augustus John*, Michael Holroyd.
46 Student Paris: *Rude Assignment*, Wyndham Lewis.
47 Gwen Salmond to Michel Salaman: *Augustus John*, Michael Holroyd.
48 Whistler on tonal modelling: *Life of James McNeil Whistler*, E. R. and J. Pennell, London 1911.
48 Whistler on G.J.: quoted in *Chiaroscuro*, A.J.
49 G.J. to A.J.: *Augustus John*, Michael Holroyd.
50 G.J. usually came with McEvoy: *ibid.*
50 G.J. bathing: *ibid.*
51 The Johns at 1 Pembroke Cottages: *Men and Memories*, William Rothenstein.
52 Le Puy: 'Le Puy 1889' from *Wanderings*, Arthur Symons, 1931
52 McEvoy to Salaman: National Library of Wales, Aberystwyth.
53 A.J. on 'sister Gwen': from unpublished working notes for an autobiography, 1923.
55 The professors' wives' offerings: *Augustus John*, Michael Holroyd.
56 G.J. and Dorelia's walking plans: Albert Rutherston to Michel Salaman, 1903, and quoted in 'Gwen John' by A.J. in the *Burlington Magazine*, vol. LXXXI, no. 475, October 1942.

Chapter 5   **Toulouse** 1903–4
57 A long letter from La Réole: G.J. to U.T., 2 September 1903.
58 Letters for the 'crazy walkers': *Augustus John*, Michael Holroyd.
59 G.J.'s accounts of Toulouse: G.J. to U.T., 1903.
60 G.J.'s five paintings at Toulouse: *ibid.*
61 A.J.'s family Christmas: Ida Nettleship to Winifred John, January 1904.
61 G.J.'s bossy side: author's interview with Romilly John, 1980.

Chapter 6   **Rodin I** 1904–6
74 Typical day in the A.J. household: Ida Nettleship to her aunt, Margaret Hinton, 1905.
79 Ida on living with A.J.: Ida Nettleship to Mrs Sampson, 1905.
79 'Ardor looking after the four' other *ibid.*, 1905.
80 'always the same reserved creature': *ibid*, undated.
81 The face of 'Lady reading at a window': G.J. to U.T., 19 October 1911.

Chapter 7   **Rodin II** 1907
98 'There is always death': Ida Nettleship to Mrs Sampson.
98 Ida's demands on Mrs Nettleship: Mrs Nettleship to U.T., March 1907.
98 A.J. on Ida's death: A.J. to Mrs Sampson, 1907, in *Augustus John*, Michael Holroyd.

99 McEvoy at Ida's memorial service: *ibid.*

104 Rodin's maxims: G.J. to U.T., 13 November 1908.

105 G.J. on having one or two canvases in reserve: G.J. to U.T., 30 April 1908.

Chapter 8 **Conversion** 1908–13

112 The Rothensteins ask G.J. to stay: G.J. to U.T., 29 May 1908.

113 G.J. scolds Rodin: G.J. to U.T., 1908.

114 G.J. reads Poe: *ibid.*

115 Losung Tiger: G.J. to U.T., 29 May 1908, 12 July 1908 and 15 February 1909.

117 G.J. avoids her rue Cherche-Midi neighbours: G.J. to U.T., 1909.

117 The move to rue de l'Ouest: G.J. to U.T., 6 May 1910.

117 G.J. enchanted by Fenella: G.J. to U.T., 30 September 1909.

118 G.J. dreams of primroses: G.J. to U.T., 15 February 1909.

119 Virginia Woolf: a lecture delivered 18 May 1924.

121 'One must paint a lot of canvases': G.J. to U.T., 3 August 1916.

121 G.J. on Puvis de Chavannes: G.J. to U.T. 28 November 1911.

121 'Love is my illness': G.J. to Rodin, 2 April 1911.

121 G.J.'s plea to be left to herself: G.J. to U.T., 30 June 1910.

122 Experiments with etching: G.J. to U.T., 21 December 1910.

123 29 rue Terre Neuve: G.J. to U.T., 21 November 1910.

124 U.T. urged to come to Paris: G.J. to U.T., 6 May 1910.

124 Edwin John's visit to Paris: G.J. to U.T., 30 June 1910.

125 Quinn's proposed visit to G.J.: J.Q. to G.J., 29 July 1910, and 16 November 1911.

125 G.J.'s spring *grippe*: G.J. to Rodin, 2 April 1911.

125 G.J. notebook confidences: see 'Gwen John: her art and her religion', unpublished M.A. report by Annella Twitchin, Courtauld Institute, 1972.

126 G.J. to Quinn: 11 August 1911.

126 Questions on the artistic scene: J.Q. to G.J., 16 November 1911 and 1 November 1912.

126 U.T. again urged to come to Paris: G.J. to U.T., 15 October 1911.

126 Quinn fails to enjoy Paris: J.Q. to A.J. 22 October 1912.

127 Quinn on 'Girl reading at the window': J.Q. to G.J., 16 November 1911.

127 G.J. on framing 'Girl reading': G.J. to J.Q., 25 January 1913.

127 'Better *without* frames': G.J. to J.Q., 20 February 1913.

128 Quinn on his own health: J.Q. to G.J., 27 March 1919; and solicitude for G.J.'s: J.Q. to G.J., 11 April 1921.

128 Quinn horribly terribly driven: J.Q. to Arthur Symons, 1920.

131 'God's spiritual child': 'Gwen John: her art and her religion', Annella Twitchin, *op. cit.*

132 G.J. on the *bonne sœur*: G.J. to U.T., 22 April 1915.

Chapter 9 **War** 1914–18

133 'the chase of the aryplanes': G.J. to J.Q., 29 September 1914.
133 G.J. on the Gare Montparnasse: G.J. to U.T., 7 September 1914.
134 Father Faber's *Creator and Created*: quoted by Annella Twitchin, *op. cit.*
135 Rodin becoming a child again: see *Rodin*, Bernard Champignelle, London 1967.
136 G.J. talks to English soldiers: G.J. to U.T., 27 September 1914
136 The curé and *The Times*: G.J. to U.T., 4 December 1914.
136 After the Ypres massacre: *ibid*.
136 A.J. in Paris: see *High Relief*, Charles Wheeler.
137 Quinn on 'Study of a woman': J.Q. to G.J. 4 September 1914.
137 The Ruth Manson drawing: G.J. to J.Q., 21 December 1914.
138 Grève des Vallées at low tide: G.J. to J.Q., 1920.
139 Paintings 'more serious' than drawings: J.Q. to G.J., 3 August 1916.
139 G.J. suggests sharing an exhibition: G.J. to U.T., 3 August 1916.
140 'A picture for every sitting': G.J. to U.T., 19 April 1917.
140 David Fraser-Jenkins: see Catalogue to the Gwen John Exhibition, National Museum of Wales, 1976.
140 Cecily Langdale: see Catalogue to the Gwen John Exhibition, Davis and Long, New York, 1975.
141 G.J. on her output: G.J. to U.T., 18 May 1917.
141 Work and pray: see Annella Twitchin, *op. cit.*
141 'Impose your style': A.J. quoting from G.J.'s notebooks in his introduction to the 1946 Memorial Exhibition Catalogue.
142 Albert Besnard on Rodin: see *Sous le Ciel de Rome*, Paris.
142 Winter 1915: see Julien Green, *Partir avant le Jour*, Paris.
143 Rodin's stroke: G.J. to J.Q., 25 March 1916.
144 Painting from photos: G.J. to U.T., 3 August 1916; and G.J. to J.Q., 26 October 1916.
145 'pleased to do another in their place': G.J. to J.Q., 13 February 1916.
146 U.T.'s clothes parcel: G.J. to U.T., 18 May 1917.
146 G.J. on the state of the war: G.J. to J.Q., 11 April 1917.
147 On Rodin's death: G.J. to U.T., 22 November 1917.
148 G.J. dines with A.J.: G.J. to U.T., 31 December 1917.
149 The bombing of Paris: G.J. to U.T., 19 May 1918.
150 Refuge in the cellar: *ibid*.
150 The armistice: G.J. to U.T., 19 August 1918.
150 11 November in Paris: G.J. to J.Q., 12 November 1918.
151 The trunk drawings: G.J. to J.Q., 13 October 1918; and J.Q. to G.J., 27 March 1919.
151 The Manoir de Vauxclair: G.J. to J.Q., April 1920.

Chapter 10 **Quinn** 1919–24

153 Symons recommends G.J. to Quinn: Arthur Symons to J.Q., 1920.
154 Answering Quinn's questionnaire: G.J. to J.Q., 4 April 1920.
155 Gerald Cumberland on Arthur Symons: *Written in Friendship*, 1923.

155 The John boys at Dane Court school: Michaela Pooley to Michael Holroyd, 1969.

156 Edwin elects to stay in France: *Seventh Child*, Romilly John, London 1932.

156 Cottage rented from M. Lesage: author's interview with Mme Lejeune, 1979.

157 A new patronage arrangement: J.Q. to G.J., 26 June 1920.

157 The advent of Mrs Foster: G.J. to J.Q., 10 July 1920.

157 The virtues of Mrs Foster: J.Q. to G.J., 26 June 1920.

157 Mrs Foster's visit to Paris: G.J. to J.Q., 18 July 1920, quoted in *John Quinn* by B. L. Reid.

158 J.Q. to Lady Gregory: 11 May 1922; and to Ezra Pound, 24 September 1920.

158 G.J. on Ford Madox Ford: G.J. to J.Q., March 1924.

159 Quinn against Rhoda Symons: J.Q. to G.J., 19 July 1921.

159 Drawings hung in sets: G.J. to U.T., autumn 1921.

159 First meeting with Quinn: G.J. to U.T., winter 1921.

160 Jam for the orphans' bread: see *John Quinn*, B. L. Reid.

160 'Mère Poussepin': see *Modern English Painters*, John Rothenstein, London; and G.J. to J.Q., 27 March 1922.

162 G.J.'s *grenier*: Mrs Foster to J.Q., 11 May 1922.

162 'Long quiet days of work': G.J. to U.T., autumn 1921.

162 The Sculptors' Gallery exhibition: J.Q. to G.J., 24 April 1922.

162 Quinn on his English pictures: J.Q. to Roché, 5 March 1922.

163 Summer of 1922: G.J. to J.Q., 12 July 1922.

165 After the party at Brancusi's: G.J. to J.Q., 29 October 1923.

165 Keeping up with Brancusi: J.Q. to G.J., 12 November 1923.

167 Rousseau's 'Sleeping gypsy': G.J. to J.Q., 22 August 1911, quoted by B. L. Reid, *op. cit.*

167 Quinn on G.J. paintings owed him: J.Q. to Roché, February 1924, quoted by B. L. Reid, *op. cit.*

167 Quinn on his cancer: J.Q. to Lady Gregory, 10 May 1924.

Chapter 11 **The Exhibition** 1925–7

170 Miss Bishop's account of her sitting: see Annella Twitchin, *op. cit.*

171 Louise Roche's memories: Louise Roche to John Rothenstein, 20 March 1947.

171 'The simplicity of the primitive Japanese prints': G.J. to U.T., 10 November 1925.

175 A.J. on the 'mere shed': 'Gwen John' by A.J. in the *Burlington Magazine*, *op. cit.*

176 Edwin John on the weather: see *Augustus John*, Michael Holroyd.

176 First sight of Yew Tree Cottage: G.J. to U.T., 23 July 1926.

176 Trying to get settled at Yew Tree Cottage: G.J. to U.T., 1 September 1927.

177 Cat in the tunnel: G.J. to U.T., 18 August 1927.

177 Return to England: *ibid.*

177 Fryern Court: see *Two Flamboyant Fathers*, Nicolette Devas.
177 Carrington on Dorelia: *Dora Carrington, Letters and Extracts from her Diaries*, ed. David Garnett.
177 Kathleen Hale and Lady Pansy Lamb on Dorelia: interviews with the author, 1980.
178 Lord David Cecil's hat: see *Augustus John*, Michael Holroyd.
178 Fanny Fletcher: *ibid.*
178 A.J. on G.J.: in the *Burlington Magazine*, *op cit.* p. 238.
179 Henry Lamb's memory of G.J.: author's interview with Lady Pansy Lamb, 1980.
179 Vivien John's memory of G.J.: quoted in 'The Fire and the Fountain', by Eric Rowan, the *Listener*, 20 March 1975, p. 362.
180 G.J.'s alleged dislike of priests: see *Seventh Child*, Romilly John.
181 'I will not be troubled by people': G.J. to U.T., 17 July 1927.
181 'We're part of each other's atmosphere': G.J. to U.T., 27 August 1927.

Chapter 12   **Véra** 1928–32
183 G.J.'s reaction to Rilke's death: see A.J. in his introduction to the catalogue of the 1946 Exhibition.
184 Inside 10 rue du Parc: see *Le Sabbat*, Maurice Sachs, Paris 1947.
184 Raïssa's diary: *Journal de Raïssa*, Paris.
185 Véra's compassion for G.J.: see *Carnet de Notes*, Jacques Maritain.
185 G.J.'s confession of love for Véra: see *Chiaroscuro*, A.J.
185 Véra's words inscribed on a tablet in G.J.'s brain: G.J. to Véra Oumançoff, quoted in the catalogue of the 1946 Exhibition.
186 'I do not want to live anymore': *ibid.*
186 Maritain denies being Y.M.: *Carnet de Notes*.
186 G.J. turns to flowers: see the catalogue of the 1946 Exhibition; and G.J. to U.T., 4 April 1925.
187 An autumn exhibition: G.J. to U.T., 17 July 1930.
188 Edwin John at twenty-two: author's interview with Lady Pansy Lamb, 1980.
189 G.J. shocked by Henry John: Louise Roche to John Rothenstein, 10 March 1947.
189 Maritain's ukase: see *Journal de Raïssa*.
190 G.J.'s work attributed to Christine van der Meer: author's interview with Antoinette Grunelius, 1979.

Chapter 13   **The Hut in the Garden** 1932–9
191 'God has taken me': Notebook, 13 March 1932.
192 Maritain's devotion to St Teresa of Lisieux: see *Journal de Raïssa*.
194 Privations take their toll: G.J. to U.T., 22 July 1936.
194 Mrs Cornelius's lack of success at rue Babie: Maynard Walker to Edwin John, 1947.
195 The exact shades of water colours: G.J. to U.T., 22 July 1936.
196 G.J.'s self-neglect: Louise Roche to John Rothenstein, 10 March 1947.

INDEX OF PAINTINGS AND DRAWINGS

Gwen John rarely dated her work. The dates supplied here are arrived at from biographical evidence and in some cases approximate only.

INDEX

13th Feb.